Software
Fortresses

Software Fortresses

Modeling Enterprise Architectures

Roger Sessions

Art Coordinated by Janet Van Sickler

✦ Addison-Wesley

Boston • San Francisco • New York • Toronto • Montreal
London • Munich • Paris • Madrid
Capetown • Sydney • Tokyo • Singapore • Mexico City

The publisher offers discounts on this book when ordered in quantity for bulk purchases and special sales. For more information, please contact:

> U.S. Corporate and Government Sales
> (800) 382-3419
> corpsales@pearsontechgroup.com

For sales outside of the U.S., please contact:

> International Sales
> (317) 581-3793
> international@pearsontechgroup.com

Visit Addison-Wesley on the Web: www.awprofessional.com

Library of Congress Cataloging-in-Publication Data
Sessions, Roger.
   Software fortresses : modeling enterprise architectures /
  Roger Sessions.
       p.   cm.
   Includes index.
   ISBN 0-321-16608-6 (alk. paper)
   1. System design. 2. Computer architecture. I. Title.
  QA76.9.S88S48 2003
  005.1—dc21   2003041454

ISBN: 0-321-16608-6
Text printed on recycled paper
1 2 3 4 5 6 7 8 9 10—CRS—0706050403
First printing, February 2003

Contents

Preface

You and I have never met. I have no idea what your business is. However, I do know what your enterprise architecture looks like. I can even show you the exact picture you use to describe your enterprise system. Take a look at Figure P.1. Look familiar?

It goes without saying that your enterprise is a perfect three-tier (or N-tier) software architecture. When describing your system, you wax poetic about your perky presentation tier, accepting HTTP requests from complacent clients and SOAP requests from congenial collaborators. You illuminate in minutiae how you manage your middle tier, running well-behaved business logic cherubs, all gleefully sharing database connections and other valuable system resources. Behind all of this, your enterprisewide database shouts encouragement from its sheltered back end.

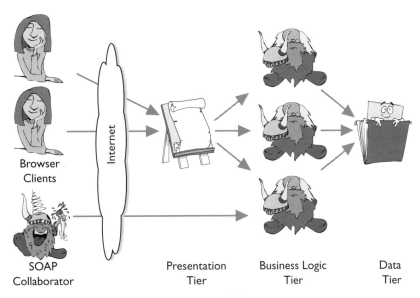

Figure P.1 The Picture You Show of Your Enterprise System

See? I told you I know what your enterprise architecture looks like. I also know one other thing. I know you lie. You lie through your teeth. Your enterprise architecture looks nothing like Figure P.1. Do you want to see the real picture of your enterprise architecture? Take a look at Figure P.2. But first sit down. It isn't pretty!

In the real world your clients are not meek, but malicious. Your middle tier is not well behaved, but made up of a disparate bunch of applications developed without regard for the needs of their stablemates. Your "database" is not an enterprisewide anything, but rather a series of disorganized data storage technologies that spend most of their time cringing from the unreasonable and often conflicting demands of the business logic.

As architects, we have two choices. We can ignore this chaos, or we can model it. When we model it, we have the opportunity to bring it under some degree of intellectual control.

Figure P.2 Your *Real* Enterprise Architecture

The Software Fortress Model

This book introduces a new approach for modeling large enterprise systems: the software fortress model. The software fortress model treats enterprise systems as a series of self-contained software fortresses. Each fortress makes its own choices as to software platform and data storage mechanisms and interacts with other fortresses through carefully crafted treaties. Without going into too much detail this early, I present in Figure P.3 a view of the same enterprise that is shown in Figure P.2, but as seen from the software fortress model. Don't worry at this point about what the cartoon figures mean; they will become familiar soon enough.

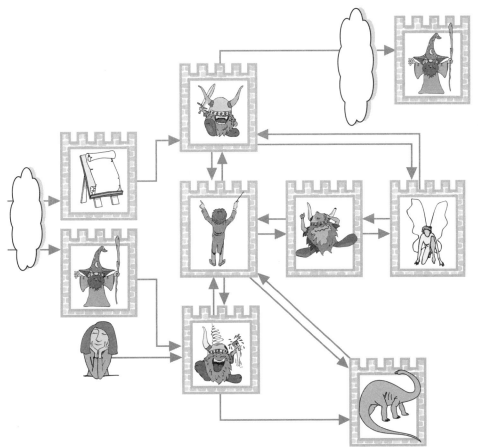

Figure P.3 The Enterprise as Seen from the Software Fortress Model

The software fortress model pushes simplification of the enterprise architecture further and further. As we use the model to decompose the enterprise, Figure P.3 becomes a series of collaborations, as shown in Figure P.4.

I will discuss what the software fortress model is throughout this book. For now, let's focus on why we need this model.

The most important reason for the software fortress model is so that we can better understand how our systems interact within our overall enterprise architecture. Even without knowing the details of how the software fortress model works, you can quickly get the sense that Figures P.3 and P.4 are a lot more approachable than Figure P.2.

We already have many good techniques for modeling software systems. The most prevalent is the Unified Modeling Language (UML). But existing systems, including UML, focus on the issues involved with designing software systems. They have little to offer the enterprise architect in modeling how the various software systems that make up the enterprise architecture relate to each other. In other words, they are fine for modeling a sales system, an inventory system, or an accounts payable system. They are not useful for showing how sales, inventory, and accounts payable systems need to work together to coordinate a customer purchase.

The software fortress model picks up where techniques like UML leave off. Or, to be more precise, UML picks up where the software fortress model leaves off. The software fortress model helps us describe and plan for the relationships between software systems. These relationships ultimately define the enterprise architecture. UML and related technologies can then be used to document how individual software systems are designed.

Who Cares about Software Fortresses?

The software fortress model has a lot to offer, especially for the high-level manager who is trying to understand the overall enterprise architecture, and for the enterprise architect who is trying to explain it.

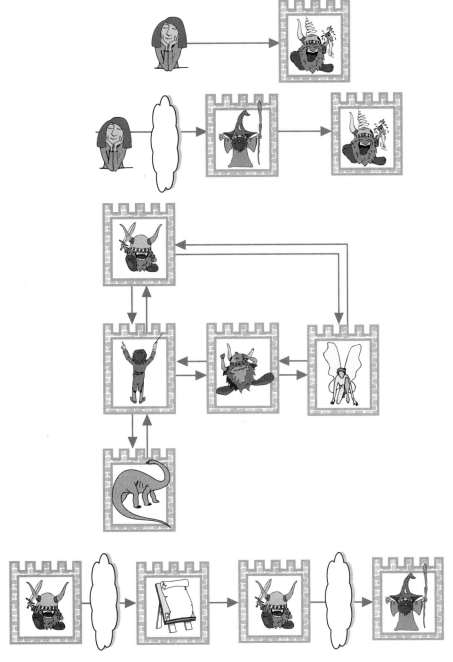

Figure P.4 The Enterprise as Fortress Collaborations

For CTOs, the software fortress model offers these immediate payoffs:

- It aligns technology boundaries with organizational boundaries within the enterprise.
- It provides an intellectual framework for modeling and managing the technical complexity of enterprise systems.
- It cleanly separates issues that *must* be decided at the enterprise level from those that *can* be decided at the local level.
- It is independent of technology and allows groups with different technology biases to discuss architectures using a common language.

Enterprise architects will appreciate the following additional benefits of the software fortress model:

- It cleanly defines *natural technical boundaries* across which autonomous groups can agree to disagree.
- It provides a methodology for achieving *interoperability* between software systems.
- It provides a methodology for defining *security* at the enterprise level.
- It provides an intellectual framework within which *different technologies can be meaningfully compared.*

But CTOs and enterprise architects are not the only ones who will gain from the software fortress model; this model has the power to transform the entire industry. For the first time, the entire industry will have a lingua franca for discussing enterprise applications. Customers and clients will be able to communicate readily with programmers and architects, Java programmers will be able to understand Visual Basic programmers, and architects from different business fields will be able to compare approaches to common problems.

Over time, the software fortress model will influence the software platforms themselves. Tools will appear to directly support the model. Platforms will evolve as the model exposes underlying platform weaknesses. New technological approaches will be explored as the model helps us better understand the needs of the enterprise.

Perhaps the most important contribution of the model is simplification: simplification of security, simplification of interoperability, and simplification of collaboration. Simple systems are inherently better than complex systems. They are cheaper to build, they are more reliable, and they are more secure. We can all get behind that.

The Goals of This Book

The software fortress model is still quite young, even by software standards. However, I have already presented the main ideas that make up this model to over 3,000 developers and conducted in-depth workshops with very high-level enterprise architects from many large companies. I have also introduced the ideas to the readership of the *ObjectWatch Newsletter*, which has more than 20,000 readers, including highly placed managers and architects at virtually all of the Fortune 500 companies.

The response to the software fortress model, even in its relative state of immaturity, has been overwhelming. Almost everybody who is exposed to the software fortress model feels a strong sense of resonance, as if this model addresses a very basic requirement at their organization: the requirement to model and simplify their enterprise.

This book is designed to meet an immediate need: to define, clarify, and explain the basics of this new approach to modeling large-enterprise software architectures. This approach will evolve, and I hope the evolution will be aided by a universal language for describing software fortresses and a universal approach to modeling them. Once we can all speak the same language, we can quickly start to learn from each other. One goal of this book is to provide this common language.

Who Should Read This Book

The software fortress model is not for everyone. If you are one of five developers working in a ten-person company, this modeling technique is overkill for anything you need to do. You don't need this methodology, and you don't need this book.

The software fortress model is for the enterprise. If you are one of a hundred or more developers, architects, or technical managers working in a large corporate IT organization, then this modeling technique will prove invaluable, and the language defined in this book will likely soon be used throughout your organization.

If you work in a large enterprise, even if you are not directly involved in defining software fortresses, it will be important that you are able to understand and contribute to discussions about them.

If you are a consultant advising large enterprises, the information in this book will be critical to you. Whether or not you believe in software fortresses will be unimportant, but you will need to be able to discuss them. You can be for them or against them, but you can't ignore them.

If you are a client paying the bill for a corporate system, the software fortress model is your best shot at making sure that software architects understand your needs and that developers implement systems you can use.

The History of the Software Fortress Model

As I look back over the last year, the time during which I formed the basic ideas of the software fortress model, I can see clearly several threads that came together to form this tapestry.

First, I have been teaching master's classes for enterprise software architects for most of the last decade. For a decade before that, I was heavily involved in building enterprise infrastructure technologies. During most of this time, I have been preaching a consistent message: The two major issues facing the enterprise are *interoperability* and *security*. I have been looking for a modeling methodology that would focus on these critical issues.

Second, I have always been interested in the modeling ideas that were known as *data silos*. Those ideas seem to capture a key idea of data ownership.

Third, the architectural ideas introduced by transaction processing monitors—namely, the three-tier architectural model—gave us some important clues to understanding what was needed to build highly scalable software systems. I have been working in the middle-tier technologies for many years now, and these ideas have been extrapolated into the software fortress model.

Fourth, Pat Helland of Microsoft has been proposing a model for autonomous computing. It is based on what he calls *software fiefdoms*, with *emissaries* linking together different fiefdoms. This model has been very influential on me, especially because it seems to capture the idea of systems working together to accomplish a higher goal. I will discuss Helland's ideas further in Chapter 10 (Internet Fortresses), where they are most relevant.

Fifth, the readers of the *ObjectWatch Newsletter*, now more than 20,000 strong, have read earlier drafts of my software fortress ideas and have written back with excellent insights.

Sixth, participants at my two-day workshop have added immeasurably to my understanding of software fortresses. I have been fortunate to work with very high-level enterprise architects, with many years of collective real-world experience in building large enterprise systems. These participants have contributed valuable insights.

Finally, I have had opportunities to present the software fortress ideas at perhaps a dozen conferences to over 3,000 enterprise architects in the last year. The feedback of my audiences has been tremendously helpful.

I am grateful to all of these sources for the insight each has contributed to the ideas discussed in this book. I am also grateful to you, the reader, who I hope will be helping to advance these ideas in the near future.

The Organization of This Book

Chapter 1 of this book is an introduction to software fortresses, discussing what they are, the terminologies we use to describe them, and how interfortress relationships work.

Chapter 2 is an overview of the various techniques we use to document fortresses, including fortress–ally–responsibility cards (based on class–responsibility–collaborator cards) and sequence–ally diagrams (based on UML's class sequence diagrams).

Chapter 3 gives an overview of transactional integrity. This is a background chapter needed to understand the many flavors of the word *transaction* and how different parts of software fortresses cooperate to coordinate their work.

Chapter 4 gives an overview of drawbridges. The two major subcategories of drawbridges, synchronous and asynchronous, are covered in more detail in Chapters 5 and 6, respectively.

Chapter 5 covers synchronous drawbridges, including component technologies on which they are based.

Chapter 6 covers asynchronous drawbridges, including the message queues on which they are based.

Chapter 7 discusses how security is implemented in software fortress architectures. It covers the two important aspects of security: keeping things out (wall technologies) and letting things in (guard technologies).

Chapter 8 discusses how software fortresses form partnerships and work together, through well-defined treaty relationships.

Chapter 9 gives a general overview of issues that are relevant to all fortress types.

Chapter 10 discusses the two Internet-connected fortresses: Web service fortresses, which accept programmatic requests over the Internet, and presentation fortresses, which interact with browsers.

Chapter 11 discusses the business application fortresses that run your mission-critical business systems.

Chapter 12 covers legacy, service, and treaty management fortresses.

Chapter 13 enumerates 25 important issues you should consider in a design review of a software fortress architecture.

Chapter 14 presents a software fortress architecture case study.

Chapter 15 gives a few (well, maybe more than a few) final thoughts on software fortresses.

Acknowledgments

I would like to thank the many people who have contributed to this book. I am especially grateful to my wife, Alice, and my children, Emily and Michael, for their support. Janet would like to thank her daughter Kate for her patience and smiles.

We would both still be half asleep if not for the continuous supply of marvelous macchiatos and luscious lattes made by the crew at our local Starbucks: Corey, Jo, Bert, Charlotte, Casey, Scott, Jay, Travis, and Z.

I have taught much of this material in one form or another to thousands of workshop participants. The discussion from these workshops has been tremendously helpful in refining these ideas. Thanks to all of the participants in these many workshops, and to the many more I hope to meet in the future.

This book has benefited from early reviews by some very talented and experienced individuals. I appreciate the feedback of the following people (company affiliations are included where allowed): Richard Campbell, Chris Corrado, Charles Erickson (VP of Development, WhisperWire), Stephen Fulcher (Principal, DeveloperLabs), Lynn Keele, Ruth Leuzinger (Senior IT Architect, Zurich Insurance Company, Switzerland), Don Pipkin, Ruben Prieto-Diaz, Carlos Recalde (Executive Director of Technology – Americas Region, KPMG. LLP), Stuart Sands (a Director of Technology Solutions at a major brokerage firm), and David L. Smith.

It has been great working with the staff at Addison-Wesley: Peter Gordon, Amy Fleischer, John Fuller, Bernard Gaffney, Karin Hansen, and unknown others. I am grateful for the careful attention of my copy editor, Stephanie Hiebert. After removing my many dangling modifiers, this book was greatly improved. (I know, I know . . . "Her removal of my many dangling modifiers greatly improved this book!")

Thanks to all of you.

—Roger Sessions
  Austin, Texas

About the Author

Roger Sessions is one of the world's leading experts in enterprise software architectures. He has extensive experience with Microsoft's .NET, OMG's CORBA, and Sun's J2EE platforms. He has written six books and dozens of articles, and he is a popular keynote speaker at conferences on enterprise software systems. He writes and publishes the *ObjectWatch Newsletter*, a widely read, highly regarded, and often hotly debated newsletter on high-end software technologies. His last book, *COM + and the Battle for the Middle Tier*, published by John Wiley & Sons, compared and contrasted Microsoft's COM + to Sun's EJB technologies.

From 1990 to 1995 Roger Sessions worked at IBM on the CORBA effort. He spent a year as a lead architect for the CORBA persistence service and four years as the lead architect for the object persistence portion of the IBM implementation of CORBA. His third book, *Object Persistence: Beyond Object-Oriented Databases*, was about the CORBA Persistence Service.

Roger Sessions started ObjectWatch, Inc., in 1995. His vision was to build a company dedicated to master's classes for enterprise software architects. ObjectWatch now has a worldwide reputation for its expertise in teaching how to build high-caliber enterprise systems. More than 50,000 people have attended his workshops in more than 30 countries.

About the Art Coordinator

Janet Van Sickler has been working as the ObjectWatch Executive Administrator and Chief Morale Officer for what appears to her to be an eternity. She is well known to readers of the *ObjectWatch Newsletter* as a personal analogy of many computer technologies. The most common question people ask her is how she puts up with

Roger Sessions and the constant abuse. She usually says that she puts up with it in return for her unlimited expense account at Starbucks. She is the mother of the incredibly adorable Kate Van Sickler.

About the *ObjectWatch Newsletter*

If you are interested in following future developments in the software fortress model, the starting point is to subscribe to the ObjectWatch Newsletter, the official publication of the software fortress movement. Past issues are kept at the ObjectWatch Web site (www.objectwatch.com). To subscribe, send an e-mail to sub@objectwatch.com, with a line of text giving your name and e-mail address, in this format:

    subscribe yourname, youre-mail

Enough background. Let's move on to the heart of the matter: the software fortress model.

Introduction

If you are one of those people who ignore prefaces and start with the first chapter, *not so fast*! Go back and start with the preface. It contains important background information.

If you have read the preface and you are still reading, you are probably doing so because you believe that your software IT structure is a mess. If it weren't a mess, you would have no reason for learning about software fortresses. The primary goal of the software fortress model is to bring order to the IT mess.

I have some good news for you. Your IT structure is probably not as bad as you think. One of the benefits of the software fortress model is that you have probably been following it fairly closely all along. You just haven't been following it closely enough. Hopefully the gap between where you are and where you need to go is not too big.

Let's see how close you are to following the software fortress model. Take the following quiz, answering *yes* for each statement that describes your situation, and *no* for each statement that does not apply to you. Every yes answer brings you one step closer to the model, but also one step closer to the need to be following the model with a little more rigor. Here's the quiz:

1. My company has dozens of disparate independently developed systems, some built, others purchased, yet others acquired through mergers. With some, we don't even know where they came from!

2. Our systems are interrelated in such complex ways that we have no way to even guess what the ramifications of a given system failure would be.

3. We often get into religious wars about technology. Some groups are committed to Java, others just as committed to Microsoft. Neither camp seems able to communicate with the other.

4. The departments within my company don't trust each other's work.

5. Our databases are a mess. Each department has its own databases, its own database administrators, and its own idea about how to manage database security.

6. My company worries about hooking up to the Internet. We have mission-critical and proprietary information that we are afraid somebody might steal and/or compromise.

7. We have legacy systems we depend on, but we are afraid to change many of them. Some we don't change because they are too fragile, some because they were purchased from companies no longer in business, some because the original developers have retired, and some because we have lost the source code.

Give yourself one point for each yes answer. How did you do? If you scored a 5 or higher, good news! You are already using many of the principles of software fortresses. Now you just need to add a few tweaks. The rest of this book is about those tweaks. So keep reading!

As you read through this book, you will notice a large number of acronyms and technical terms. Those that are part of the software fortress model are always defined in this book. But if you run into a term that is unfamiliar, whether from the software fortress model or elsewhere, use the glossary at the end of the book. The glossary includes every technical definition and acronym used in this book.

1.1 Definitions

The software fortress is the basis for the software fortress model, so I'll start by defining that:

Definition: Software Fortress

A *software fortress* is a conglomerate of software systems serving a common purpose and typically owned by a cohesive group of individuals. These software systems work together in a tight trust relationship to provide consistent and meaningful functionality to a hostile outside world.

As you can see, the definition of a software fortress includes both technical and organizational aspects. From the technical perspective the software fortress is a collection of systems. This collection can consist of many different types of software systems, including but not limited to processes, system services, component-packaged business logic, and databases.

From the organizational perspective, the software fortress encompasses people who work together, have a reasonably clear sense of what each other is doing, have a fair amount of trust in each other's systems, and are probably separated by no more than two levels of management (i.e., their managers all report to the same person). In my experience these people are often part of the same department. In some companies, the software fortress organization may consist of informal relationships. The personnel probably include developers, architects, managers, quality assurance specialists, deployment specialists, and often technical writers.

This book will look at the technical aspects of software fortresses. However, the political boundaries within the company should somewhat reflect the organizational boundaries of the software fortresses, at least at a given point in time. If you find yourself spending a great deal of time on unproductive squabbles, you probably have a misalignment between the organizational and technical boundaries.

Given this definition of a software fortress, we can now consider a software fortress architecture:

Definition: Software Fortress Architecture

A *software fortress architecture* is an enterprise architecture consisting of a series of self-contained, mutually suspicious, marginally cooperating software fortresses interacting through carefully crafted and meticulously managed treaty relationships.

Finally, we have the definition of the software fortress model:

Definition: Software Fortress Model

The *software fortress model* is a methodology consisting of specific algorithms, categories of technologies, and documentation techniques that together can be used to model and build enterprise systems as software fortress architectures.

As we will see, the software fortress model includes techniques for describing how systems interoperate, maintain proper trust relationships, and pass information back and forth. The model also gives strong clues about which technologies are appropriate to use for connecting software fortresses, which technologies are appropriate to use within the software fortress, and which technologies map well to specific fortress types.

1.2 Software Fortress Organization

A software fortress is not just a hypothetical concept. It is a specific, concrete collection of software systems that work together as an integrated whole within the organization. Pictorially, a software fortress looks like Figure 1.1. Let's examine the archetypical software fortress, as well as the various software fortress artifacts that are common to all software fortresses.

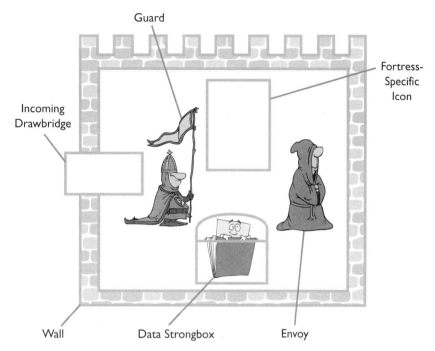

Figure 1.1 The Archetypical Software Fortress

The *walls* of the fortress are designed to prevent any communications from coming into the fortress except through approved channels. The approved channels are the *drawbridges*. The drawbridges are protected by *guards*, whose job it is to ensure that only approved communications are accepted from the untrusted outside world. *Envoys* prepare communications for other fortresses. A *data strongbox* represents a collection of persistent data that is used by the systems that make up the fortress.

A *fortress-specific icon* is used to indicate pictorially the general category of fortress under consideration. I will discuss the different categories later. The fortress-specific icon represents the *workers* inside the fortress that implement the internal fortress responsibilities—say, inventory control. The different fortress-specific icons that I use to represent workers are shown in Figure 1.2.

Figure 1.2 Fortress-Specific Icons

I will discuss what each of the icons in Figure 1.2 represents soon. For now, think of them as icons telling us what type of fortress we're looking at. These icons are just examples of what you might choose. If you like these specific icons, they are part of the Art Explosion collection by Nova Development Corporation (**www.novadevelopment.com**).

It is not important that you use the same icons I use, but it is helpful if you choose specific icons and stick with them. Such consistency will allow people in your organization to internalize a common pictographic shorthand. If everybody in your organization uses, say, Vikings, conductors, and fairies for business application, treaty management, and service fortresses, respectively, then you can put a slide up like the one shown in Figure 1.3, and everybody can quickly come to a common understanding of the picture.

Icons are used mainly to maximize the information content of your PowerPoint presentations and internal documents while still keeping

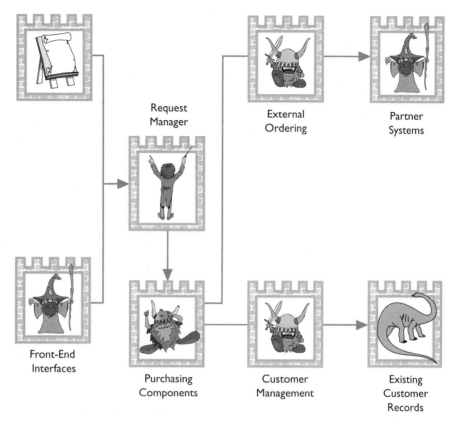

Figure 1.3 Sample Fortress Architecture

the material light and interesting. However, nobody expects you to draw fairies on a whiteboard. I will describe whiteboard-compatible documentation techniques in Chapter 2. For those of you who just can't stand a little beauty in your lives, feel free to ignore the icons completely and use only the whiteboard-compatible equivalents.

1.3 Typical Technologies

Although we're just scratching the surface of software fortresses, we can already discuss how some common technologies might be used within the software fortress architecture. Here are just a few obvious technology mappings. I will discuss them and others in detail later:

- Data strongboxes, the repositories of fortress data, are often implemented as physical databases, especially in business application fortresses.

- Workers inside the business application fortress are often implemented as distributed components.

- Walls, the parts of the fortress that keep out the riffraff, are often implemented with physical firewalls and/or operating system security services, such as access control lists (ACLs).

- Guards, the parts of the fortress that approve requests from the outside world, are often implemented through the use of cryptography APIs of whatever underlying operating system is used as the fortress foundation.

- Drawbridges, the channels through which outside communication passes, are often implemented through message queues.

It might be tempting to think of a fortress as an operating system process, a specific computer, or a physical location. None of these notions are correct. Fortresses often consist of multiple processes running on many machines distributed over a geographically disperse area.

1.4 The Fortress as a Trust Boundary

Above all, remember this: The fortress represents a trust boundary. This is the fundamental principle of software fortresses. The fortress represents not only a technical trust boundary, but usually an organizational trust boundary as well. Here I will focus on the technical idea of the trust boundary, formulated as the *trust rule*:

Definition: Trust Rule

Everybody inside a fortress trusts everybody else inside the fortress, and nobody inside the fortress trusts anybody outside the fortress.

The trust rule tells us that within a fortress there is complete trust, kind of a technical utopia. This concept is perhaps the most radical idea of the software fortress model. Consider, for example, a data strongbox implemented as a database. One implication of the trust rule is that the database applies no security at all to data update requests. No security at all! Can you believe it?

Actually it isn't quite that bad. It isn't that the database will have no security constraints, just that the constraints will serve only to ensure that update requests are coming from within the fortress. After convincing itself that a particular update request originated from within the fortress, the database will accept the request. No more questions asked.

This is not to say that we do not restrict who can update data. It is just that the database is not where we enforce the restrictions. But if not the database, then where?

In the software fortress model, security is the responsibility of four units working together. The wall keeps the hostile world at bay. The drawbridge allows controlled access from those few members of the outside world that this fortress is willing to trust. The guard makes sure that requests coming through the drawbridge are from authorized sources. And the envoy ensures that communications heading to other fortresses meet the security requirements of those fortresses' guards.

If the wall is doing its job, ultimately the guard controls access to the fortress. Once you gain access to the fortress interior, the trust rule says that you can access anything inside the fortress, including the database. With regard to database security, it isn't that we don't control who can access the database; it's just that we don't give the responsibility for controlling that access to the database. We give that responsibility to the guard.

This access control is applicable not only to the data strongbox, but to the different software systems within the fortress. If we have a software system in, say, a banking fortress that can take money out of your savings account, the scary truth is that *anybody* can withdraw money from your savings account. Anybody, that is, who can get past the guard.

Given that we place no security in either the database or the individual software systems within the fortress (other than ensuring that requests originate from within the fortress), you might expect the software fortress architecture to be inherently insecure. Not so. Security is a major focus of the software fortress model. The removal of security responsibilities from the individual entities doesn't weaken the overall security of the fortress; it actually strengthens security.

Security is strengthened because it is consolidated in a single location. If you think about it, you will realize that very few programmers have the knowledge needed to build a truly secure system. Database administrators think they know a lot about security, but in fact they know very little.

By making one well-defined entity within the software fortress responsible for security, you can consolidate your scarce security resources to the one spot that will benefit everybody in the fortress. The software fortress model tells you to invest your domain expertise in the business application implementations, your database expertise in the back-end data strongboxes, and your security expertise in the implementation of the guard.

Some people mistakenly think that this security model allows anybody from outside the fortress to do anything they want inside the fortress, once they have gotten past the guard. This idea is incorrect on many fronts. First, nobody from outside the fortress "gets inside" the fortress at all. Even the drawbridge request does not enter the fortress.

The only one who ever sees the outside request is the guard. The guard receives the request. The guard determines both the identity of the sender and what the sender wants to do. The guard then decides whether or not to allow that particular sender to make that particular request. If the guard accepts the request, the guard then makes its own request to workers inside the fortress. The request the workers see will be from the guard (or from other workers inside the fortress). Fortress workers never see the original request.

Obviously, getting the guards and walls right is critical to the well-being of the entire fortress. Chapter 7 (Guards and Walls) covers this topic.

1.5 The Main Fortress Types

There is a potentially endless variety of fortresses. Historically I have focused on five main types. At some recent workshops I have conducted, participants have reached a consensus that one more type would be useful, so now we are officially up to six. Some organizations may find it convenient to add types I have not considered. So don't consider this a final list, but rather a collection of software fortress patterns.

In any case, here is my current list of the six "standard" fortress types, along with the responsibilities of each and the abbreviations I use to refer to them throughout the book. I will give only an overview here:

1. **Business application fortress (BAF)**. Represented in my illustrations as the fuzzy Viking, the BAF is the most common fortress type. The BAF is the fortress that runs your business. When it is working hard, you are making money. When it is idle, you are not making money. Because no doubt you prefer to be making money rather than not making money, you want to make sure this fortress is capable of working as hard as possible. Typically the BAF runs transactions against high-end databases. An example of a business application fortress is inventory control.

2. **Treaty management fortress (TMF).** Represented in my illustrations as a conductor, the TMF is a fortress that manages relationships between other fortresses. These relationships are called treaties. I will explain the treaty concept shortly.

3. **Legacy fortress (LF)**. Represented in my illustrations as a dinosaur, the LF is a fortress that wraps a legacy system. Wrapping a legacy system allows that system to participate in the overall software fortress approach without your having to rewrite working, mission-critical systems.

4. **Presentation fortress (PF)**. Represented in my illustrations as an artist's drawing board, the PF is responsible for dealing with browser clients over the Internet. It accepts HTTP requests and delivers HTML-like responses. It does not run any business logic, but typically interacts closely with business application fortresses to fulfill client requests.

5. **Web service fortress (WSF)**. Represented in my illustrations as a wizard, the WSF is responsible for dealing with programmatic requests over the Internet. It accepts SOAP requests delivered over HTTP and delivers SOAP-style responses. Like the presentation fortress, it runs no business logic but has a fairly intimate relationship (for software fortresses!) with one or more back-end business application fortresses.

6. **Service fortress (SF)**. The SF is the most recent addition to the fortress collection. It is represented in my figures as a fairy and is a fortress that provides services to other fortresses. Such a service might be a wrapping around a standard operating system service, such as .NET's Active Directory, or it could be your own implementation of a service that several fortresses will need, such as a compensatory transaction manager.

Certain fortress types may overlap somewhat. A business application fortress might manage some simple treaties. A presentation fortress might contain some minor business application functionality, as long as that functionality has minimal security requirements. Treaty management fortresses often include service functionality.

1.6 Treaty Relationships

If an organization's overall architecture could be described as a single fortress, we wouldn't need the software fortress model. We could use simple three-tier (or N-tier) diagrams to explain our architecture. The reason we need the software fortress model is that enterprises are not monolithic. They have many software fortresses. It is the relationship between these different fortresses that we are trying to model and understand.

When one or more fortresses work together to accomplish a higher-level activity, we say that the fortresses are *allies* of each other. They coordinate their work through *treaty* relationships.

The fact that the cooperating fortresses are allies doesn't mean that they trust each other. They still communicate using drawbridges, and those communications are still closely monitored by guards. Other than the specific relationship defined by the treaty, the fortresses still consider each other hostile entities.

There are two types of treaties: simple and complex. A *simple treaty* can be implemented directly between two fortresses, with one fortress making requests to the other through an approved drawbridge channel. A common example is the treaty between a presentation and a business application fortress, allowing, say, Web clients to process banking transactions.

A *complex treaty* requires a treaty management fortress. A treaty management fortress may be required for any number of reasons. It may be required because many fortresses are involved in the treaty. For example, a customer order may require several business application fortresses to work together (one authorizing credit cards, another updating inventory, yet another processing the shipment). A treaty management fortress may be required because of incompatibilities in the ally drawbridges, such as one using Microsoft's MSMQ and the other using J2EE's RMI/IIOP.

Figure 1.4 pictorially differentiates between simple and complex treaties.

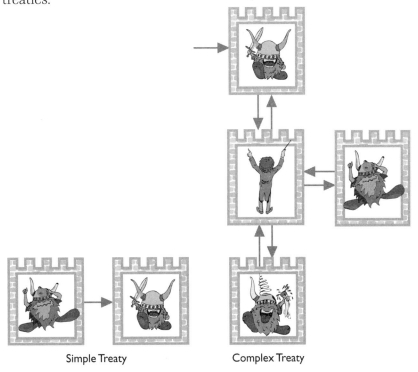

Simple Treaty   Complex Treaty

Figure 1.4 Simple versus Complex Treaties

1.7 The Fortress as a Unit of Interoperability

The software fortress is a natural unit of interoperability. Software fortresses are connected through drawbridges. Drawbridge technologies are independent of the technologies used inside fortresses. Drawbridges thus shield each fortress from technological decisions made by other fortresses, even when the fortresses have treaty relationships with each other. Organizations are therefore free to choose fortress technologies solely on the basis of the specific needs of the fortress for which they will be used.

Many organizations, for example, are debating between using Java and .NET technology. Each has strengths and weaknesses, yet Java and .NET do not play together well. Enterprise JavaBeans, for example, do not interoperate well with either COM + components or Microsoft presentation technologies. How does an organization choose between Java and .NET?

The answer is to use both. Use Java technologies where they make sense and .NET technologies where they make sense. I will discuss the advantages of each throughout the book. The important point here is that the choice between Java and .NET need not be made at the organizational level; it can be made at the fortress level. At the organizational level, choose drawbridge technologies that will connect to either Java or .NET fortresses. As long as the Java and .NET systems are encapsulated in a fortress architecture, interoperability becomes a matter of choosing appropriate drawbridges.

1.8 Objects, Components, and Fortresses

Considerable confusion exists in our industry on the relationship between objects and components. Throwing software fortresses into the fray, which share characteristics of both objects and components, is likely to add to the confusion. So let me take a moment to clarify how these three loosely connected ideas are related.

Objects are implementation details of a larger body of software. They are created with object-oriented programming languages, such as C# or Java. A typical program may be composed of hundreds or even thousands of interacting objects. Object interfaces are typically made up of many fine-grained methods. They run inside the process of their callers. Security is not an issue for objects.

Components are coarse-grained blobs of software that make up distributable units. They are created with some distributed-component technology, such as Enterprise JavaBeans. A typical distributed application may have several components working together. Component interfaces are typically made up of a small number of methods, each about the granularity of a tightly coupled transaction. They typically run outside the process of their callers. There are many security options for components, but the overall security *model* for components is undefined.

Fortresses are entire systems, each probably consisting of several fully functional applications. They are built according to the principles of the software fortress model. The equivalent of an interface for a fortress is a drawbridge. Drawbridges usually have only one allowable request, and that request is of a granularity coarse enough that probably several tightly coupled transactions will be required to fulfill it. The security model is highly defined for fortresses, making extensive use of walls to keep requests out and guards to let requests in.

Figure 1.5 pictorially shows how objects, components, and fortresses are related.

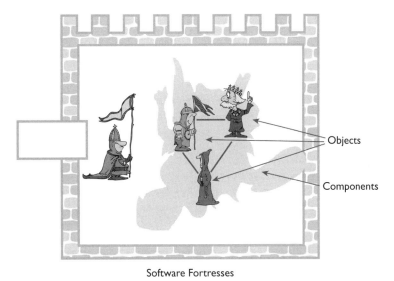

Software Fortresses

Figure 1.5 Objects, Components, and Software Fortresses

Summary

I said at the beginning of this chapter that you are probably already using something close to a software fortress architecture. I even had you take a quiz to prove it. Let's go back and score your yes answers.

1. If, in the quiz, you said that your systems are developed independently, this is exactly how software fortresses are built. You just need to learn to apply some design discipline to this independence.

2. If you said that your systems are interrelated in complex ways, then I have good news. This is the assumption of the software fortress model. You just need to start thinking of the interrelationships as treaties among allies, apply a little methodology, and start making better choices about how you connect these systems.

3. If you said that your organization often gets into religious wars about technologies, perfect! The software fortress model gives permission for people to disagree.

4. If you said that departments within your organization don't trust each other—for technical, political, or organizational reasons—then you are well on your way to understanding the basic trust boundaries that form the heart of the software fortress architecture.

5. If you said that your databases are not coordinated at the enterprise level, no problem. In the software fortress model, we *expect* each fortress to be responsible for the organization, maintenance, and administration of its own data strongbox.

6. If you said that you are concerned about connecting your systems to the Internet, you are well on your way to understanding why we are so careful to separate the functionality of a presentation fortress from that of a business application fortress.

7. If you said that you have critical legacy systems that you don't want to touch, voilà! Welcome to the world of the legacy fortress!

The major points you should remember from this chapter are these:

- The software fortress is a trust boundary of like systems developed by a cohesive group of individuals, kind of an atomic unit of trusted processing.

- The software fortress architecture builds enterprise systems as a collection of software fortresses held together in treaty relationships.

- All software fortresses have walls, guards, drawbridges, and data strongboxes. If they send messages to other fortresses, they have envoys as well.

- The main fortress types (at least so far) are presentation, Web service, business application, legacy, treaty management, and service fortresses.

- Fortresses are quite different from either objects or components.

Now we're ready to start looking at software fortresses in more detail.

Diagramming Software Fortresses

Up to now I have been using an informal documentation style consisting primarily of cartoon characters. These work for high-level presentations of the PowerPoint variety, but as we move into serious discussions at the architect level, we need something a little more formal. In this chapter I'll present the main documentation techniques I have found helpful in describing software fortress architectures.

My philosophy in choosing documentation techniques has been to borrow wherever possible from existing techniques, especially UML, adapting them as little as possible to make them work for software fortresses.

2.1 Basic Software Fortress Diagram

The basic picture of a software fortress is somewhat similar to the UML class diagram. The software fortress version uses a double-lined box to indicate the fortress itself. Drawbridges are indicated either by single-lined boxes or, in some diagrams, by labeled arrows entering the fortress. Rather than use a cartoon figure to indicate the type of the fortress (such as the Viking to represent the business application fortress), I give the name of the fortress followed by a double colon followed by the fortress type (e.g., presentation).

Several features are conspicuously missing from the fortress diagram. For example, there is no diagrammatic counterpart to the guard, the envoy, or the strongbox, all of which are assumed to be present. Unlike a UML class diagram, the fortress diagram does not include

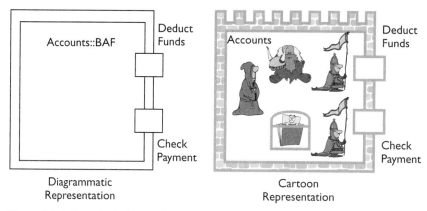

Figure 2.1 A Sample Software Fortress Diagram

the interface to the fortress. The interface to the fortress is equivalent to the drawbridge, which, at the fortress level, is complex enough to require a specialized documentation technique, which I will discuss shortly.

Figure 2.1 shows a diagrammatic representation of a business application fortress, contrasting it to its cartoon counterpart.

2.2 Fortress–Ally Diagram

A single fortress by itself is not very interesting. It is the relationship between fortresses that defines the enterprise architecture. A *fortress–ally diagram* (*FAD*) shows all of the enterprise fortresses and the ally relationships between them. Figure 2.2 shows an example of a FAD for a bill payment system.

The important features of a FAD are as follows:

■ Each fortress should be identified with a name and a type in the format name::type so that the appropriate fortress overview can be consulted for more detail.

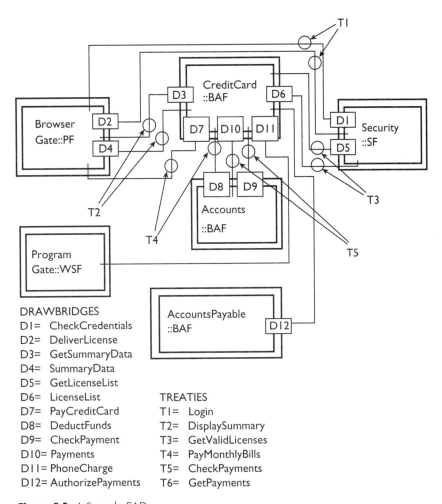

DRAWBRIDGES

D1= CheckCredentials
D2= DeliverLicense
D3= GetSummaryData
D4= SummaryData
D5= GetLicenseList
D6= LicenseList
D7= PayCreditCard
D8= DeductFunds
D9= CheckPayment
D10= Payments
D11= PhoneCharge
D12= AuthorizePayments

TREATIES

T1= Login
T2= DisplaySummary
T3= GetValidLicenses
T4= PayMonthlyBills
T5= CheckPayments
T6= GetPayments

Figure 2.2 A Sample FAD

- Each drawbridge should be identified (with either labeled arrows or boxes) so that the appropriate drawbridge overview can be consulted for more detail.

- Each treaty should be identified so that the appropriate treaty overview can be consulted for more detail.

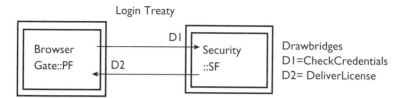

Figure 2.3 A TAD for the Login Treaty

2.3 Treaty–Ally Diagram

Usually the entire enterprise architecture is a bit much to digest at once. If we take a subset of the architecture showing only those fortresses involved in a particular treaty, the FAD reduces to a *treaty–ally diagram* (*TAD*). A TAD is easier to work with than a full FAD. The TAD in Figure 2.3 diagrams one of the treaties (Login) from Figure 2.2.

2.4 Sequence–Ally Diagram

FADs and TADs are good for getting a high-level view of fortress relationships. They do not go into detail about the sequence of events that link fortresses as a treaty unfolds. To see better how the allied fortresses coordinate their workflow to fulfill the overall treaty requirements, we use a *sequence–ally diagram* (*SAD*).

SADs are adaptations of the UML construct called class sequence diagrams. A SAD gives an overview of a single treaty. In a SAD, the heading of the card gives the name of the treaty. Within the treaty, each ally fortress is represented by a vertical line. Interactions between the fortresses are shown with one of three arrows, following conventions similar to those used in UML's class sequence diagrams. Full solid arrowheads show use of a synchronous drawbridge. Full hollow arrowheads show a synchronous drawbridge returning information. Half solid arrowheads show use of an asynchronous drawbridge. Underneath each arrow is the name of the gate.

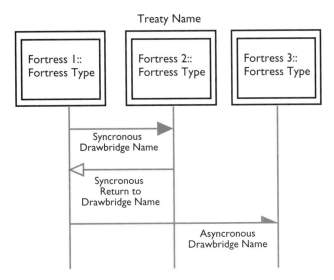

Figure 2.4 Prototype of a SAD

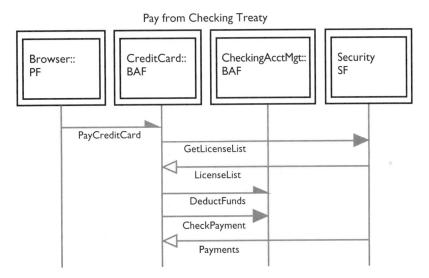

Figure 2.5 A Sample SAD

Figure 2.4 shows a prototype of a SAD; Figure 2.5, an example. For now, don't worry about the details of synchronicity versus asynchronicity. I will cover that distinction in detail in coming chapters.

2.5 Fortress–Ally–Responsibility Cards

Sometimes all the labeled drawbridges and fortresses in a TAD can seem daunting. You may feel that you just want to hold a treaty in the palm of your hand, literally. That is the time for *fortress–ally–responsibility (FAR) cards*. FAR cards are a way of boiling down the fortress relationships to the most essential details.

FAR cards are an adaptation of a design technique called *class–responsibility–collaborator (CRC) cards*. CRC cards were first described at an OOPSLA (Object-Oriented Programming, Systems, Languages, and Applications) conference by Ward Cunningham and Kent Beck in 1989, and they became popularized most notably by Rebecca Wirfs-Brock, Brian Wilkerson, and Lauren Wiener in their book *Designing Object-Oriented Software* (1990, Prentice Hall). CRC cards, though more than a decade old, have aged gracefully. I have used them in my past life as an object-oriented designer; as a fortress architect, I find that their adaptation as FAR cards works equally well.

FAR cards are even more low-tech than whiteboards. They use only two pieces of hardware: 3×5 cards and pencils. If you're unfamiliar with this particular hardware combination, think of a 3×5 card as a small computer monitor and a pencil as a keyboard. I have noticed two significant advantages of 3×5 cards over monitors: (1) They are small (3 inches by 5 inches, coincidentally). (2) They seem to have an amazingly long battery life. In fact, I have never seen a 3×5 card run out of power, even after years of storage.

A given FAR card tells us three things about a fortress:

1. The name and type of the fortress
2. The responsibilities of the fortress
3. The allies with which the fortress must collaborate to fulfill its responsibilities

Figure 2.6 shows a prototype of a FAR card; Figure 2.7, an example. The top region of the FAR card tells the name and type of the fortress (in pseudo-UML syntax). One line for each major responsibility of

Fortress Name::Fortress Type	
Responsibility 1	Ally 1
Responsibility 2	
Responsibility 3	Ally 2
Responsibility 4	

Figure 2.6 Prototype of a FAR Card

Accounts::BAF	
Manage Checking Accounts	
Deduct Payments for Credit Cards	
Check Payments	Credit Card

Figure 2.7 A Sample FAR Card

that fortress follows. To the right of the responsibility block is the ally block, where all the allies that this fortress must rely on to fulfill its responsibilities are listed. Responsibilities are grouped by ally, and double lines separate ally blocks.

A FAR card provides a good overview of a particular fortress and its allies. FAR cards are particularly useful for helping fortress architects remember what commitments they have made to others.

2.6 Treaty–Ally–Responsibility Cards

When treaties are very simple (one fortress interacting with one other, no intermediaries, no third parties), FAR cards may be all that are necessary to provide an architecture overview. In many real-life

Treaty Name	
Ally 1	Responsibility 1
Ally 2	Responsibility 2

Figure 2.8 Prototype of a TAR Card

Treaty::PayCreditCard	
Browser Gate	Collect Information from Browser
Credit Card	Process Payment Request

Figure 2.9 A Sample TAR Card

scenarios, however, the overall treaties that define the enterprise architecture are more complex. In these cases you may find yourself chaining together a large sequence of FAR cards to get a good architectural overview. Those itty-bitty tables at Starbucks (where else would one do an architectural review?) may not have enough room for the entire treaty, if diagrammed exclusively with FAR cards.

When you need more than two or three FAR cards to keep track of all the treaty responsibilities, it is probably time to switch to *treaty-ally–responsibility (TAR) cards*. Like FAR cards, TAR cards are small and concise. But whereas FAR cards are fortress centric, TAR cards are treaty centric. TAR cards provide an overview of exactly which fortresses are part of which treaties and what the responsibilities of those fortresses are.

Figure 2.8 shows a prototype of a TAR card; Figure 2.9, an example.

2.7 Fortress Overview Document

A *fortress overview document (FOD)* is a detailed description of a specific fortress, including any information that a fortress outsider might find helpful to know, such as information about the data strongbox, the drawbridges, the high-level algorithms that the fortress implements, and the major technologies that are used inside the fortress. The FOD does not include implementation details of the fortress. It is used primarily to communicate information to people outside the fortress.

2.8 Treaty Overview Document

A *treaty overview document* (*TOD*) is a detailed description of a specific treaty that includes any information that a participant in the treaty might need to know, such as sequences of fortress interactions, security requirements, transactional expectations, and asynchronous versus synchronous messaging. A TOD does not include information about the fortresses themselves. It focuses on describing how the fortresses work together.

Summary

Confused by all the acronyms? Don't forget the glossary!

Don't feel that you need to use all of these techniques. Just use the documentation techniques that work well for you, feeling free to invent others. Here is a reminder of the techniques that I find useful:

- FAD (fortress–ally diagram), which shows all of the enterprise fortresses and their allies with drawbridges and treaties labeled.
- TAD (treaty–ally diagram), which shows the subset of a FAD that is relevant to a particular treaty.
- SAD (sequence–ally diagram), which shows the sequence of interactions between fortresses necessary to implement a particular treaty.
- FAR card (fortress–ally–responsibility card), which shows, for a given fortress, all of its responsibilities and the allies with which it collaborates directly.
- TAR card (treaty–ally–responsibility card), which shows, for a given treaty, all of the participating fortresses and the responsibilities each has in relationship to this treaty.
- FOD (fortress overview document), which gives a detailed look at a fortress from an outsider's perspective.
- TOD (treaty overview document), which gives a detailed look at a treaty from the perspective of a fortress participant.

CHAPTER 3

Transactions

One of the issues we run into when differentiating among different technologies used in software fortress architectures is transactions. So before I look too closely at software fortresses, I will spend some time on transaction basics.

According to Microsoft's Encarta computer dictionary, a *transaction* is "a discrete activity within a computer system, such as an entry of a customer order." This is an overly simplistic definition, making a transaction sound like little more than a read request to a disk drive. Transactions are much more important and a lot more complex than Microsoft's Encarta, or even most database folks, would have you believe.

Transactions come in three standard varieties: (1) tightly coupled single-resource, (2) tightly coupled multiple-resource, and (3) loosely coupled multiple-resource. These three varieties differ in how they coordinate updates across different transactionally aware resources.

3.1 Transactionally Aware Resources

A *transactionally aware resource* is a system with all of these characteristics:

- It can accept some update requests.
- It can group a collection of update requests into a set, called a *transaction*.

- It can guarantee that when processing a transaction's worth of update requests, either the entire transaction collection is processed or none of the transaction collection is processed.

- It can guarantee that, once that transaction has been processed, there is no likely scenario under which any of the updates included in the transaction will be lost.

The most common transactionally aware resource is a database. We'll run into other transactionally aware resources shortly, but for now I'll limit my discussion to databases.

3.2 Tightly Coupled Single-Resource Transactions

I'll start with the simplest transaction variety, the tightly coupled single-resource transaction. Because all single-resource transactions are tightly coupled, I'll simplify the terminology by calling them *single-resource transactions*. Let me take you through a typical single-resource transaction involving a database.

Consider writing an application to withdraw money from a checking account. Let's say that "withdrawing money from a checking account" means the following:

1. Finding the specific account record in the CheckingAccount table.
2. Reading the CurrentBalance field.
3. Deducting the amount from the current balance.
4. Logging the withdrawal in a Logging table.

Imagine the problems that would be caused by any of the following events:

- We read the balance from the account record, but before we have a chance to deduct the withdrawal amount, the account is closed by another program.

- We deduct the amount from the current balance, but we are unable to log the withdrawal in the Logging table.

- We log the withdrawal, but we are unable to deduct the amount.

This is just a sample of the things that can go wrong. When all of these updates are heading toward a single transactionally aware resource (i.e., a database), the resource itself can prevent any of these scenarios.

With a transactionally aware resource, we can enclose all of these withdrawal database activities inside a single transaction. We can then ask the database to process that transaction as a whole. The database will then process either all or none of the transaction updates. The database gets to choose which. Further, the database guarantees that if it does process the entire transaction, it will do so without consistency errors (such as the account being closed after the balance has been read) and without any chance of losing the updates after the fact (say, because the disk drive happened to choose that inopportune moment to disintegrate).

How the database makes these guarantees is a secret known only to the database. We don't care. We care only about deciding which updates to bunch together into the transaction and about letting the database know where the transaction boundary begins and ends.

Several techniques are available for letting the database know about the transaction boundaries, but most use some transaction boundary-marking APIs, such as BeginTransaction and Commit (the standard name for EndTransaction). Any database updates issued after BeginTransaction and before EndTransaction are assumed to be part of the same transaction collection. The checking account system then looks something like this:

1. Issue a BeginTransaction request.
2. Issue a Read request to get the CurrentBalance field from the appropriate account record.
3. Do whatever programming is necessary to update the account balance.
4. Issue an Update request to the database to store the new account balance.
5. Issue an Append request to the database to log the withdrawal in the Logging table.
6. Issue a Commit request, signaling to the database that you have reached the end of the transaction.

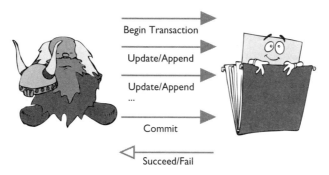

Begin Transaction

Update/Append

Update/Append
...

Commit

Succeed/Fail

Figure 3.1 Flow in a Tightly Coupled Single-Resource Transaction

Once the database knows that the transaction has been concluded, it will attempt to apply all of the Update and Append requests en masse. If, by some horrible chance, the database concludes that one or more of the updates or appends is impossible, it will toss out the whole collection and notify you, giving you time to drown your sorrows at the local pub or take other appropriate remedial action.

Figure 3.1 illustrates the flow in a tightly coupled single-resource transaction.

3.3 Multiple-Resource Transactions

The next degree of complexity enters when updates span more than one transactionally aware resource. Going back to the checking account example, imagine that the Logging table is in Database A and the rest of the tables are in Database B. Neither database can now guarantee that all of the updates can be done en masse. Database A can guarantee that its updates are done (or not done), but it has no idea what Database B's opinion is on the subject. Database B is equally ignorant about how Database A feels about the situation.

When we have updates spanning two different transactionally aware resources, we have what I call a *multiple-resource transaction*. There are two types of multiple-resource transactions: tightly coupled and loosely coupled.

3.3.1 Loosely Coupled Multiple-Resource Transactions

In a *loosely coupled multiple-resource transaction*, we are willing to give the transactionally aware resources (databases) a bit of slack and "loosen up" on our expectations of the transaction guarantee.

Here is our compromise: as long as all of the updates to Database A are tightly coupled *and* all of the updates to Database B are tightly coupled, *and* as long as we can figure out a protocol for the software systems using Databases A and B to let each other know whether or not their respective transactions succeeded, then, *and only then*, we are willing to live with a decoupling (or loosening) of Database A's collection of updates from Database B's collection of updates.

In other words, we are willing to allow the possibility that Database A's collection of updates will succeed and Database B's collection will fail, or vice versa, *as long as* the failing systems using those databases let the other systems know of their failures (or even better, of their successes).

Figure 3.2 illustrates the flow in a loosely coupled multiple-resource transaction.

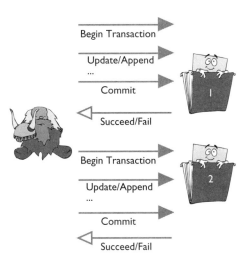

Figure 3.2 Flow in a Loosely Coupled Multiple-Resource Transaction

3.3.2 Tightly Coupled Multiple-Resource Transactions

There are two problems with loosely coupled multiple-resource transactions.

First, they have no standard protocol for the software systems to brag back and forth about their successes or commiserate about their failures (at least, as of press time). So guess who gets to design this protocol? You!

Second, imagine you are the system using Database A. Your transaction succeeds. Your buddy system, the one using Database B, is not so lucky. Its transaction fails. Your buddy sends you the bad news. Now what? Given that you have already completed your updates, what are you supposed to do about it? Good question!

Both of these problems can be solved if instead of using a loosely coupled multiple-resource transaction, we go with a tightly coupled multiple-resource transaction.

In a *tightly coupled multiple-resource transaction*, even though we know we are sending updates to two different resources, we still want the updates coordinated. We expect the underlying infrastructure to come up with some way of doing so.

The transaction is tightly coupled, meaning that all the updates must be treated as a single tightly coupled collection, with all being done or none being done (exactly the same semantics as we expected from the single-resource transaction). The updates to Database A are thus tightly coupled to those of Database B, even though Databases A and B are (obviously) different databases.

To achieve this tight transactional coordination across multiple resources, we need to involve a third party. This third party is usually referred to as the *distributed transaction coordinator*, affectionately known as *DTC*.

DTC's algorithms were first introduced by the technologies we know as *transaction processing monitors* (*TPMs*). In the IBM space, this functionality is contained within WebSphere. Within the Microsoft space, this functionality is part of MS DTC (you can guess what this acronym stands for).

3.4 The Distributed Transaction Coordinator

To represent DTC, I use a cartoon figure of a wise woman in a Zen meditative state who sees everything happening around her and is not distracted by the flotsam of life. You need this kind of focus to implement DTC's demanding algorithms. Meet DTC in Figure 3.3.

DTC manages the tightly coupled multiple-resource transaction by creating a higher-level supertransaction that oversees transactions at the resource (database) level.

From a software system perspective, tightly coupled multiple-resource transactions using DTC look identical to tightly coupled single-resource transactions. In both cases, we issue a BeginTransaction request, a bunch of Update requests, and a Commit request. Then, magically, either the entire bunch is processed or none of the bunch is processed. However, to coordinate the transaction across the various databases, DTC takes a direct role in managing the transaction.

DTC can find herself in any of four states, each with different algorithmic responsibilities. Her states, and the conditions under which she moves from one to the other, are as follows.

The first state is the *sleep* state. This is DTC's default state. Vacation state. The state she stays in when there is nothing better for her to do.

When somebody issues the BeginTransaction request, DTC transitions from the sleep state to the *meditative* state. In the meditative state she starts paying attention to which databases are getting Update requests. When she notices a database—say, Database A—getting its first Update request, she makes a mental note that Database A is

Distributed Transaction Coordinator
(DTC)

Figure 3.3 Introducing DTC, the Distributed Transaction Coordinator

part of this transaction. This is when she needs her full Zen focusing powers. If even one database update sneaks past her, the whole algorithm will fall apart.

When we issue the Commit request, DTC transitions from the meditative state to the *consensus* state. She assumes that the transaction has concluded and starts trying to achieve consensus among the involved databases as to whether the transaction should be accepted or rejected in its entirety. To do this, she asks each database in turn if it would be willing to accept its portion of the updates. Each database gives her an answer but holds its updates in a state of limbo until hearing further from DTC.

When DTC gets an answer from the last database that had been part of this transaction, she transitions from the consensus state into the *final* state. What she does in the final state depends on the answers she got from the various databases in the consensus state. If they all indicated a willingness to accept the updates, she goes back to each database and tells each to "commit" the changes. If any database in the consensus state indicated an unwillingness, or even a mild trepidation, about accepting its updates, then in this final state DTC tells all the databases to forget the whole deal and discard their update requests.

When DTC has told the last database what to do, she transitions from the final state back into the sleep state. DTC's state transitions are shown in Figure 3.4.

You might think that DTC has the last word in transactional coordination, combining the best capabilities of single-resource transactions (tight coordination) with the best capabilities of multiple-resource transactions (no restrictions as to the number of players). For all her charm, however, DTC has her own set of problems.

Her first problem is communication. She needs to know how to chat with the databases. If she can't have the discussions with the databases that are required in the consensus and final states, she can't orchestrate this algorithm. Her ability to coordinate is dependent, therefore, not just on her willingness to work with the databases, but on the databases' willingness to work with her.

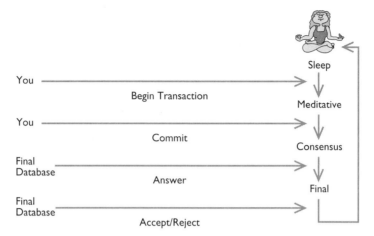

Figure 3.4 DTC's States

DTC's second problem is performance. She needs not just to communicate with the databases, but to communicate frequently. Even worse, most of this communication requires synchronous protocols. The dependence on synchronous communication protocols means that the rest of the world (including the rest of the databases that DTC is coordinating) is blocked, waiting for her expensive communications to complete.

To see the relative cost of the three approaches to transactions—tightly coupled single-resource, loosely coupled multiple-resource, and tightly coupled multiple-resource—consider the checking account update described in this chapter. Remember, this example involved a balance read, a balance update, and an activity log. I'll consider three cases. In Case 1, shown as a SAD (sequence–ally diagram) in Figure 3.5, both accounts and activity logs exist in a single database (single resource, tightly coupled). In Case 2, shown as a SAD in Figure 3.6, accounts and activity logs are separated into two loosely coupled databases. In Case 3, shown as a SAD in Figure 3.7, accounts and activity logs again are separated into two databases, but now the databases are tightly coupled, so DTC is involved.

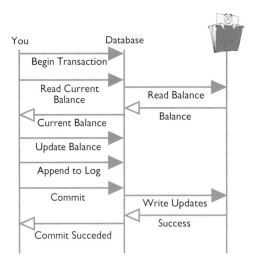

Figure 3.5 SAD for a Tightly Coupled Single-Resource Transaction

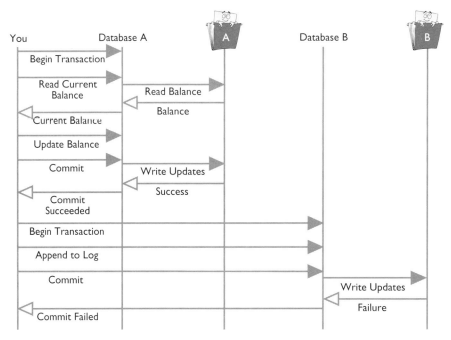

Figure 3.6 SAD for a Loosely Coupled Multiple-Resource Transaction

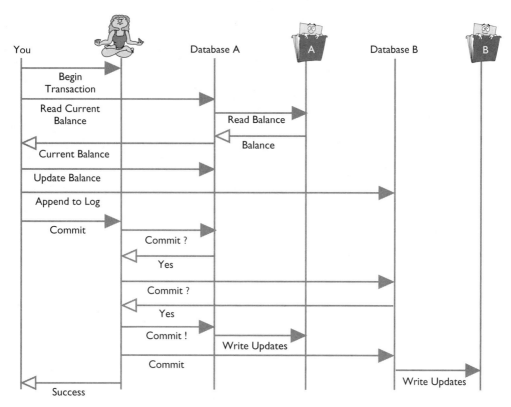

Figure 3.7 SAD for a Tightly Coupled Multiple-Resource Transaction

The SADs for the three types of transactions show how much more communication is required for the tightly coupled multiple-resource case. The SADs also show how much of that additional communication is synchronous. It's pretty SAD.

Summary

This chapter may seem to have very little to do with software fortresses. In fact, however, transactional coordination is a major issue for software fortresses. Different technologies have different support for different flavors of transactions. The support that these technologies offer for transactions often influences our choice of which technologies to use in which fortress situations.

In a business application fortress, for example, it is important to be able to coordinate the work of different entities within a single, tightly coupled transaction, even when each of those entities is updating different transactional resources. Therefore, for a business application fortress we need intrafortress communication technologies that support tightly coupled multiple-resource transactions.

The main points of this chapter are these:

- A transaction is a way of grouping together access requests to transactionally aware resources.

- A transactionally aware resource is something that knows how to accept groups of updates and how to guarantee that those updates are done or not done en masse. A transactionally aware resource is often described simply as a transactional resource.

- Tightly coupled single-resource transactions encompass only a single transactional resource.

- Loosely coupled multiple-resource transactions encompass more than one transactional resource, but they do not attempt to coordinate their transactional updates across resources, although each individual resource coordinates its part of the transaction.

- Tightly coupled multiple-resource transactions encompass more than one transactional resource and are coordinated across all of the transactional resources. These types of transactions require the help of a distributed transaction coordinator (DTC).

This chapter has introduced the fundamentals of transactions. I will expand on these basic concepts throughout the rest of the book.

CHAPTER 4

Drawbridges

Drawbridges are the information pipeline for the enterprise architecture. They are the basis for fortress interoperability. They carry messages from one fortress to another.

Many companies treat drawbridges as second-class citizens that take a back seat to the higher-profile fortress technologies. For example, I have seen many companies worry ad nauseam about whether to use J2EE or .NET for a particular software fortress, a decision that has relatively little long-term impact. The same companies then spend very little time worrying about their drawbridge technologies, even though bad choices here have serious long-term ramifications on the overall enterprise architecture. Drawbridge choices affect not only interoperability, but also scalability, reliability, security, transaction support, and overall system responsiveness.

In this chapter I give an overview of drawbridges. I will discuss the different types of drawbridges in more detail, as well as how to choose among them, in Chapters 5 and 6.

As always, if you find yourself having trouble with specific terms or acronyms, refer to the glossary.

4.1 Drawbridge Overview

A drawbridge is a gateway into a fortress. A drawbridge allows something outside of the fortress to pass information into the fortress. I call a unit of information that passes over a drawbridge an *infogram*.

The drawbridge specification defines both the format of the info-grams and the protocol used for their delivery. An infogram is a complete and self-contained information packet that meets the format and protocol requirements of a specific drawbridge.

Because what is outside the fortress is in a different process than anything inside the fortress (for trust boundary requirements, if nothing else), we can assume that a drawbridge will require some form of interprocess communication. Depending on the drawbridge technology, an infogram could take the form of a remote method invocation, a text string delivered over a message queue, or a SOAP call over HTTP, all of which are forms of interprocess communication. We would not expect to see an object method invocation used for a drawbridge because object method invocations are strictly intraprocess.

A fortress may have multiple drawbridges. In Figure 4.1, for example, a business application fortress can accept infograms from either a presentation fortress or another business application fortress, with drawbridges designed to meet the specific needs of each fortress.

Infograms must come from somewhere, and usually that somewhere is an envoy in another fortress. The envoy, remember, is the specific fortress entity responsible for placing infograms on the drawbridge for delivery to the ally fortress. I refer to the fortress that is creating and sending the infogram as the *donor* fortress and the one receiving the infogram as the *recipient* fortress.

I use the term *homogeneous* to describe a situation in which both the donor and the recipient fortresses are on a common technology base (such as both .NET) and *heterogeneous* to describe a situation in which the two fortresses are on different technology bases (such as one on .NET and the other on J2EE).

It is helpful to know whether we are facing a homogeneous or heterogeneous situation because we can optimize our drawbridges in the homogeneous case. However, this optimization is usually not worth forcing both software fortresses to use a common technology. It is merely an optimization that we can apply opportunistically when we happen to find ourselves in a homogeneous situation.

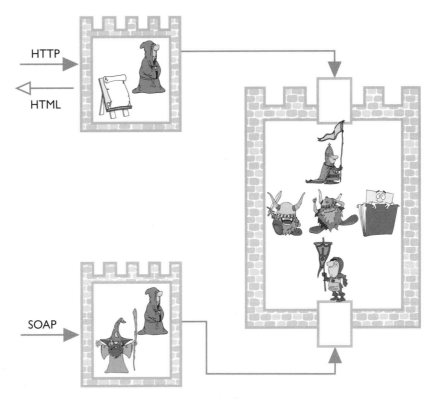

Figure 4.1 One Fortress with Two Drawbridges

Some people advocate designing all drawbridges for the heterogeneous situation, assuming that these drawbridges can be used for
new treaty relationships in the future. In my experience, recipient
drawbridges are usually hardwired for only one treaty relationship,
and it is not common that more than one donor fortress will be sending infograms through a single drawbridge. Should an existing fortress
need to accommodate a new treaty, it will likely need a new drawbridge for that new treaty relationship, and that drawbridge can be
optimized at that time. This situation is depicted in Figure 4.2.

Although I often talk about a message being received into a fortress,
in fact messages from outside the fortress never pass the guard. I will
talk more about guard implementations in Chapter 7 (Guards and

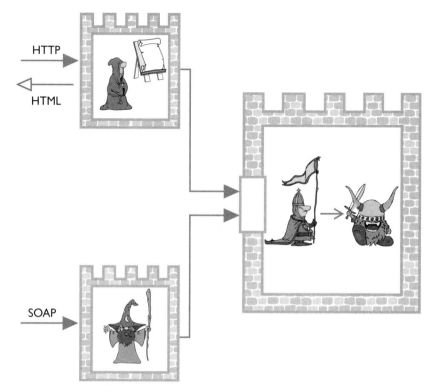

Figure 4.2 An Unlikely Scenario

Walls). For now, assume that the infogram flow will go through the following typical sequence, as illustrated in Figure 4.3:

1. The infogram is created by the envoy of the donor fortress. In Figure 4.3 the donor fortress is a business application fortress.

2. The infogram is sent to a compatible drawbridge in the recipient fortress, which in this case is also a business application fortress.

3. The infogram is received by the recipient fortress guard.

4. The guard is highly suspicious and subjects the infogram to stringent security tests.

5. The guard decides that the infogram is from a trusted source, and that it meets all other security requirements.

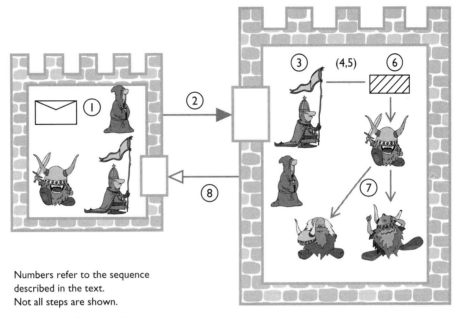

Numbers refer to the sequence
described in the text.
Not all steps are shown.

Figure 4.3 Infogram Flow

6. The guard pulls apart the infogram and transforms it into a
   form that is useful within the fortress. Because the fortress in
   Figure 4.3 is a business application fortress, a reasonable internal
   form might be a distributed component method invocation,
   à la COM+ or Enterprise JavaBeans.

7. Information passes freely within the fortress without further
   need for security analysis until the fortress has fully processed
   the infogram.

8. If the recipient fortress needs to communicate back to the
   donor fortress, it does so through one of the donor fortress's
   drawbridges.

An infogram is therefore a packet of data that is intended for interfortress communication. It is targeted at the guard and usually does
not correspond to data formats used within the fortress.

There is no standard for infograms, either for the format of the information they carry or for the communications protocols over which

that information is delivered. However, there are some general categories of drawbridges, each with, if not a standard for infograms, at least some strong hints about the nature of the infograms they will accept. I will discuss these categories in Chapters 5 and 6.

Drawbridges can be either synchronous (blocking) or asynchronous (nonblocking), and either heterogeneous (connecting fortresses with different technologies) or homogeneous (connecting fortresses with the same technology). Because these characteristics are independent of each other, we can theoretically have four basic types of drawbridges: heterogeneous synchronous, homogeneous synchronous, heterogeneous asynchronous, and homogeneous asynchronous. In Chapters 5 and 6 I will cover synchronous and asynchronous drawbridges, respectively.

Summary

The information in this chapter is relevant for both synchronous and asynchronous drawbridges. Here are the main points:

- Drawbridges are gateways into fortresses.
- Drawbridges can be either synchronous or asynchronous.
- Infograms are packets of information passing over the drawbridge.
- Infograms are created by envoys and received by guards.

CHAPTER 5

Synchronous Drawbridges

In a *synchronous drawbridge*, the donor fortress is blocked until the infogram has been received by the recipient fortress *and* the recipient fortress guard has sent a reply back to the donor. In fact, however, the donor fortress is probably not totally blocked. The donor fortress is most likely doing a lot of work for many different users. But at least the particular instance of the envoy process assigned to handle this particular infogram of the donor fortress is blocked, as are possibly some workers waiting on that particular envoy.

5.1 Components

The standard synchronous drawbridge technologies are all based on component technology. Component technology is somewhat based on object-oriented technology. Let me start, then, by giving the briefest of introductions to object-oriented technology as it applies to component technology.

An *object* is a little blob of software functionality that can do something for you if you know how to ask. A request to an object to do something is referred to as a *method invocation*. Theoretically, an object has an interface. That *interface* defines what, exactly, you can ask the object to do, how you must ask, and what, if anything, the object will return in response. In reality, most object-oriented languages support but do not require interface definitions for objects. For the purpose of this discussion, I will assume that all objects are defined by interfaces.

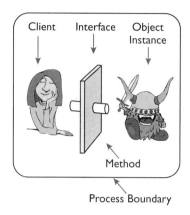

Figure 5.1 Client–Object Relationship

Figure 5.1 shows the relationship between the client (you) and the object instance.

A given interface definition can have many implementations. A specific interface implementation is called a *class*. You can actually write code knowing only what interface you're using and having no idea what implementation class you're using. You can do this because the object-oriented system chooses an appropriate class (implementation) at runtime to serve as the recipient of the method invocation.

The ability to define one interface, implement it many times, and then have the system choose the most appropriate of those implementations on the basis of clever heuristics goes by the term *polymorphic method resolution*. Polymorphic method resolution is the basis for framework architectures and is therefore an important feature of object-oriented programming languages.

Components are a lot like classes; each component is an implementation of an interface. The interface implemented by a component is called a *component interface*. Like their object-oriented counterparts, component systems typically support polymorphic method resolution. The blob of software on which you can make requests, analogous to an object, is a *component instance*. The requests are described as *method invocations*.

So what's the difference between objects and components? They sure look alike. There is really only one major technical difference.

Objects always reside within the process from which they are called. Components do not. You can probably sense why I'm so interested in components. One process is making requests of another process. It sounds a lot like the makings of a drawbridge, doesn't it? But I'm getting a little ahead of myself.

How do you communicate to a component in a far-off process? Either you need to have a lot of knowledge about communicating over distributed protocols (not likely), or you need to have something in your process that communicates on your behalf. That something is called a *component surrogate* because it is a local surrogate for a component that is really someplace else, in a different process. Some people prefer the term *proxy* to *surrogate*.

The far-off process in which the component instance really lives is called the *component process*. The component process also needs help with communication. Its helper is called a *client surrogate* because it is a surrogate for something (you) that is actually in another process (your process, the client process).

Figure 5.2 shows the relationship connecting the client (you), the two surrogates, the component interface, and the component instance. Technically this relationship is known as remote method invocation (RMI). If you have used remote procedure calls (RPCs), this will all look familiar. You might think of components as remote procedures plus polymorphic method resolution.

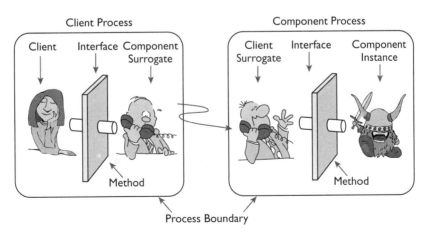

Figure 5.2 Client–Component Communications

Figure 5.3 RMI Implementation of a Drawbridge

The client of a component can be almost anything, including another component instance. If the client were another component instance, we could naively implement a drawbridge directly as a remote method invocation. Figure 5.3 illustrates such an implementation.

There are two things wrong with this naive implementation of a drawbridge as a remote method. The first is that we are missing the guard function on the recipient side. No guard, no security! The donor fortress may have a high opinion of itself, but the recipient fortress should be more cautious. The second thing wrong is that if the recipient fortress returns any information to the donor fortress (as would be normal in a component method invocation), there is no security in that direction either.

Does all this seem overly paranoid to you? Probably, but paranoia is a good trait when we are dealing with software fortresses. Without any guard function, we have many opportunities for a miscreant, represented here by Bart the bad guy, to stick his nose where it doesn't belong. Figure 5.4 shows some of the ways that Bart might try to take advantage of this unguarded system.

Unguarded fortresses may not be as vulnerable as they seem. Some synchronous drawbridge protocols have built-in guard and/or wall functionality. In general, drawbridge protocols that have such

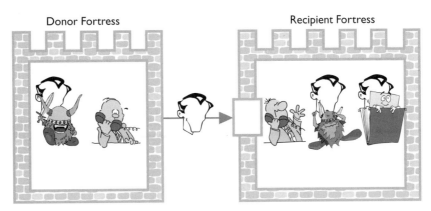

Figure 5.4 Points of Vulnerability in an Unguarded Fortress

built-in functionality fall into the category of *homogeneous synchronous drawbridges*. Drawbridge protocols that, at least today, have little or no built-in guard and/or wall functionality generally fall into the category of *heterogeneous synchronous drawbridges*. I will discuss these two drawbridge types in Sections 5.2 and 5.3, respectively.

A fully secure architecture should use a guard for all incoming communications. This is true even when that incoming information is being returned as a result of an outgoing synchronous request. When fortresses are connected through synchronous drawbridges, the guard of the receiving fortress is effectively an envoy of the return information, and the envoy of the donor fortress is also effectively a guard when that result returns.

Here, then, is my preferred architecture for all synchronous drawbridges: The donor fortress uses the envoy half of an envoy/guard to post the infogram to the recipient fortress. The recipient fortress receives the message with the guard part of an envoy/guard. When it is ready to respond, it uses the envoy part of the envoy/guard to do so. The responding infogram is received by the guard part of the envoy/guard in the original donor fortress. This arrangement allows both the original infogram and the responding infogram to be subjected to whatever security inspections are deemed necessary. This configuration, without the surrogates, is shown in Figure 5.5.

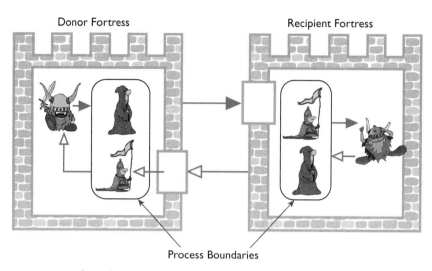

Donor Fortress   Recipient Fortress

Process Boundaries

Figure 5.5 Preferred Security Configuration for Synchronous Drawbridges

5.2 Homogeneous Synchronous Drawbridges

A homogeneous synchronous drawbridge is designed to connect two fortresses, both built on similar technology bases (e.g., both .NET or both WebSphere). In contrast, heterogeneous synchronous drawbridges allow any two fortresses to work together, whether they are on similar technologies or not. Why, then, should we bother with homogeneous synchronous bridges at all?

Homogeneous synchronous bridges have two redeeming features that make them worth considering. First, homogeneous synchronous bridges are faster than heterogeneous synchronous bridges. Second, at least today, they have more built-in functionality, especially in the security area.

The reason they are faster is that they are hardwired to the underlying component model. Remember that all modern synchronous drawbridges are based on remote method invocations on components. When the donor and recipient fortresses are using the same component model, both the infogram and the transport protocol can be optimized for the component technology of the two fortresses (say, .NET).

When both fortresses are built on a J2EE system (such as WebSphere), the homogeneous synchronous drawbridge usually uses a variant of RMI/IIOP (pronounced "RMI over IIOP"). RMI stands for Remote Method Invocation. IIOP stands for Internet Inter-ORB Protocol. (ORB, by the way, stands for object request broker.) IIOP is the old CORBA (Common Object Request Broker Architecture) component protocol. It is owned by the OMG (Object Management Group).

The fact that RMI and IIOP appear together in the same term suggests a relationship between the J2EE and CORBA protocols. And in fact there is—at least a political relationship. Originally, the Java-Sun folks came up with their own component protocol, which they called simply RMI. As originally conceived, RMI had nothing to do with CORBA. However, Sun was also a leading member of the OMG, which was officially pushing the CORBA IIOP protocol. The fact that the OMG-Sun folks were advocating one protocol and the Java-Sun folks were advocating another was quite embarrassing to all involved. Eventually these two protocols came together in a shotgun marriage orchestrated primarily by IBM. The combined protocol was called RMI/IIOP.

RMI/IIOP was supposed to be a Java standard that could link together any two Java vendors, and even Java and CORBA vendors. In fact, however, each vendor evolved its own proprietary version of RMI/IIOP, and the modern perspective is that two different Java vendors are no more homogeneous than a Java vendor and Microsoft are. If you need to synchronously link two or more fortresses that are built with different Java implementations (say, WebSphere and WebLogic), I recommend that you link them using heterogeneous synchronous drawbridges, which I will cover in Section 5.3.

The major competition to RMI/IIOP in the homogeneous synchronous drawbridge space is Microsoft. Microsoft really has two homogeneous synchronous drawbridge technologies. The older technology is known as DCOM (for Distributed Component Object Model, whatever that means!). The newer technology is known as .NET Remote Binary Protocol, which does not seem to have, as yet, attached itself to an acronym. (I know, it's hard to imagine Microsoft passing up an acronym opportunity!)

Homogeneous synchronous drawbridges have three unique capabilities not found today in heterogeneous synchronous drawbridges:

1. Autosecurity
2. Instance management
3. Transaction flow

Autosecurity refers to the ability of the system to automatically provide some security features administratively. Because this capability is more relevant to the discussions of guards and walls, I will cover autosecurity in Chapter 7 (Guards and Walls).

Instance management refers to the ability of the system to provide for the sharing of component instances (and the resources they require) among many clients. This capability can be useful if your architecture makes extensive use of rich clients. Fortress architectures are less likely to use rich clients, favoring instead thin clients, so I won't be covering instance management in this book.

Transaction flow refers to the ability to carry a transactional context across process boundaries. From a fortress perspective, this means that work done by the donor fortress can be transactionally coordinated with work done by the recipient fortress.

As I pointed out in Chapter 3 (Transactions), there are three types of transactions: (1) tightly coupled single-resource, (2) tightly coupled multiple-resource, and (3) loosely coupled multiple-resource. Transaction flow across drawbridges is most relevant to tightly coupled multiple-resource transactions. Loosely coupled multiple-resource transactions can also be coordinated across a homogeneous synchronous drawbridge, but transactional flow is not relevant to this type of coordination today, although this may change in the future. For now, you will be doing any loosely coupled coordination yourself. I will discuss the coordination of loosely coupled multiple-resource transactions in Section 12.2.4, on loosely coupled transaction managers.

Figure 5.6 shows a tightly coupled multiple-resource transaction crossing a homogeneous synchronous drawbridge. As discussed in Chapter 3, DTC (the distributed transaction coordinator) is managing the overall transaction coordination.

Distribution Transaction Coordinator (DTC)

Figure 5.6 Tightly Coupled Multiple-Resource Transaction Crossing a Homogeneous Synchronous Drawbridge

All homogeneous synchronous drawbridge technologies allow you to flow the transaction from fortress to fortress. However, just the fact that you *can* flow a transaction across fortresses does not mean that you *should*. The problem with flowing transactions across fortresses has to do with the relationship between database locks and trust boundaries.

To guarantee consistent updates, databases use database locks extensively. Database locks prevent users from updating records until those record updates can be done safely—in other words, until existing transactions already accessing those records have completed.

When the transaction spans fortresses, one fortress is forced to hold onto its database locks until the other fortress is ready to complete its transaction. Unfortunately, this means that the donor fortress is at least partially blocked until the recipient fortress completes its updates.

This is a violation of the basic trust rule, the rule that states you trust your fortressmates and nobody else. In particular, you never allow anybody outside your fortress to dictate how long you will hold database locks, and you can't have tightly coupled transactions across fortresses without holding locks. Ergo, we don't like transactions across fortresses.

This is not to say that flowing transactions across distributed components is a bad idea. In fact, that capability is used extensively inside fortresses, a topic I will discuss further in Chapter 11 (Business Application Fortresses). It is fine to have components blocked on other components, as long as those two components are in the same fortress and therefore, by definition, trust each other. So transaction flow *within* a fortress is fine. Transaction flow *across* fortresses is a no-no.

You might think that I am against the use of homogeneous synchronous drawbridges. After all, their built-in security offers nothing at the drawbridge level. Their instance management is useful only for rich clients. Their ability to flow transactions is a violation of the trust rule. What's left?

One thing that's left is speed. If response time is your name, then homogeneous synchronous drawbridges are your game. But do be careful here. Speed is generally overrated. *What* you do is usually more important than how fast you do it. If the recipient fortress is going to do any substantial amount of work (and if it isn't, you have a poor software fortress architecture), then even relatively slow drawbridge traversal times will usually be white noise in the background. Speed usually doesn't matter as much as size—at least, the size of the workload.

The autosecurity features should also not be dismissed lightly. They may have little to offer at the drawbridge level, but they have quite a bit to offer in constructing guards and walls. I will come back to that topic in Chapter 7 (Guards and Walls).

5.3 Heterogeneous Synchronous Drawbridges

Heterogeneous synchronous drawbridges differ from their homogeneous cousins in that they are designed to link fortresses built on different technology bases—for example, .NET and WebSphere.

Many organizations standardize on heterogeneous synchronous drawbridges because such drawbridges can accommodate requests from both homogeneous and heterogeneous fortresses, or even from fortresses outside the organization. I usually do not recommend standardizing all drawbridges as heterogeneous. The homogeneous performance optimization is worth using, where you can. As far as external fortresses go, you will never accept an external request through a heterogeneous synchronous drawbridge. Instead you will insist that such requests go through a Web service fortress, a topic I will discuss in Chapter 10 (Internet Fortresses).

To improve your understanding of the technology underpinning the heterogeneous synchronous bridges, it is helpful to spend a moment thinking about why homogeneous synchronous drawbridge technologies fail in the heterogeneous world. Remember that all synchronous drawbridges (both homogeneous and heterogeneous) are based on component systems. The homogeneous flavor is based on proprietary protocols, such as .NET Remote Binary Protocol or Java RMI/IIOP.

The proprietary remote method invocation protocols are what make heterogeneous systems incompatible. Most people assume that the incompatibility is caused by incompatibility of the platforms themselves (e.g., .NET or WebSphere). In reality, the vast majority of the .NET and WebLogic platforms have nothing whatsoever to do with remote method invocation.

There are only two "features" of the .NET and WebLogic platforms that prevent clients on one platform from communicating with components on the other. One is the mapping algorithm that the two surrogates use to map back and forth between byte arrays and method or return values. The second is the communications protocols used by the two surrogates to transfer those byte strings.

The momentum toward agreement in the industry as to both the mapping/unmapping algorithm and the transport protocol is building. The mapping/unmapping algorithm is called SOAP. SOAP originally stood for Simple Object Access Protocol, a rather odd acronym, given that SOAP is anything but simple, has nothing whatsoever to do with objects, and is not an access protocol. SOAP defines the standard mapping between component method requests and a very specific kind of byte array: XML strings. The communications protocol on which the industry has settled for moving the XML string from surrogate to surrogate is HTTP.

HTTP may seem like an odd choice for a communications protocol, given that it was originally intended (and is still largely used) to carry requests from browsers to Web servers for HTML pages. But HTTP requests and HTML pages are both just strings, like XML. Because HTTP is good at carrying strings, it was seen as a reasonable candidate for carrying SOAP requests and replies—just another kind of string.

Two features of HTTP made it attractive as a likely SOAP communications protocol. One is the fact that it is widely supported by Web servers. The other is that most firewalls, the membranes protecting enterprises from the Internet, are configured to be HTTP permeable.

Ironically, neither the ubiquitous Web server HTTP support nor the firewall permeability has, as yet, turned out to be particularly useful to SOAP applications. The Web server support has fizzled because generally the servers that process standard HTTP requests are not the same as those that process SOAP/HTTP requests. The firewall permeability has fizzled because despite the industry propaganda, very few SOAP requests *need* to cross a firewall.

Why don't SOAP requests typically need to cross a firewall? SOAP/HTTP needs to cross a firewall when a request needs to cross the protective membrane of the enterprise. In other words, SOAP usually crosses a firewall only when it is being used for *inter*company collaboration (in which case, it will probably cross not just one, but two, firewalls).

In the real world, few companies are using SOAP/HTTP for intercompany collaboration. Most companies have a much more pressing need than intercompany collaboration—that is, *intra*company collaboration. Intracompany collaboration is the business of the heterogeneous synchronous drawbridge. In my experience, this is the most important use of SOAP today—not for allowing companies to talk together, but for allowing a company to talk to itself. The other use of SOAP, intercompany communication, is a topic that I will cover in Chapter 10 (Internet Fortresses).

Summary

In this chapter I have covered the basics of synchronous draw-bridges, which are sometimes referred to as blocking drawbridges. Here are the most important points to remember about synchronous drawbridges:

- They can be optimized for the homogeneous case. Homogeneous synchronous drawbridges use native component protocols.

- They can also be designed for the heterogeneous case. Heterogeneous synchronous drawbridges are usually based on SOAP messages delivered over HTTP.

- The same SOAP/HTTP that is used for heterogeneous synchronous drawbridges is the basis for intercompany collaboration, a topic I consider to be a Web service fortress.

- Homogeneous synchronous drawbridges can support transaction flow across drawbridges. You should not use this feature.

CHAPTER 6

Asynchronous Drawbridges

You might think that most interfortress communication would occur across synchronous drawbridges. What is there not to love about synchronicity? It is the world of immediate gratification. You want an answer, you get an answer. But it turns out that, at least in the fortress world, patience pays. Asynchronicity has many benefits, but it does require a mind shift. That's the goal of this chapter: to shift your mind.

The history of *asynchronous drawbridges* is quite different from that of synchronous drawbridges.

Synchronous drawbridges, as I discussed in Chapter 5, are all based on component technology. In that discussion, components were seen as just one part of a larger software platform, whether it was WebSphere, WebLogic, or .NET. It should be no surprise, therefore, that synchronous drawbridges favor the homogeneous (single-platform) world.

Asynchronous drawbridges evolved differently. They are based on message queues. Message queues have been around for a long time, although they are underappreciated by today's developers, most of whom grew up in an object-oriented culture. Objects are the ultimate in immediate gratification: They live in your process, and they do what you want them to do when you want them to do it.

Unlike components, message queues were intended, from the very beginning, to be *independent* of the underlying software platform. Thus it is not a coincidence that whereas synchronous drawbridges, with their component heritage, favor the homogeneous case, asynchronous drawbridges, with their message queue heritage, favor the heterogeneous case.

Most large enterprises do not standardize on a single technology platform. Therefore the more flexible heterogeneous communications technologies are more important for most organizations than are the relatively limited homogeneous communications technologies. For this reason, if for no other, we will want to pay close attention to asynchronous drawbridges.

Just to make sure we are "in sync" on asynchronicity, let me review the basics. Assume that a donor and a recipient fortress are connected by an asynchronous drawbridge. When the donor wants to communicate with the recipient, it creates an infogram. For an asynchronous drawbridge, the infogram takes the form of a message queue message. The donor now sends the infogram to the recipient.

The fact that the drawbridge is asynchronous has at least three implications. First, the donor does not know when the recipient will get the message and therefore does not know when the recipient will start the requested workload. Second, if multiple messages are being sent, the donor does not know the order in which they will be delivered. Third, the donor does not expect any information to be returned from the recipient.

6.1 Message Queues

As I have said, message queues are the basis for asynchronous drawbridges. This situation is changing, but that's where we are today. So an overview of message queues is a good starting point for understanding asynchronous drawbridges.

A *message queue* is like a postal service. Someone puts messages into a receiving mailbox. Someone else takes them out of a delivery mailbox. Messages are not sent to a person, but rather to a specific delivery mailbox. Anybody who can access that mailbox can receive the message. How the postal service chooses to route the message from one mailbox to the other is not your problem. You care only that when you send a message, somehow it gets there.

Whereas a message queue overall is like a postal system, an individual queue is like a mailbox. Queues have names that uniquely identify them, and when we send or remove messages, we do so to specific named queues, just as we send and receive mail to and from specific mailboxes. In the software fortress architecture, a named queue typically maps to a specific drawbridge used to connect two fortresses.

The time required to deliver a queued message is indeterminate for two reasons. First, like the postal service, the message queue doesn't make any guarantee about how long it will take to move messages from one end to the other. Second, even if the queue has the message ready for delivery, it has no authority over when that message will be read. Just as the postal service cannot force you to check your mailbox, the message queue cannot force you to check for queued messages.

6.2 Implementation of Asynchronous Drawbridges

Knowing that asynchronous drawbridges use message queues is only part of the problem. We still have to decide on these issues:

- On the donor fortress side, what, exactly, will be technically responsible for inserting messages into the queue?
- How will other workers inside the donor fortress communicate with the message inserter?
- On the recipient fortress side, what, exactly, will be technically responsible for receiving the message? We know a guard will receive the message (because the message is being transferred across a trust boundary), but how will that guard be implemented?
- How will other workers inside the recipient fortress receive their marching orders from the guard?

On the donor side, the envoy deals with the message queue. The envoy acts as a single exit point that deals with all the ugly details

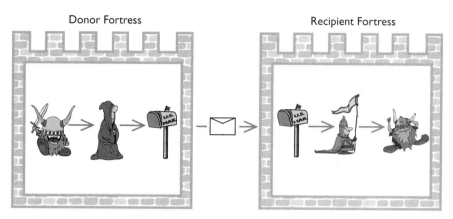

Figure 6.1 Asynchronous Drawbridge Architecture

of formatting the infogram, setting up any security requirements, and handling error conditions. This architecture is shown in Figure 6.1.

When a subsystem within the donor fortress needs to communicate with the recipient fortress, that subsystem makes a request of the envoy. The envoy is built in an appropriate native (for that fortress) technology, and requests to the envoy use native communications. If the donor is a business application fortress built on .NET, the envoy will probably be either a COM+ component or a .NET class, and the internal communications to that envoy will probably be transported via the .NET Remote Binary Protocol or a variant of RMI/IIOP.

On the recipient fortress side, the guard is often implemented as a dedicated process, one whose only purpose is to execute a tight loop in which it waits for a message to appear on the queue, grabs the message, and passes it on to a guard component. If the recipient fortress is a business application fortress, the guard process will probably invoke a component-style method on the guard component. The guard component will check the message for appropriate security clearance, tease out its data, and repackage it for consumption by other business components inside the fortress.

6.3 **Persistence and Transactions in Queues**

Queues can be configured as persistent or transient. A *persistent queue* is stored on disk and is therefore protected against system failure. A *transient queue* is not protected against failure, but because it requires no disk access, it can run faster. I assume that persistent queues will be the norm for drawbridges. Drawbridges are a lot like databases; we almost always trade performance for reliability.

Queues can also be configured as transactional or nontransactional. A *transactional queue* acts as a transactional resource. A *nontransactional queue* does not. I talked about transactional resources back in Chapter 3 (Transactions), but let me give a brief refresher here. A transactional resource is a system that knows how to converse with DTC (the distributed transaction coordinator), and thereby participate in what, in Chapter 3, I called a *tightly coupled multiple-resource* transaction.

A tightly coupled multiple-resource transaction has special characteristics when one of the transactional resources is a database acting as a data strongbox and the other is a message queue acting as a drawbridge. Consider a business component inside the donor fortress that first updates its data strongbox and then makes a work request of another fortress. The following sequence occurs:

1. The business component starts a new transaction. This transaction is intercepted by DTC (as discussed in Chapter 3), who goes into her meditative phase.

2. The business component updates the strongbox. DTC notices the update.

3. The business component makes an envoy request. The transaction flows to the envoy, meaning that any work the envoy does will be done within the same transaction as the work done by the business component.

4. The envoy creates an infogram and places it in the drawbridge (message queue). DTC notices that a message has been placed in the queue.

5. The envoy receives confirmation from the message queue that the message has been received.

6. The envoy returns control to the business component.

7. The business component commits the transaction, letting DTC know that the end transaction boundary has been reached. DTC enters the consensus phase.

At the end of this sequence, DTC is ready to coordinate the transaction between two transactionally aware resources: the database (representing the data strongbox) and the message queue (representing the drawbridge).

DTC now asks both the database and the message queue (all of the transactional resources that she noticed when she was in the meditative state) whether they are willing to accept the updates that each of them has received during this transaction.

When DTC gets an answer from the last resource (either the database or the message queue; we don't know the order in which she will ask), she switches to the final state. If both the database and the message queue were willing to "commit" to commit, then in the final state, she tells them to go ahead and do the commit. If either is unwilling to commit to commit, she tells them both to forget it.

All transactionally aware resources know how to process the Commit request. This is part of the requirement of being a transactionally aware resource. However, the resources can decide for themselves what it means to commit. The database interprets a Commit request as a request to process the transaction in an all-or-nothing fashion.

The message queue interprets the Commit request differently. If the message queue is asked to insert a message, then *commit* means accepting the message and "guaranteeing" delivery. As I mentioned earlier, however, the message queue can't really guarantee delivery. All that it can guarantee is that it will hold the message for delivery until somebody (namely, the recipient guard) gets around to reading the message.

Suppose DTC decides that she can't safely commit the transaction—for example, because the donor strongbox, in a grumpy mood, refuses to commit to commit. What does she do with the message queue? She says to forget it. "Forget it," in formal lingo, is known as a rollback.

When a message queue is told to roll back, it ejects the message. This means that the drawbridge is returned to the state it was in before the infogram was inserted. If the recipient guard were to check for a message after a rollback, it would find none.

If the message queue is asked to deliver a message, as would be the case on the recipient fortress side, then *commit* means "giving up" the message and *rollback* means taking the message back into the message queue. When a message queue rolls back, it is as if the guard never read the message in the first place. The next time the guard method loop executes, it will find the very same message waiting patiently.

An odd transactional relationship exists between the workloads in the donor and the recipient fortresses. Each fortress works within its own independent transaction, but the two transactions are related. The first (donor) transaction coordinates the work done by the donor fortress with the placement of the infogram into the drawbridge. The second (recipient) transaction coordinates the receipt of the infogram by the recipient fortress with the work that the recipient fortress needs to do to fulfill that request. These relationships are shown in Figure 6.2.

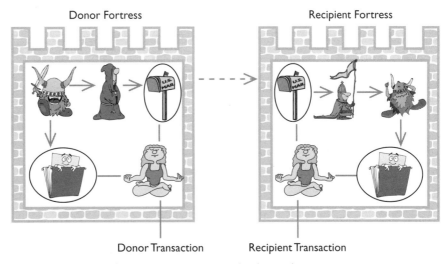

Figure 6.2 Donor and Recipient Transactional Relationships

The donor and recipient transactions are related to each other in two ways. The first relationship is one of sequence. The recipient transaction cannot begin until the donor transaction has committed because the infogram is not really placed into the message queue until then.

The second relationship is one of a loose guarantee. The fact that the drawbridge is a transactional resource more or less guarantees that either both the donor and the recipient transactions will commit or neither of them will. What is somewhat remarkable is that this coordination occurs without DTC. She is needed to coordinate each transaction individually, but she is not needed to coordinate the two together.

To see how this works, let's consider the possibility that the donor transaction fails. We won't worry about a business failure (e.g., insufficient balance to make the withdrawal), but a failure because either the message queue (drawbridge) or the database (strongbox) declines to make the commitment to commit. In this case, both the drawbridge and the strongbox will be told by DTC to roll back. If this happens, the message will be ejected and not delivered. When the recipient guard looks for a message, it won't be there, and nothing will happen in the recipient fortress. So both transactions will effectively fail—the first because it is rolled back, and the second because it never starts.

Now let's consider the possibility that the donor transaction succeeds but the recipient transaction fails, again because either its strongbox or its drawbridge declines to commit to commit. In this case, both the recipient strongbox and the drawbridge will roll back. When the drawbridge rolls back, the message will be sucked back into the message queue.

At this point the donor transaction has committed (it must have, or the recipient guard never would have seen the infogram), but the recipient transaction has rolled back. Notice that even in this scenario, we have a loose guarantee of transaction coordination between the donor and recipient fortresses because even though the recipient has rolled back, the infogram is still in the drawbridge. The next time the guard checks, it will still be there. If the recipient transaction fails again, then once again the infogram is sucked back into the drawbridge. In theory, sooner or later whatever is causing the problem (probably the strongbox, since strongboxes cause most transactional problems in this world) will relent and the transaction will succeed.

In practice, the recipient transaction may still fail. Failure could result for two reasons. First, if the recipient transaction failed repeatedly, sooner or later the message queue underneath the drawbridge would lose interest in the message and move the erstwhile infogram to a limbo no-man's-land. The second way the transaction could fail is that the recipient fortress could, in its business logic, decide to discard the request and still commit the transaction.

In this case the drawbridge would consider its duty to deliver the infogram as having been fulfilled. So the coupling of the donor and recipient transactions is loose in the sense that the system will do its best to accomplish both or neither transaction, but it can't make an absolute guarantee in the same way that DTC can when she has full control of all the transactional resources. However, the coupling is still much tighter than most people realize.

In any case, DTC is not an option for coordination of the donor and recipient transactions. Remember, DTC requires the holding of database locks and the flowing of transactions across drawbridges. As I discussed in Chapter 5, we don't flow transactions across drawbridges, regardless of the functionality that the vendors provide.

In light of this background on asynchronous drawbridges, let's look more closely now at the heterogeneous and homogeneous varieties.

6.4 Heterogeneous Asynchronous Drawbridges

As in all other heterogeneous cases, the heterogeneous asynchronous drawbridge situation occurs when we have two fortresses working together that are each built on different technology bases. And, as in the synchronous situation, we have two issues to deal with: the delivery engine and the infogram format.

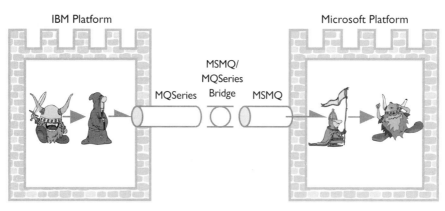

Figure 6.3 Drawbridges Using Message Queue Bridges

The delivery engine is not necessarily a problem because at least some message queues run across different platforms. IBM's MQSeries, for example, falls in this category. Other platforms, such as Microsoft's MSMQ, do not. Even when the message queue is platform limited, good bridge products exist that can be used to link different message queues together.

So we can handle asynchronous heterogeneity in one of two ways. We can run a cross-platform message queue product on both platforms, or we can use native message queues on each platform and then use a message queue bridge to move infograms from one message queue to the other. The latter case is shown in Figure 6.3.

We also need to worry about the infogram format. Because the infogram format is really part of the formal treaty between the two fortresses, it is reasonable to deal with this issue as a treaty-specific issue. But we can also make use of a ready-made infogram format.

One obvious choice for a ready-made format is the same format that we use for heterogeneous synchronous drawbridges. Do you remember what that is? SOAP! Recall that SOAP doesn't care about delivery channels. It is just as happy to ride over a message queue as to ride over an HTTP request. This is not to say that you must use SOAP. It is just one of the work request formats (which is all an infogram is) that is widely understood. And over time, it is a format for which vendors are likely to offer increasing support.

That pretty much covers the heterogeneous case. The nice thing about drawbridges based on message queues is that they are inherently fairly heterogeneous.

6.5 Homogeneous Asynchronous Drawbridges

In addition the heterogeneous asynchronous drawbridge technology, both Microsoft's .NET and Sun's Java support a *homogeneous* asynchronous drawbridge technology. In essence, it is a component veneer on top of a message queue. Microsoft calls this technology *queued components* and Sun calls it *message-driven beans*. The goal in both cases is to allow the use of a message queue to look as much as possible like an invocation of a method on a native component. I refer to both Microsoft's queued components and Sun's message-driven beans as *asynchronous components*, which is what they really are.

Remember from the discussion of homogeneous synchronous drawbridges that component technologies use surrogates in both the client and the component process to deal with the ugly details of communications. As shown in Figure 6.4, asynchronous components work in the same way, but their surrogates use a message queue

Figure 6.4 Asynchronous Component

rather than either a proprietary synchronous transport protocol (as do the homogeneous synchronous components) or HTTP (as do the heterogeneous synchronous components).

The thin veneer that asynchronous components add to the underlying message queue changes nothing about the characteristics of the message queue itself. The discussion about transactions is therefore just as relevant to asynchronous components riding over message queues as it is to message queues used directly.

In general, I don't like asynchronous components—either the Sun or the Microsoft flavor. You lose the flexibility of heterogeneity and get nothing in return other than not having to learn the message queue API. Given that use of the message queue API is limited to the envoy, having to learn the API does not seem too onerous.

6.6 Advantages of Asynchronous Drawbridges

Asynchronous drawbridges have four important benefits over synchronous drawbridges:

1. They have nonblocking workflow.
2. They give pseudoreliability.
3. They provide workload averaging.
4. They can be used to implement a poor-man's cluster.

I'll describe each of these in Sections 6.6.1 through 6.6.4.

6.6.1 Nonblocking Workflow

The nonblocking characteristic of asynchronous drawbridges is probably the most familiar. Once an infogram has been placed in the asynchronous drawbridge, the donor fortress can go on its merry way. No waiting. If it takes two hours for the recipient fortress to get around to receiving the infogram and another two hours for the work to complete, it shouldn't matter. If it does matter, then you probably should have been using a synchronous drawbridge.

6.6.2 Pseudoreliability

Wouldn't it be great if you could take off in the middle of the day whenever you wanted? The problem, of course, is that people expect you to be working in the middle of the day. But suppose you had a cardboard cutout of yourself that you could leave at your desk, so that everybody would assume you were working hard while, in reality, you were floating on a river in your kayak.

That is essentially what an asynchronous drawbridge does for a recipient fortress. The fortress can take off whenever it feels like it. Nobody can really tell that it's gone. As long as the fortress comes back online often enough to process its infograms in a reasonable time period, nobody knows if the fortress is at its desk or floating in the middle of a lake. The result is that even the most shiftless, irresponsible fortress in the world can be made to look like a fine, upstanding citizen. All that's required is an asynchronous front end!

6.6.3 Workload Averaging

If the whole world were composed of nothing but software fortresses, life would be grand and predictable. Unfortunately, it isn't. The world also has people. People, as any software architect knows, are the big problem.

One of the problems with people is that they clump together, like lemmings. They wake up at the same time. They go to work at the same time. They take their lunch breaks together. If they are women, they even go to the bathroom at the same time!

The result of all this clumping is huge variances in workload over time. At some times everybody in the world will seem to be beating on your poor, defenseless fortress. At other times your fortress will wonder if it is the last living being on Earth.

For most fortresses, especially those involved with the Internet, the difference between average workflow and peak workflow is large. I frequently find a tenfold difference between the two, meaning that if a fortress is asked to process, on average, 10,000 requests per minute, at peak it will be asked to process 100,000 requests per minute.

This huge difference between average and peak request flow can seriously affect the overall cost of a system. If your fortress is going to receive 100,000 requests per minute, you must make sure it can process 100,000 requests per minute. How will you do this? If these requests come over a synchronous drawbridge, you have only one choice. You must build your fortress big—really big.

The way you build a fortress really big is simple: You spend money, lots of money. In the best case, hardware costs tend to be linear with workload. Suppose that the hardware necessary to process 10,000 requests per minute costs 1 million dollars. You can assume, then, that the hardware needed to process 100,000 requests per minute will cost 10 million dollars.

Nobody minds spending a lot of money on hardware if that hardware is being used effectively. After all, when you process requests, you are presumably *making* money. What is annoying is spending a lot of money on hardware that then sits around doing nothing for much of the day.

This is exactly what your hardware will be doing if it is supporting a fortress accessed through synchronous drawbridges. On average, it will be processing the average workload (that's why they call it *average*!). On average, your very expensive hardware system will be utilized at only 10 percent capacity—probably even less, since you need to allow some buffer to handle *peak* peaks. This means that if you're using synchronous drawbridges, on average you will be wasting at least 9 out of every 10 hardware dollars you spend.

Building an asynchronous drawbridge to your fortress is far more cost-effective. Now you just need to buy enough hardware to process your average request flow. When the peak load hits, you just put off some of the processing until you reach the next lull. Sooner or later you will get it all done.

The result is a big difference in hardware costs between fortresses accessed with synchronous versus asynchronous drawbridges. Fortresses accessed with synchronous drawbridges require expensive hardware platforms that are used lightly most of the time. Fortresses accessed with asynchronous drawbridges can be built on cheap hardware platforms pushed to their limits.

Expensive hardware or cheap hardware . . . guess which one the bean counters are going to prefer!

6.6.4 Poor-Man's Clustering

When you build a large commerce system, you hope more and more people will use your system because this is where your profit comes from. But success also means your system must be able to scale gracefully to handle the increased workload. How will it do this?

There are generally three approaches to planning for increases in workload. First, you can build your system big enough from the beginning to handle the maximum workload it will ever face. I call this approach *build-big*. Second, you can plan on replacing your system with a bigger system once you exceed the capacity of your existing system. Most people call this approach *scale-up*. Third, you can build your system from the beginning using a clustered architecture and then plan on adding more systems to the cluster as your appetite for processing power increases. This last approach is known as *scale-out*.

Let me digress for a moment to give you a quick introduction to clusters. A cluster architecture is one in which workload can be evenly distributed among a collection, or *cluster*, of machines. If one machine goes down, the other machines can take over the remaining workload. If workload exceeds the capacity of the cluster, new machines can be added to the cluster without existing machines having to be taken offline.

There is a clear preference in how to choose among build-big, scale-up, and scale-out.

Scale-out is always the first choice. This approach allows you to add processing power to your system with little or no disruption to existing workflow. It allows you to use much cheaper hardware. And it dramatically increases your overall system reliability by providing built-in redundancy.

When you can't scale out, the second choice is scale-up. This approach still allows you to build small and handle increased workload if it actually materializes.

Your last choice is to build big from the beginning. The build-big approach forces you to try to predict your maximum system workload before you have processed your first work request, and it requires you to spend a lot of money on hardware at a time when you neither need nor can afford it.

In reality, often you will be using all three approaches: scale-up, scale-out, and build-big.

The database hosting machine is most compatible with build-big. The existing cluster algorithms for databases are not very good, so scale-out is out. Taking a database offline for the many days that will probably be required to migrate your database to new hardware is not very appealing, so scale-up is out. The only option you are left with is build-big. So if you have a fortress with high demands from its data strongbox, such as some business application fortresses, spend your extra money on the machine hosting the database. Mitigate the situation by limiting the build-big architecture to one machine and one machine only: the one housing the data strongbox.

Scaling *out* a legacy fortress is difficult. A scale-out architecture is easiest when the fortress is built from the beginning with a cluster architecture. So legacy fortresses typically scale *up*, not out.

New fortresses should be built from the beginning to scale out. The fortress architecture is especially amenable to a cluster architecture, so take advantage of it!

One way you can build a fortress to scale out is to plan on using asynchronous drawbridges (whew, finally, back to the topic of this chapter!). Because asynchronous drawbridges are typically built through the use of message queues, you can take advantage of the fact that multiple processes in multiple machines can all be pulling messages off of the same named message queue.

One simple architectural approach to clustering a business application fortress via asynchronous drawbridges is illustrated in Figure 6.5. Here we have a guard process and a business application component

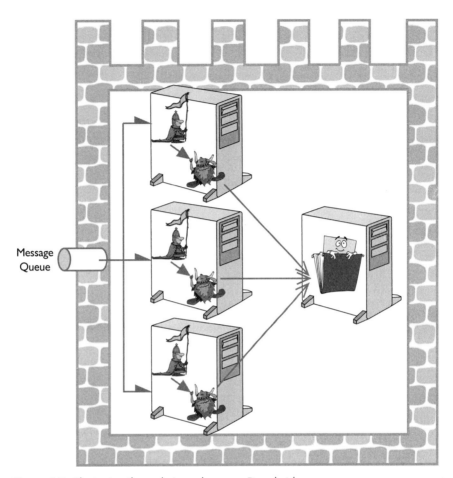

Figure 6.5 Clustering through Asynchronous Drawbridges

process, both running on the same machine. When the guard receives an infogram from the drawbridge, it invokes a remote method invocation on the business application component that is running on the guard's machine (albeit in a different process). This basic machine configuration is then duplicated as necessary to form the cluster. The clustered machines share a single data strongbox implemented as a shared database on a dedicated machine.

Using asynchronous drawbridges to implement a clustered architecture is not a complete cluster solution. The message queues that are the basis for the asynchronous drawbridges do not support many of the administrative tools one needs to manage a cluster environment, which is why I call clusters implemented with asynchronous draw-bridges *poor-man's clusters*. Nevertheless, in many fortress environments, asynchronous drawbridges will provide all the clustering you need.

6.7 Performance Problems of Asynchronous Drawbridges

Now that I have convinced you to use asynchronous drawbridges based on message queues, I will take the opposite viewpoint: I'll tell you why you shouldn't.

The biggest problem with asynchronous drawbridges based on message queues is that they force you to involve our old friend DTC, the distributed transaction coordinator. Remember DTC? She's the one required when a transaction involves more than one transactional resource—say, a database and a message queue. These are the types of transactions we're using when our donor fortress both updates a local database and makes an asynchronous interfortress request from within the same transaction.

There is a huge difference between a tightly coupled multiple-resource transaction (one involving DTC) and a tightly coupled single-resource transaction (one that doesn't require DTC). You can see the distinction easily in a sequence diagram showing the communication that must occur among the various parties in both the multiple-resource case (Figure 6.6) and the single-resource case (Figure 6.7).

The question is, can we eliminate the cost of DTC without giving up either the coordination between the donor transaction and the insertion of the infogram or the coordination between the receipt of the infogram and the recipient transaction? And the answer is, sometimes.

The way to eliminate DTC is to get rid of all but one of the transactional resources involved in the transaction. Who can we eliminate? We have only two transactional resources: the database and the message queue. The database isn't going anywhere, so that leaves only

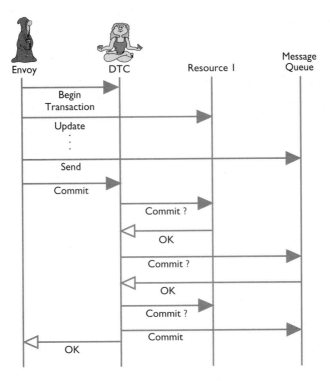

Figure 6.6 Sequence Diagram for Multiple-Resource Transactions

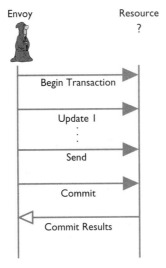

Figure 6.7 Sequence Diagram for Single-Resource Transactions

one candidate: the message queue. How do we get rid of the message queue? We have two options.

The first is to have the message queue vendors replace the underlying data storage that is now used by the message queue with a database. And not just any database, but the one we are using for the donor and recipient fortresses. Consider, for example, Microsoft. If Microsoft rewrote MSMQ (its message queue technology) to use SQL Server (its database technology) rather than MSMQ's native data store, then any fortress that used SQL Server as its data strongbox would be able to use MSMQ without having to involve DTC. IBM could take a similar approach with its message queue and database.

In fact, most of the major database vendors have announced plans to do exactly this. But until this work is completed, we have to follow the second approach to banishing DTC. In this approach we build our asynchronous drawbridges on top of the database instead of on the message queue.

Building an asynchronous drawbridge on top of a database is more difficult than building one on a message queue, but it is not an impossible chore. For example, I could allocate a table named ProcessPayment that represents the ProcessPayment drawbridge used by the CreditCard fortress to make requests of the Payment fortress. The rows in ProcessPayment could include these fields:

- CreditCardNumber
- PaymentAmount

The envoy implemented in the CreditCard fortress would append a new record to the ProcessPayment table. The guard implemented in the Payment fortress would check to see if there is a row in the Process-Payment table. If there is, the guard would read the first such record, process it, and delete the row. Not too horrible, all things considered.

The major problem with the database approach is that it pays the jackpot only when both fortresses are using the same database as their data strongbox. If one fortress is built on Microsoft's .NET and the other is built on IBM's WebSphere, the two fortresses will probably not be using the same database. Even if both fortresses are using

Microsoft technology, they will often be using their own private versions of SQL Server. Which one, then, becomes the holder of the message table?

The use of a database as an asynchronous drawbridge technology could be criticized as violating trust laws. Remember, the fundamental idea of a software fortress is that is represents a trust boundary. One can argue that the sharing of a database between two different fortresses requires a higher-than-reasonable degree of trust between the two fortresses.

My own opinion on this subject is that a data strongbox does not necessarily need to be a fully self-contained database. Using a logical partition of a database is an acceptable implementation of a data strongbox. What is critical is that the database be configured so that the logical partition is accessible only to the processes within that fortress.

If you accept this argument, you can use a single physical database to implement not only the data strongboxes in two different fortresses, but also the asynchronous drawbridge tying the two together. From a security perspective, we would logically divide the database into three pieces, as shown in Figure 6.8. Only the donor fortress would be

Figure 6.8 Logical Partitioning of a Database

able to access the portion allocated to the donor strongbox, and only the recipient fortress would be able to access the portion allocated to the recipient strongbox. Both fortresses would be able to access the portion allocated to the drawbridge.

I can't say I'm delighted with having to implement an asynchronous drawbridge myself. I would prefer to have someone else—such as Microsoft, Oracle, or IBM—physically unify the various storage technologies.

Even when the vendors unify their storage technologies, new problems will be created. Let me take Microsoft as an example. Sooner or later, we can expect the different groups in Microsoft to unify all storage under the umbrella of SQL Server. This unification will allow the different systems to work together much more efficiently (no DTC!).

But what happens, in this new Microsoft world, when we need to tie in an Oracle database to a fortress that is otherwise built on Microsoft technology? You guessed it: Suddenly DTC is crawling out of the woodwork. So in the Microsoft world, the cost of using Oracle for some specific applications will be much higher than the cost of using SQL Server for those same applications. Presumably you will not have the choice about whether or not you use SQL Server because every Microsoft application, including the operating system, will depend to some extent on SQL Server. Your only choice will be whether or not to introduce Oracle (and therefore DTC) into the fray.

The fact that DTC is required with the Oracle implementations is a powerful incentive to ban Oracle from the Microsoft fortresses. Not only will Oracle be much slower than SQL Server (through no fault of Oracle's), but Oracle may potentially slow down Microsoft applications that have little to do with Oracle other than having the misfortune to be somehow transactionally related to the Oracle-based work.

Clearly there is no cut-and-dried solution. Every fortress and every drawbridge has a unique problem that requires a unique solution. That's why you, Mr. or Ms. Enterprise Architect, are paid the big bucks.

Summary

Here's a review of the most important points of this chapter:

- Whereas synchronous drawbridges are based on component technologies, asynchronous drawbridges are based on message queues.

- The message queues that are used for asynchronous drawbridges are both persistent and transactional.

- The insertion of an infogram is transactionally coordinated with work being done by the donor fortress by DTC, the distributed transaction coordinator.

- The receipt of an infogram is also transactionally coordinated by DTC, this time with work being done by the recipient fortress.

- Sending of the infogram is fairly well coupled with receipt of the infogram.

- Homogeneous asynchronous drawbridges are based on a configuration in which a component veneer is placed over a message queue architecture. They are not recommended.

- Asynchronous drawbridges have four main advantages over their synchronous counterparts: they are nonblocking, they give pseudoreliability, they provide workload averaging, and they provide a poor-man's cluster architecture.

- Asynchronous drawbridges based on message queues can have performance problems resulting from the use of DTC to coordinate transactions. Sometimes these problems can be reduced if the message queue is replaced by a homegrown asynchronous system built on a database.

I hope this chapter has whetted your appetite for investigating opportunities to use asynchronous drawbridges in your enterprise architecture.

Guards and Walls

At first glance, guards and walls seem to have paradoxical functions. Walls are designed to *block* access to the fortress. Guards are designed to *allow* access to the fortress. These two functions, however, are actually complementary. The efficacy of the walls is what makes the guard's job necessary. After all, if outsiders could send requests into the fortress any which way they wanted, there wouldn't be much incentive to use approved and guarded drawbridges.

Although charged with allowing access to the fortress, the guard is very selective. The fortress architect is responsible for deciding just how selective the guard will be and which technologies can be used to implement this selectivity.

In this chapter I discuss some of the issues involved with designing and implementing walls and guards. I will focus on three main fortress types: presentation fortresses, Web service fortresses, and business application fortresses. These three fortress types represent a good cross section of available guard and wall design and implementation strategies.

For the purposes of this discussion, I will assume a simple configuration of two fortresses wanting to communicate over a drawbridge and a bad guy who is up to no good. Shown in Figure 7.1, this setup consists of the following characters:

- Ed, the envoy in the donor fortress
- Gwen, the guard in the receiving fortress
- Bart, the bad guy

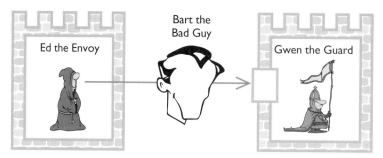

Figure 7.1 Two-Fortress Configuration

There are eight security issues we generally worry about when planning our fortress walls and guards:

1. Fortification
2. Validation
3. Auditing
4. Authentication
5. Privacy
6. Integrity
7. Nonrepudiation
8. Authorization

I'll go through these one by one, discussing each problem more fully and offering some likely solutions.

7.1 Fortification

Fortification refers to the ability of the fortress walls to prevent entry into the fortress (except, of course, through the drawbridge). If the fortress is well fortified, then the only way Bart the bad guy is going to get into it is by somehow tricking Gwen the guard into letting him in. Figure 7.2 illustrates the concept of fortification.

In the case of an Internet fortress (Web service or presentation), Bart will attempt to break into the fortress using an unexpected entry point, such as FTP or remote login. Once Bart has penetrated the

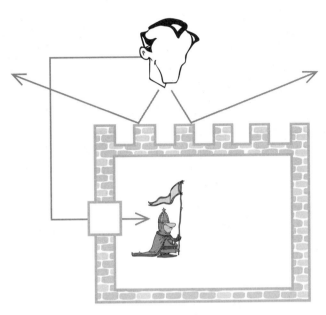

Figure 7.2 Fortress Fortification

Internet fortress, he may be able to erase or modify binaries, reboot the system, copy sensitive files, or set up his own privileged accounts, depending on the authorization level he manages to gain.

The most common way of fortifying the Internet fortress walls is with firewalls. Firewalls are a common fortification technology for many fortresses, but especially those connected to the Internet. Firewalls can restrict all but a select group of users from remote access. This small, select group is part of the fortress community (remember, a fortress is a group of people as well as a group of systems). Bart, needless to say, is not part of this select group.

Bart might also try to break into the fortress through the data strongbox. Data strongboxes are usually implemented with databases. If Bart can gain direct access to the database, he has effectively circumvented Gwen and can access all of the critical fortress data.

The database should be configured so that only user IDs associated with the owning software fortress are allowed to read, write, or modify data. Those user IDs, as trusted members of the fortress, should be allowed to do pretty much whatever they want.

Although proper configuration of the database is an important part of the fortress fortification, that configuration is much less complex for the software fortress architecture than for most N-tier architectures. N-tier architectures often require sophisticated database security configurations, with specific users allowed to access specific tables in specific ways that change as implementations of the business logic change. For a software fortress, database configuration boils down to a simple rule: If you are a member of the fortress, you can do what you want; if not, you can't. The configuration is very simple, it is easy to set up, and it doesn't change as implementations inside the fortress change.

Although all fortresses can avail themselves of firewalls and database security, business application fortresses have another trick up their sleeves: a mechanism called *role-based security*.

As I will discuss in Chapter 11 (Business Application Fortresses), business application fortress infrastructures are based on a technology that I refer to as *component-oriented middleware* (*COMWare*). COMWare is a technology closely associated with components, which I have discussed in the context of synchronous drawbridges.

Component systems transmit requests from a caller (the client) to a callee (the component instance) as a remote method invocation. The client lives in one process (the client process) and the component instance lives in another process (the component process).

Don't confuse the idea of a caller and client with a drawbridge. When we're looking at components as used within a business application fortress, the caller and the callee are part of the same fortress (although probably not part of the same process). As part of the same fortress, they do not go through drawbridges to get to each other, even though the technology is similar to some of the drawbridge technology.

Both the caller and callee processes have a specific associated user ID. In role-based security, each of these user IDs is assigned one or more roles by a component administrator. Examples of roles could be company managers or bank tellers.

Once the component administrator has given each client user ID one or more roles, that same component administrator sets up component access rights. The administrator decides which roles can access which methods in which components. For example, it might be appropriate to give either tellers or managers access to the updateAccounts method but only managers access to the addNewAccount method.

Role-based security was originally designed to deal with two security issues: authorization and authentication (I will discuss these issues in more detail later in the chapter). When role-based security was first introduced, it received a flurry of interest. It seemed attractive because it was an administrative model (one that can be totally managed by an administrator) rather than a code-based model (one that requires a programmer). All things being equal, administrative models are always preferable over coding models because they are easier to maintain. Besides, nobody believes that coders care all that much about security anyway.

However, role-based security turned out not to live up to its promise. The reason is that relatively few problems can be dealt with through role-based authorization. Let me give an example of a common problem that is not amenable to a role-based solution.

Consider a bank wanting to let clients check their balances online. The bank wants to make sure the clients are authorized to access the requested balances. This is a two-part problem. First, the clients must be authenticated (we know who they really are). Second, the bank is going to let clients access only their own bank balances. Using role-based security, we can say that only users in the client role can access the checkBalance method, but there is no way to specify that they can do so only when requesting to check their own account balances.

The problem we run into here is that limiting a client to only a specific account means that authorization is based not only on a specific method, but also on specific parameters to that method (e.g., accountID). Even the parameters don't give the full story. To really verify the user's access right, we probably need to check information in the database to be sure this particular account ID is associated with this particular client. Such a task is way beyond the capabilities of role-based security.

Why, you might ask, am I spending so much time on role-based security if it is so limited? It turns out that fortress architectures may be the redemption of role-based security. Although role-based security is relatively useless in run-of-the-mill authorization problems, it can provide one important capability for software fortresses: fortification.

In the same way that we can fortify the fortress by locking foreign users, such as Bart the bad guy, out of the database, we can also fortify the fortress by locking foreign users out of the components. We do this by using role-based security. We define each process in the fortress as being a member of the role of, say, this-fortress. All components that are part of the fortress are then configured to allow access by members of the this-fortress role. If your user ID is associated with this-fortress, then you can ask any of your fortressmates to do whatever you want. If your user ID is not associated with this-fortress, then don't even bother asking for the time of day. And that includes you, Bart!

7.2 Validation

Validation refers to the checking and rechecking of user input. One of the tricks that Bart learns in bad-guy school is how to exploit weaknesses in the guard, especially guards in Internet fortresses. In this scenario, Bart doesn't try to bypass Gwen the guard; he tries to trick her into doing something she shouldn't do. There are two ruses Bart will use to try to trick Gwen into becoming his willing accomplice.

In the first approach, Bart tries to overwhelm Gwen with large amounts of data, hoping to overwrite her allocated memory buffers. Bart sends much more data to Gwen than she is expecting. If Gwen doesn't check for this data excess, Bart can turn Gwen into his personal zombie. Gwen will now do anything Bart asks! And since Gwen is a trusted member of the inner sanctum, whatever Gwen asks, the rest of the fortress, having no idea that Gwen is now under the hypnotic spell of Bart, will do. Effectively, Bart has control of the entire fortress.

The technical term for Gwen's zombielike condition is a *buffer overflow*. Buffer overflows are probably the most common approach used by hackers to attack both presentation and Web service fortresses. The attacker enters large amounts of data into form fields, hoping to overwrite the memory addresses that control program flow. This approach allows a hacker to hijack the presentation (or Web service) fortress processes.

If Bart is thwarted in his attempt to cause Gwen's memory buffers to overflow, his next approach will be to send in scam data. Scam data is data that Bart hopes Gwen will pass to the inner fortress workers as real data, and that he further hopes will convince those workers to do something they normally wouldn't do.

For example, let's say that one of the parameters Gwen is expecting is an account ID. Gwen will pass that account ID on to an inner worker—say, Walt—who will subtract an amount from that account. Assume that Walt will find the account in the database using the SQL statement "Select * from accounts where accountID = account", where *account* is the parameter that Gwen passed through.

Bart is expected to pass in a string like "12345", which then will be passed through Gwen. But we know what Bart is like. Suppose that instead of passing in "12345", Bart passes in the string "1@". Now the SQL statement becomes "Select * from accounts where accountID = 1@". If the database interprets the @ character as a wildcard, then Bart will be able to subtract money from every account in the database. This is not exactly something that Walt would willingly do.

It is Gwen's responsibility to worry about unexpected characters in input fields. Unexpected characters are the sign of scam data attacks. If Gwen finds, for example, a quotation mark within a field that is expected to contain a user name, she must assume that she is under scam data attack. If user names should contain only letters, numbers, and underscores, then Gwen must treat *any* character that is not one of these as signaling a scam data attack.

Gwen needs to be highly suspicious of all user input. She must check each string character by character. She must examine the length of every string to be sure it meets length constraints. Gwen can never know what input is coming from a bona fide user and what input is coming from Bart the Bad.

If Gwen finds herself under attack, either by attempted buffer overflow or by scam data, she should take appropriate actions. She should *not* try to fix the data and then send it on to Walt the worker. She should reject the infogram containing the scam data in its entirety. If possible, she might want to take evasive actions to guard against further attacks. In an extreme case, she might even want to shut herself and her fortress down, sacrificing her own life to protect the greater good of the enterprise.

7.3 Auditing

Auditing refers to the ability to track all changes to the internal state of a fortress. Because the state of the fortress is effectively the content of the data strongbox, we can say that auditing is the ability to track all changes to the data strongbox.

There are four things we want tracked in an auditing system:

1. The fortress that made the request resulting in the change.
2. The exact request the fortress made.
3. The data that was sent with the request.
4. The time the request was made.

Other bits of information may be included in the audit trail, but these are the main points.

Hypothetically, auditing could be done in several places. It could be done at the worker level, with each worker in the fortress, when asked to do something, logging that request. It could be done within the database itself, which is where the database vendors, with their egocentric view of the world, recommend it be done. It could be done by Gwen. Where should it be done?

In my view, auditing at either the worker or the database level makes no sense. The workers have no way of knowing which fortress originated the request, what the original request looked like, what data was sent in, or even when the request was made. The database is even further removed from this information. So neither the worker nor the database is in a good position to take on serious audit responsibility.

The only one who has access to the exact information we want audited is good old reliable Gwen. Gwen is not only the obvious candidate for auditing; she is, in my view, the *only* candidate. Not every fortress may need to have requests audited. For those that do, Gwen is our girl.

Auditing is not only useful for security purposes; it can also be useful for debugging. At the enterprise level, debugging often requires careful workflow tracking, as one tries to determine when an error first occurred. The ability to dynamically turn on auditing at the fortress level can be a big help in these unpleasant situations.

7.4 Authentication

Authentication refers to the procedure we go through to convince ourselves that somebody is who he or she claims to be. We have two fortresses in a trust relationship: Ed the envoy's fortress and Gwen the guard's fortress. Neither fortress wants to talk to Bart the bad guy. But how does Gwen know that she is talking to Ed, and not to Bart pretending to be Ed? For that matter, how does Ed know that he is really talking to Gwen, and not to Bart pretending to be Gwen? It is just one more task we're going to add to Gwen's ever expanding list of responsibilities: to be sure that when she thinks she is talking to Ed, she really is talking to Ed. Depending on how paranoid Ed is, he can also take on the problem of being sure that Gwen is really Gwen.

There are generally two approaches to authentication: (1) through a shared key (symmetrical encryption) or (2) through a public/private key (asymmetrical encryption). Both are based on encryption/ decryption algorithms; let's look at this class of algorithms.

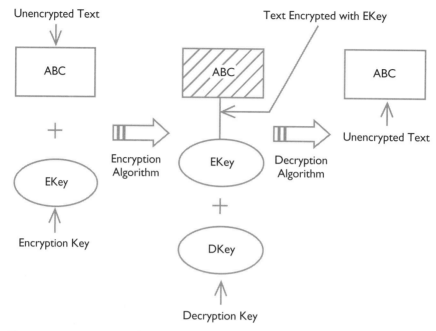

Figure 7.3 Encryption and Decryption Phases

Encryption and decryption are mirror images of each other. Encryption means taking some text and an encryption key and returning garbled text. Decryption means taking that same garbled text along with a decryption key and returning the original text. The two processes are illustrated in Figure 7.3.

The difference between a shared-key system, like Kerberos, and public/private–key systems, like secure sockets, is whether or not the decryption key is the same as the encryption key. For shared-key systems, the two keys are the same. For public/private–key systems, the two keys are different, although algorithmically related.

For shared-key systems, both parties (in this case Ed and Gwen) store a secret key (often corresponding to a password) with a trusted third-party authenticator, whom I will call Al. Both Ed and Gwen trust Al to keep each of their secret keys a secret.

When Ed wants to talk to Gwen, he asks Al the authenticator for a "ticket" to use Gwen. In response, Al gives Ed a ticket to use Gwen.

The ticket contains information about Ed and a temporary key called a *session key*. That ticket is encrypted with Gwen's secret key, which only Gwen and the authenticator (Al) know. Notice that the ticket is useless to Ed; Ed can't read it. Only Gwen, who knows the decryption key (which is, after all, her secret key), can read the ticket. About the only thing that Ed can do with the ticket is send it on to Gwen.

Al gives Ed one more thing. He gives him a package containing the session key, the same one contained in the ticket. That package is encrypted with Ed's secret key, which only Ed and the authenticator know.

Now Ed has two things. He has the ticket, which only Gwen can read, and he has the package containing the session key, which only he can read. So both Gwen and Ed now have the session key, albeit encoded with different secret keys.

Now Ed and Gwen are ready to prove to each other their respective identities. Ed sends the ticket to Gwen. Gwen reads it with her secret key, thereby convincing herself that only Al could have prepared the package. She opens (decrypts) the package and gets both the session key and the information about Ed. This convinces her that Al has authenticated Ed, and she trusts Al.

This algorithm is very close to the one used by Kerberos, and in fact a Kerberos authenticator could be used as the trusted third party Al.

There are at least four disadvantages to this algorithm. First, both parties need to trust the same third party with their secret keys. Kerberos relaxes this requirement slightly by providing a fourth party, but the effect is the same.

Second, the trusted third party, Al, can be a bottleneck for the algorithms because he is needed for every communication initiation. For fortresses, this probably means that Al must be consulted with every use of the drawbridge.

Third, the algorithm is susceptible to compromise. The algorithm can be compromised if Bart (the bad guy; remember him?) steals a ticket. Bart can then use brute force to guess Gwen's private key. Once he knows Gwen's private key, there is nothing to stop him from impersonating her. Similarly, Bart can steal the package (the one encrypted with Ed's private key) and use a similar brute-force approach to guess Ed's private key, with similar consequences.

The fourth disadvantage of the algorithm is a particular problem for Web service and presentation fortresses, the very fortresses that are most likely to want to use this algorithm. To understand this problem, we need to follow the algorithm from Gwen's perspective.

Gwen gets a message from somebody who claims to be Ed. She believes it really is Ed if her secret key can be used to decrypt the data. Besides herself, only Al the authenticator knows her secret key, so Al must have sent Ed the package containing the session key. To prove that Ed is who he says he is, Gwen must decrypt the ticket. And to decrypt the ticket, she must use her secret key. This need implies that Gwen is storing her secret key someplace in her fortress, someplace where she can get to it easily.

In Chapter 10 (Internet Fortresses) I will discuss some of the security guidelines for building Web service and presentation fortresses. One of these guidelines is to be careful not to store confidential information in the fortress. A great example of confidential information that should not be stored in the presentation fortress is Gwen's secret key, the very key she needs to prove that Ed is Ed. This is a fundamental problem with the shared-key algorithm. Without her key, Gwen can't securely prove that Ed is Ed. But if anybody steals her private key, then she is really in trouble. Now Bart can impersonate her at will.

All of these disadvantages can be eliminated with public/private–key systems. In these systems, each player (Ed and Gwen, in our drama) has both a public and a private key. The public key is readily available to anybody who wants it. The private key is kept secret. The only one who knows Ed's private key is Ed.

Either the public or the private key can be used to encrypt, and whichever one is used, the other one, and only the other one, can be used to decrypt. So if the private key was used for encryption, only the public key will decrypt. If the public key was used to encrypt, only the private key will decrypt.

We still need a trusted authenticator, Al, but he plays a much smaller role here than he does in the shared-key system. First of all, Al doesn't need to know anybody's secret key (as he does with the Kerberos-like system). Second, Al is not consulted on every communications initiation. In fact, the only role Al plays is to guarantee that Ed's and Gwen's public keys are really Ed's and Gwen's.

The way that Al guarantees that Ed's public key is really Ed's is to create a package containing Ed's public key and identification information about Ed. Al then encrypts this package with his own private key. This encrypted package is called a *certificate*. Al sends this certificate to Ed. Ed can now send the certificate to Gwen.

How does Gwen know that Al certified Ed's public key, the one that is contained in the certificate? She decrypts the certificate with Al's public key. This decryption will work only if the certificate was originally encrypted with Al's private key. Gwen doesn't know Al's private key, but she does know his public key (so does everybody else). Anything that Al's public key decrypts must have been encrypted with Al's private key, and she trusts Al to keep his private key private.

Most of the disadvantages of the shared-key (Kerberos-like) algorithm are eliminated or greatly reduced with the public/private–key system. First, nobody needs to trust Al with a secret key (except Al, and if Al can't trust Al, who can?). Second, Al is not needed on an ongoing basis—only once in a while for approving certificates. The third disadvantage is still there; that is, Bart can still potentially guess Gwen's secret key by brute force, but in this case even if that happened, Gwen would just need to create a new secret key and reregister its public counterpart with Al.

The final disadvantage of the shared-key system—the fact that Gwen is forced to store her private key in her own fortress—is completely eliminated with public/private–key systems. Gwen now no longer needs her own private key, at least to prove to herself that Ed is really Ed. She may need her private key to prove to Ed that she is really Gwen, but Gwen can also provide such proof by having another fortress that she trusts do the encryption on her behalf.

One final note: None of these authentication schemes work well for the typical presentation fortresses that must deal with very large numbers of browsers. Private-key systems don't work because no third parties are widely trusted. Private/public–key systems don't work because the credentials are too difficult to manage effectively. But for presentation fortresses that deal with only a limited number of browsers, or Web service fortresses, these systems usually work fine.

This is a fairly high-level look at the main issues involved with fortress authentication, but it should start you thinking.

7.5 Privacy

Privacy refers to the ability to send information in such a way that it cannot be read by unauthorized users. When privacy is implemented, Bart can still read the infograms, but they will all appear as garbled, unintelligible text, much like the user manuals you get with your operating system.

Privacy is usually accomplished with secret-key encryption. Ed and Gwen share a secret key that only they know about. Ed uses this key to encrypt data before he sends it. Gwen uses the same key to decrypt data after she receives it. To anybody in the middle, the data appears as garbled text.

This secret key is not either of their private keys. That would be a violation of the fortress trust rule. Instead, they share a temporary session key, a key that only the two of them know and that is valid only for a limited duration (probably minutes).

The trick is to exchange this secret key in such a way that even if Bart eavesdrops, he won't be able to read the key and thereby read the transmitted data. There are two ways that Ed and Gwen can exchange this secret key. The first way to share the key is as a side effect of the private-key algorithm. Remember, I said that one of the items in the Kerberos-like ticket is a session key. This session key is exactly the kind of secret key that Ed and Gwen need.

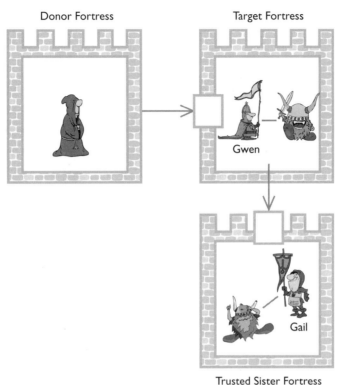

Figure 7.4 Gwen's and Gail's Fortresses

The other way to share the key is by using a public/private–key pair. In the public/private–key scheme, Ed creates a session key and encrypts it using Gwen's public key. He sends the encrypted session key to Gwen. Only Gwen's private key will decrypt the session key.

As I mentioned earlier, if Gwen is guarding a Web service or presentation fortress, she herself will not store her private key. It will instead be stored in a closely trusted sister fortress, guarded by Gail, as shown in Figure 7.4. Gwen trusts Gail's fortress to store her private key and decrypt information on her behalf. Gwen can then either ask Gail's fortress for the session key (if that does not introduce an unacceptable security risk) or have Gail's fortress do all encrypting and decrypting on her behalf.

7.6 Integrity

Integrity means preventing Bart the bad guy from changing infograms en route. Most fortress implementations deal with integrity as a side issue of privacy. The assumption is that if Bart can't read the message, he can't change it. Even more secure algorithms exist that can ensure that Bart can't even randomly change the infogram, but I won't cover those here. These are standard security algorithms that are not specific to fortresses.

7.7 Nonrepudiation

Nonrepudiation refers to the ability to prove at a later time that an infogram came from Ed the envoy. Suppose that we get a message from Ed asking that a savings account be decremented. Gwen's fortress decrements the account. Later, Ed says he never made the request. How can Gwen's fortress prove that Ed asked for the account to be decremented?

The easiest way to do this is with public and private keys. Gwen can insist that the decrement request be encrypted with Ed's private key. Gwen can decrypt this request with Ed's public key. After arranging to have the account decremented, Gwen then permanently logs the encrypted infogram. She might even want to log Ed's public key as well, just in case Ed later decides to change it. Should Ed ever deny sending the infogram, Gwen can retrieve the logged infogram and show that she can decrypt it with Ed's public key. If she can decrypt the infogram with Ed's public key, then it must have been encrypted with Ed's private key. Because only Ed knows Ed's private key, Ed must have sent the infogram. Nice try, Ed!

If Gwen is guarding a presentation or Web service fortress, she probably won't log the encrypted infogram herself because that would involve storing valuable data (the infogram log) on a nonsecure fortress. Instead she will use a trusted service fortress to do the logging for her.

7.8 Authorization

Authorization refers to the ability to determine, *not* on the basis of the fortress making the request but on the basis of the information in the request itself, whether the request being made is allowable. As a simple example, imagine Bart the bad guy is sitting at a browser and asks that 1,000 dollars be removed from Alice's account. He knows Alice's account number but not her password. This request should be rejected. The reason for rejecting the request is not that Bart's browser is an untrusted source. Gwen, sitting in a presentation fortress, has no problem with Bart's browser. The request should be rejected because there is a problem with the data in the infogram.

Solving authorization problems generally requires deferring to the business logic. Theoretically Gwen could check the database to see if the password matched the password for Alice's account. But such checking is difficult, for different reasons, depending on what kind of a fortress Gwen is guarding.

If Gwen is guarding a presentation fortress, she has no access to the database containing account IDs and passwords. This information is obviously highly confidential, and as I have hinted at and will discuss in more detail in Chapter 10 (Internet Fortresses), we don't store confidential information in a presentation fortress.

If Gwen is guarding a business application fortress, then for performance reasons we want to minimize database access. If she has to access the database to check the password and then a business application worker has to access the same database to do the account update, we have two database accesses. If the worker does both the authorization check and the account update, we can eliminate half of the database accesses.

The bottom line is that authorization, not to be confused with authentication, is usually not a guard issue, but a business application worker issue, based on application-specific algorithms.

Summary

This chapter has shown that there is quite a bit to creating guards and walls. This is the reason I emphasize making the creation of guards and walls a specialized task within your organization.

Here are the major lessons of this chapter:

- The walls are primarily responsible for fortification.
- Three technologies are typically used to build walls:
    1. Firewalls
    2. Database security configuration
    3. Role-based security
- All data coming into the fortress must be validated. Validation includes
    - Checking for string length violations
    - Checking for unexpected characters
- Auditing is important if you need to track fortress changes.
- Authentication is needed to verify that requests are coming from approved sources. Authentication is done with encryption/decryption algorithms based on either secret keys (in the shared-key system) or public/private keys (in the public/private–key system).
- Privacy is about hiding data from prying eyes, which is accomplished by encryption/decryption.
- Integrity means keeping data from changing as it passes through the drawbridge, which also makes use of encryption/decryption.
- Nonrepudiation means being able to prove, at a later date, the source of an infogram. This is usually done with public/private–key systems.
- Authorization, although it seems like a guard/wall issue, is usually done by a business application worker.

Treaties

Treaties are the formal agreements between fortresses that define how those fortresses will work together. No standard technologies today correspond directly to treaties (other than written documents), so it is hard to give more than guidelines about how to approach the treaty documentation process. To simplify the discussion, I'll consider a nonsoftware system.

8.1 A Treaty between Two Fortresses

My morning usually starts at my local Starbucks. I am often there at 5:30 A.M. In fact, I am often there earlier, but until 5:30 A.M., I am forced to sit outside looking pitiful. When I get in, I need my doppio macchiato, I need it bad, and I need it made without mistakes.

Thinking of Starbucks in terms of fortresses, the counter forms a natural boundary between me and the Starbucks corporation. Starbucks is one self-contained fortress, and I am another. We interact across the counter. Each interaction goes through a drawbridge, and the sequence of interactions is defined by a treaty. I'll call this treaty the *Purchase* treaty.

Because both Starbucks and I are self-contained fortresses, we don't ask each other a lot of stupid questions. Starbucks doesn't ask me how I got the money I am about to hand over. I don't ask Starbucks who fixes the espresso machine. Our relationship is simple. They want my money; I want their doppios.

As we look more closely at the interactions between Starbucks and me that are needed to fulfill the requirements of the Purchase treaty, we see a carefully orchestrated dance. If any one of the interactions fails, the relationship disintegrates. Let's go through the different moves.

First is the order interaction. This interaction is followed soon (hopefully) by the delivery interaction. Several other possible interactions have to do mostly with error control.

The order interaction can be divided into these lower-level interactions:

1. The Roger fortress (that's me) verbally places the order. The order has four components: item (macchiato), size (doppio), quantity (one), and frills (one brown sugar and extra foam). Note that only two of these (item and size) are defined by the menu.

2. The Starbucks fortress verbally tells the Roger fortress how much money is owed. This is essentially an error control mechanism. The Roger fortress (having ordered thousands of doppio macchiatos) knows exactly what the cost should be ($1.87). If the Starbucks fortress responds with any other price, the Roger fortress will go into error correction mode.

3. The Roger fortress authorizes a payment from his American Express account. To prove that he has the right to authorize the payment, he hands over an American Express credit card.

4. The Starbucks fortress verifies that the American Express card is valid and then returns it and a receipt to the Roger fortress.

5. The Roger fortress verifies that the amount on the receipt is accurate and signs it. His signature can later be used to prove that he has seen and accepted the amount of the debit, should he try to deny it.

6. The order is delivered.

It is worth taking a look at the overall asynchronicity of this system. Recall from Chapter 6 (Asynchronous Drawbridges) that we always want our interfortress interactions (as opposed to intrafortress interactions) to be as asynchronous as possible. Asynchronous interactions are more reliable, easier for balancing workload, and naturally amenable to workflow averaging. Synchronous interactions, in contrast, are generally unreliable, difficult for balancing workload, and downright hostile to workflow averaging.

How much of the Purchase treaty is being done asynchronously? I have identified six discrete interactions between the Roger and Starbucks fortresses, not including error control. Each one of these will require a dedicated drawbridge. A sequence–ally diagram (SAD) for our current version of the Purchase treaty is shown in Figure 8.1.

Five of the six interactions between the Roger and Starbucks fortresses are synchronous. And this doesn't include error handling. This is not a good situation. But what are we to do? We are forced into these synchronous flows by the nature of our drawbridge designs.

This treaty analysis has pointed out some weaknesses in our drawbridge design, as is typical of software fortress architectures. The design of the treaty reveals drawbridge weaknesses and forces further work in the design of the drawbridges. Once the drawbridges have been redesigned, the treaty is reconsidered and may point out new problems in the drawbridges.

Let's redesign the Starbucks fortress so that all of the synchronous interactions are collapsed into a single megainteraction, preferably an asynchronous one. To do this, we replace the human interaction

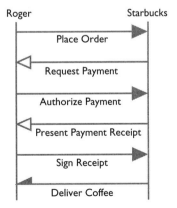

Figure 8.1 SAD for Purchase Treaty

Starbucks Order Form

Your Name: _____

Drink	Size	Frills	Quantity

1. ....
2. ....
3. ....
4. ....
5. ....
6. ....

Payment (check one)

☐ Cash

☐ Credit Card

☐ Starbucks Card

(Please enclose your cash or credit card in payment envelope.)

Figure 8.2 The New Improved Starbucks Order Form

at the counter with a stack of order forms. To order my doppio mac-chiato, I grab an order from, fill it out, throw my payment in the payment envelope, and hand it to the counter person. Figure 8.2 shows an example of such an order form.

We can even throw in error management at a low cost by creating another drawbridge for the Starbucks fortress (one designed to accept complaints) and another form—say, the one shown in Figure 8.3.

Notice in Figure 8.4 how much simpler the SAD has become, even with error management thrown in!

Of course, I don't expect Starbucks actually to implement this new system. The folks at Starbucks probably think we all want the warm and fuzzy face-to-face experience. But if this system were implemented, you wouldn't ever have to wait on another around-the-block Starbucks line. You could simply walk into the Starbucks, hand in your form, sit down, relax, read the paper, and wait for your coffee to appear. Maybe warm and fuzzy is overrated!

Starbucks Error Report

Your Name: _____

Type of error (please check all that apply)

☐ Order not delivered

☐ Wrong order delivered

☐ Card not returned

☐ Incorrect change

☐ Incorrect charge on card

Figure 8.3 The New Improved Starbucks Error Form

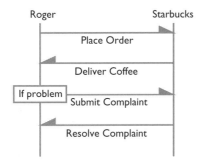

Figure 8.4 The New Improved SAD

Several intrafortress events probably will occur within the boundaries of the Purchase treaty. For example, the Starbucks fortress will probably debit Roger's American Express account. It will probably do so in a transactionally protected manner. The order will probably initiate a request from the cashier guard to the espresso machine worker. None of these events, however, are relevant to anybody but those implementing the Starbucks fortress. Similarly, the Roger fortress may drink the macchiato on the spot or in his car. He may add more sugar, add chocolate, dump it into a thermos, throw it away, or give it to the next person he sees on the street holding a "will work for doppio macchiatos sign." None of these are the concern of the Starbucks fortress. It got what it wanted from the collaboration—namely, a buck eighty-seven.

8.2 Treaty Considerations

The Starbucks example illustrates the two main considerations of treaty design:

1. **Workflow**. How does work flow from one fortress to another?
2. **Error management**. How does one fortress report an error to another fortress?

You might expect security to be part of the treaty. In the Starbucks/ Roger collaboration, I had to hand over my American Express card to prove I was authorized to make a charge on that particular account. It is reasonable to think of security as part of the treaty, but I think of it as a feature of the drawbridge rather than of the treaty, and I recommend documenting the drawbridge in the fortress documentation. Either approach is fine, though.

Treaties are spelled out in treaty overview documents (TODs), as I discussed in Chapter 2 (Diagramming Software Fortresses). The exact format of a TOD can be defined on an institutional basis because, at least for now, TODs are used by human beings, not software systems. If we ever reach the point where TODs become data digested by software infrastructures, we will need to develop standard representations of TODs. That day is still in the future. For the moment, we will be more than satisfied if we can come up with a technique that allows people to communicate with other people. For human beings, the most important information in the TOD is probably the collection of SADs.

The difficult part of documenting a treaty is knowing how much detail to include. A good test is reimplementability: If any party of the treaty were to be reimplemented from scratch, the treaty, in conjunction with the fortress documentation, must contain sufficient detail for the reimplementors to understand how to fulfill their responsibilities with respect to the other fortresses in the treaty.

It's hard to give much more guidance than this. Treaties tend to be very specific to the work being coordinated. I hope this gives you some ideas on how to proceed.

Summary

Here is a summary of the main points of this chapter:

- Treaties define interactions between fortresses.
- When we think about treaties, we are thinking about two closely related issues: workflow control and error management.
- As you document your treaties, you will often find weaknesses in your drawbridge definitions. When you find those problems, don't ignore them. Solve them!
- The SAD is one of the best tools for documenting treaties.

CHAPTER 9

General Fortress Issues

It is helpful to think of a fortress as being a certain type because the type immediately suggests specific design patterns, implementation algorithms, and appropriate technologies. Some goals are common to all fortresses, regardless of type. Four that come up repeatedly are security, scalability, reliability, and integrity. Security I have already discussed, in Chapter 7 (Guards and Walls). Here I will discuss the other general fortress topics.

9.1 Scalability

A fortress is *scalable* if it fulfills three criteria. First, the fortress's unit-of-work cost (i.e., the cost of processing a work request over a drawbridge) must be low enough for you to make a profit. It if costs you $1.50 to process a request for which you will charge $1.00, you are out of the race before you start.

Second, a path must exist by which you can increase the workload you process in a given time period up to at least the maximum workload you will ever need. You can increase your processing rate by replacing small boxes with big boxes (a *scale-up* approach) or by adding boxes (a *scale-out* approach), but one way or the other, it must be possible to increase fortress throughput. I first introduced this topic in Chapter 6 (Asynchronous Drawbridges).

Third, as you trudge along the path of increasing your fortress through-put, your workload costs must do no worse than remain constant. In other words, if it costs you $1.00 to process a work request when you're processing 100 requests per hour, it should cost you no more than $1.00 to process a work request even when you're processing 10,000 requests per hour. The total system cost will go up, of course, but the cost per request should remain constant. If your workload costs increase as your throughput increases, then a fortress that was profitable when servicing a small number of requests can lose money when processing a large number of requests.

Calculating the workload costs is not trivial, but it is necessary. It requires you to calculate your fortress costs on an annual basis, figure out your average workload throughput (for asynchronously accessed fortresses) or your peak throughput (for synchronously accessed fortresses), reduce those numbers to cost per unit of workload, and then, finally, watch what happens to these costs as you increase your workload potential.

Why do we figure *peak* workload when using synchronous draw-bridges and *average* workload when using asynchronous drawbridges? If you don't know the answer to this question, go back and review the material on asynchronous drawbridges (Chapter 6).

Keep in mind that there are always two approaches to adding work-load processing power to your fortress. You can scale up—that is, replace your small machine with a large machine. Or you can scale out—that is, add more small machines to your cluster. I'll discuss the trade-offs when I discuss reliability in the next section.

9.2 Reliability

Fortress *reliability* refers to how much I can trust the fortress to be there for me when I need it. There are two types of reliability. There is what I have previously termed *pseudoreliability*, which means that the fortress appears to be up and running when in reality it is off sucking down doppio macchiatos at Starbucks. This topic I discussed in the chapter on asynchronous drawbridges. The other type of reliability could be described as *true reliability*.

True reliability means that the fortress is honest to goodness up and running when I ask it to do something. No excuses. No doppio macchiatos. Some people call this *availability*.

There are two approaches to building true reliability. One is to build the fortress on expensive machines that never go down. The other is to build the fortress on clusters of inexpensive machines. We achieve cluster reliability by having enough machines in the cluster so that even if some of them go down, workflow can continue.

Reliability is somewhat related to scalability. Remember, there are two approaches to achieving scalability: scale-up or scale-out. These two choices parallel the choices you make to achieve reliability. The theory goes that scale-up—buying a big, expensive machine—also buys you a more reliable machine. Supporting evidence is mostly anecdotal, but the scale-up approach is certainly widely trumpeted by makers of big, expensive machines.

Where possible, I favor the scale-out approach to both scalability and reliability over the scale-up approach. Scale-out, in my experience, gives better results at a lower cost. In certain limited situations, however, scale-up is the only realistic alternative. First let me briefly explain why scale-out is such an attractive approach to reliability.

In general, small cheap machines (typically Windows-based machines) are cheaper than big expensive machines (typically mainframe-type machines). This seems reasonable. What is not so obvious is that this is true even when one takes into account the differences in the processing power between the small, cheap machine and the big, expensive machine. Most benchmarks show about a fivefold unit-of-work price differential between the small, cheap Windows-type machines and the big, expensive mainframes. This means that if it costs one dollar for a fortress to process a request on a Windows platform it will probably cost about five dollars to process that same request on a mainframe platform.

The mainframe vendors always argue that the extra cost is worthwhile for two reasons. First, mainframes can process more work requests than Windows machines can—an argument that is valid only for architectures that cannot take advantage of a cluster approach. Second, mainframes are more reliable. This argument is more complicated, so let's take a closer look.

Let's consider some representative numbers. Suppose that it costs 10,000 dollars to build and maintain a fortress on a Windows platform that can process 1,000 requests per minute. If we're using a cluster architecture, it is safe to assume that we can build and maintain a fortress that can process 10,000 requests per minute on the Windows platform for about 100,000 dollars. Ten times the workload for ten times the cost. This is standard cluster scale-out analysis.

Now let's assume that a mainframe-based fortress that can process 10,000 requests per minute will cost about 500,000 dollars, since, as I mentioned, the cost per request is typically five times higher on mainframe systems. What do you get for your extra 400,000 dollars? According to the mainframe vendors, substantially higher reliability. But the math doesn't hold up here.

For the sake of argument we'll assume that mainframe computers are 10,000 times more reliable than Windows computers. This is highly unlikely, but I'm using extreme numbers to give the mainframes every possible benefit of the doubt. I'll assume, further, that the mainframe computer fails one day out of 100,000, giving it a 0.00001 chance of failure, or a 99.999 percent reliability rating. If the Windows machine is 1/10,000 as reliable, then it is predicted to fail one day out of 10, giving it a 0.1 chance of failure, or a 90 percent reliability rating.

Let's say we have a cluster of M machines, each with a probability P of failure. What are the chances that F of those M machines will fail at the same time?

Choose one machine in the cluster. The chances of its failing on any given day are P. The chances of its next-door neighbor failing on that day are also P because they are the same basic machines. The chances of both machines failing on the same day is $P \times P$, or P^2, because the two events are probabilistically independent. The chances of F machines failing is thus P^F. If P is equal to 0.1 (our highly pessimistic initial assumption), we can calculate how many failures (F) would match the reliability of the mainframe, which had a P of 0.00001. In this case F must be 5, because $0.1^5 = 0.00001$.

In other words, if we make the cluster 5 machines bigger than is necessary to handle the workload requirements, we get about the same reliability as we have with the large mainframe. We need 10 machines to handle the workload (on the basis of initial assumptions) and 5 more to achieve mainframe reliability.

If the machines cost 10,000 dollars each, our highly reliable (by mainframe standards) cluster will cost 150,000 dollars. Of that, 100,000 dollars is the cost to process workload and 50,000 dollars is the cost for the needed reliability. To process the same workload with the same reliability on the mainframe, we will have to spend 500,000 dollars, more than three times as much. And for a mere 20,000 dollars more, we can get 100 times *more* reliability than the mainframe can offer.

All of this assumes that the mainframes are 10,000 times more reliable than the Windows-platform machines. In fact, however, if there is any difference in reliability, I suspect it is much closer to 10 times than 10,000 times.

Those of you very familiar with probability theory will realize that I have simplified the equations slightly, but the overall numbers are close to accurate.

This whole argument assumes that a cluster architecture is actually possible. There is one area in which clustering is very difficult: the data strongbox. Data strongboxes are not amenable to running on clusters (at least, not clusters in the sense that I am using the term here). I discussed this issue in Chapter 6 (Asynchronous Drawbridges).

For most fortresses, the difficulty in clustering the data strongbox is not a problem. We generally solve this problem by dedicating one machine to the data strongbox. This machine we make as big as is necessary to handle the expected data workload, a technique I described in Chapter 6 as build-big. The rest of the fortress we design with a cluster architecture. In other words, we scale *up* (or build big) the data strongbox, and we scale *out* everything else in the fortress.

Very few fortresses need particularly large data strongboxes. The data strongbox of a presentation fortress, for example, needs to hold little more than the state of the browsers it is currently processing. By database standards, this isn't a whole heck of a lot of data.

9.3 Integrity

Integrity means a lack of damage. A fortress that is designed to provide high integrity is one that does its work so that nothing is damaged or left in an incomplete state, even when failures occur within the fortress. Database folks often call this *consistency*. This topic is highly fortress specific, so I will discuss it along with specific fortress types in Chapters 10 through 12.

Summary

This chapter introduces concepts that are important to all fortresses. I have defined three important terms:

1. *Scalability*, which means that the fortress workload can be increased as necessary.
2. *Reliability*, which means that the fortress is up and running when I need it.
3. *Integrity*, which means that the fortress always leaves itself in a consistent state.

Now let's move inside the actual fortresses.

CHAPTER 10

Internet Fortresses

Presentation fortresses and Web service fortresses can both be categorized as Internet fortresses. Internet fortresses are the no-man's-land between your enterprise and the Internet. Internet fortresses have two main purposes. First, they mediate interactions between the outside world and your enterprise dominion. Second, they provide a security buffer between the outside world and the restricted world of the corporate computing grid. Both of these functions are depicted in Figure 10.1.

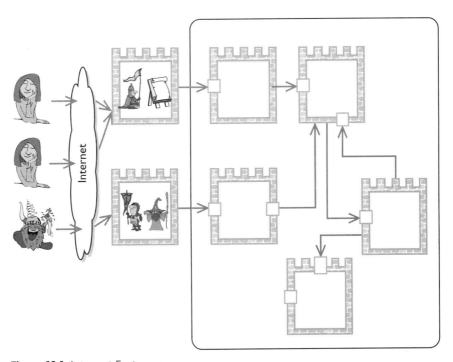

Figure 10.1 Internet Fortresses

There are two types of Internet fortresses: presentation fortresses and Web service fortresses. Presentation fortresses are specialized to deal with the browser, or thin, clients. Web service fortresses are specialized to deal with code-based clients. Web service fortresses are used relatively infrequently in today's enterprise systems; however, if one is to believe advance hype, they will become much more prevalent in the future.

I'll start by looking at the presentation fortresses because their architectures have been around the longest and are therefore the best understood. Most of what we know (or think we know) about Web service fortresses has been extrapolated from our knowledge of presentation fortresses.

10.1 Presentation Fortresses

Presentation fortresses receive HTTP requests from thin clients and deliver HTML pages in response. This simple-sounding task is complicated by numerous factors, most prominently these:

- Determining exactly what the client did (push a button? choose a menu item?) is often a nontrivial programming task.
- Managing the client's state—in other words, determining how the client's current request relates to previous requests from that same client—is often done in ways that severely restrict later scalability.
- Creating the best possible client experience regardless of client device often requires device-specific code that is difficult to maintain.
- Planning how the presentation fortress will fulfill the client request (e.g., make a purchase) requires an understanding of the overall enterprise fortress architecture.

10.1.1 J2EE versus the .NET Approach

For the presentation fortress, the technology battle is between J2EE's JavaServer Pages (JSP) and Microsoft's ASP.NET/Visual Studio.NET.

JavaServer Pages is very similar to Microsoft's pre-.NET technology, known as ASP (Active Server Pages).

JSP and ASP both make the presentation fortress implementor responsible for determining what the client did, managing the client's state, and creating a device-specific experience—three difficult tasks. A typical flowchart for a JSP or ASP presentation fortress looks something like Figure 10.2.

The new ASP.NET programming model is much simpler because most of the fortress responsibilities are managed automatically by the presentation fortress infrastructure. A typical ASP.NET flowchart is shown in Figure 10.3, which, as you can see, is a huge reduction in complexity over Figure 10.2.

The reason ASP.NET achieves such a huge simplification is not that issues like state management, browser interactions, and device dependencies have gone away. Rather, ASP.NET automatically handles these issues on your behalf.

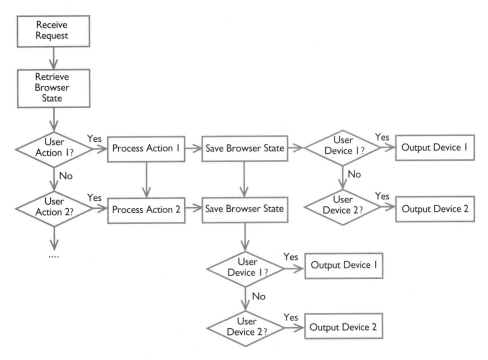

Figure 10.2 JSP or ASP Presentation Fortress Flowchart

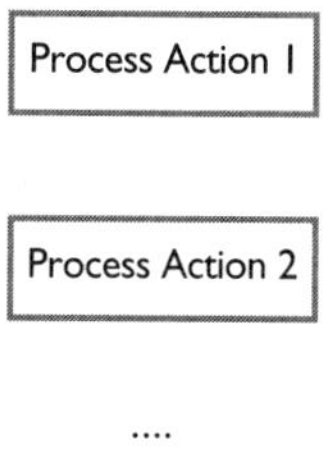

```
┌─────────────────┐
│ Process Action 1 │
└─────────────────┘


┌─────────────────┐
│ Process Action 2 │
└─────────────────┘


     ....
```

Figure 10.3 ASP.NET Presentation Fortress Flowchart

The JSP technology does have some features in its favor, primarily the support for non-Windows platforms. ASP.NET works only if your presentation fortress is built on the Windows platform. If you must run your presentation fortress on a different platform—say, Linux or a mainframe—ASP.NET won't help you. In this case you either use a particular vendor's implementation of JSP or come up with a proprietary solution.

The other differentiator between ASP.NET and JSP is language. Like all the J2EE technologies, JSP is hardwired to Java. The entire .NET platform is much more accommodating as far as languages are concerned. This topic is more relevant to the business application fortress, so I will postpone this discussion until Chapter 11 (Business Application Fortresses).

As far as presentation fortress technologies go, then, .NET wins on the simplicity of its programming model and its broad-based language support. J2EE wins on its broad-based platform support and Java support. Clearly both technologies have advantages. These are the main issues that differentiate J2EE's JSP and .NET's ASP.NET. The remaining issues are similar for both platforms, so I will discuss them generically.

10.1.2 Scalability

As usual, my preferred approach to scalability as it applies to presentation fortresses is to use a cluster (scale-out) architecture. For presentation fortresses, clusters are based on HTTP routers that balance the workload across a cluster of machines.

As Figure 10.4 illustrates, when a request comes in from a browser, it goes through a sequence of events like this:

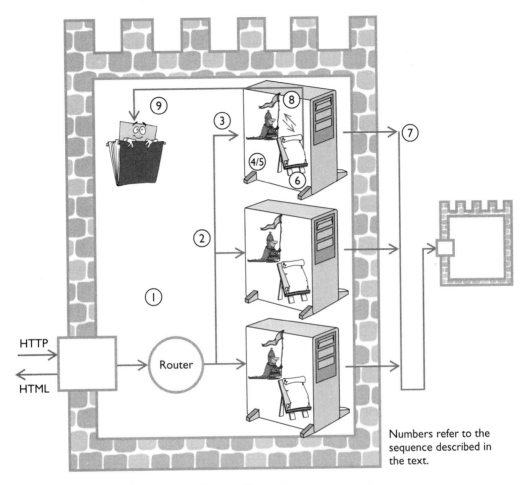

Figure 10.4 Routing of Presentation Fortress Requests

1. The request passes through the drawbridge and is picked up by an HTTP/IP router.

2. The router chooses one of several similarly configured machines to process the request. It can do this either randomly or on the basis of its own workload tracking.

3. The router sends the request to the chosen machine.

4. The request is passed to the guard on that machine.

5. The guard decides whether to accept the request, possibly on the basis of the previous history of this browser session.

6. The request is passed to a worker, who figures out what, exactly, the user sitting at the browser wants to do, possibly using the previous history of this browser session.

7. The worker coordinates through envoys (not shown) with other fortresses to fulfill the request.

8. The worker prepares the HTML response and delivers it back to the browser.

9. The worker may need to update the history of this browser session to reflect the new work.

Notice that I haven't discussed how browser state, or session history, is maintained. The browser state can be stored in any of three places: on the browser, in the shared presentation fortress data strongbox, or on the guard/worker machine. I think of these options as more relevant to reliability than to scalability, so I will wait until the reliability discussion (Section 10.1.4) to compare these options.

10.1.3 Security

The presentation fortress is the most vulnerable part of your entire enterprise system. The only other fortress that is even close to it in terms of vulnerability is the Web service fortress, and Web service fortresses are not used widely. For a presentation fortress, security means two things. First, you must do everything possible to protect the fortress from malicious attack. Second, you must assume that you will ultimately fail and that, despite your best efforts, the horrible "they" will break in anyway.

Here are my major rules for protecting the presentation fortress. There are no guarantees in the world of security, but if you diligently follow these 11 rules, you will eliminate the vast majority of system compromises that occur today. The first seven rules have to do with trying to prevent fortress break-ins:

Rule 1: Put a firewall in front of the fortress. This firewall can be thought of as part of your fortress wall fortification. This is your first line of defense against *them*.

Rule 2: Put a firewall between the presentation fortress and the rest of the enterprise. When *they* do break into your presentation fortress, this additional firewall buys you a little more protection. Don't get too excited about this. If *they* can break through the first firewall, *they* can probably break through the second one as well.

The combination of Rule 1 and Rule 2 creates what is often referred to as a demilitarized zone (DMZ).

Rule 3: Keep up with security patches from your vendor. Most enterprise systems are compromised through known vulnerabilities with available patches that were never applied.

Rule 4: Run the presentation fortress on a minimal system. Disable any capabilities you do not need. Every capability available within the fortress is a potential vulnerability for *them* to attack. If you don't need to allow FTP or remote login, disable these options.

Rule 5: Validate all user input. I discussed this topic in Chapter 7 (Guards and Walls). Check for both buffer overflows and illegal characters.

Rule 6: Never assume that an HTTP request is coming from where you think it's coming from. *They* can create an HTTP request that looks exactly like one coming from your own form.

Rule 7: Guard the connection between the browser and your fortress. Even if perfectly respectable clients are running on the browser, *they* may be eavesdropping and even changing data as it moves back and forth between the browser and the fortress. Secure Sockets Layer (SSL) is a good candidate technology for this kind of duty.

Rules 8 through 11 exist because we assume the first seven rules will fail. These "fallback" rules are about minimizing the damage *they* can do once *they* have succeeded in breaking into your precious presentation fortress.

Rule 8: Run the presentation fortress with minimal permissions. A common attack is one in which *they* hijack one of the presentation fortress processes (e.g., the guard/worker process). If the process is running with just enough permissions to do its job, then the hijackers are limited in terms of how much damage *they* can do.

Rule 9: Stage the presentation fortress on a system that is not connected to the Internet. This staging machine has the official version of your presentation fortress, and when *they* break into your online presentation fortress and corrupt your files (not if, but when), you can re-create them from your staging machine. If your staging machine is not connected to the Internet, then it can't easily be corrupted from outside your organization. Of course, you still have the disgruntled employees *inside* your organization to worry about.

Rule 10: Don't store anything you care about anywhere in the presentation fortress, including the data strongbox. The data strongbox, after all, is part of the presentation fortress and therefore trusts any process that is a cohabitant of the fortress. The strongbox doesn't distinguish between hijacked and nonhijacked processes. Do not store credit cards, passwords, secret keys, sensitive customer information, or proprietary algorithms in the presentation fortress. This rule applies not only to data in the data strongbox, but to confidential information anyplace in the fortress, including files, executables, virtual memory, or system registries. Do not allow your presentation fortress to share a resource with any other fortress unless you can absolutely guarantee complete isolation (and you probably can't).

Rule 11: Use a software fortress architecture. This rule may seem odd. If you have read this far, you have presumably bought into the software fortress approach. This just seems like a good place to reiterate the importance of the trust boundary in maintaining overall enterprise security. Your business logic, living as it does in a business application fortress, does not trust your presentation logic, which lives in an alien and highly suspect presentation fortress. The software fortress architecture *assumes* that when you move from a presentation fortress to a business fortress, you are crossing a trust boundary. Even when *they* break into your presentation fortress, *they* still have a long way to go before *they* can compromise mission-critical systems and data.

Many of these rules are fortress adaptations of recommendations made by the CERT/Coordination Center (formally known as the

Computer Emergency Response Team Coordination Center) for any Internet-connected enterprise system, whether or not it is built with fortresses. These rules, with a few adaptations, just happen to fit especially well with the software fortress approach.

10.1.4 Reliability

Reliability means that you can count on a fortress to be there when your browser clients look for it. There is true reliability and pseudo-reliability, the latter based on asynchronous drawbridges and discussed in Chapter 6 (Asynchronous Drawbridges). The input to a presentation fortress is an HTTP request, which is synchronous. HTTP may not be exactly a poster child for a synchronous messaging system, but it is synchronous nevertheless. Pseudoreliability is therefore not an option for the presentation fortress. We must look for true reliability.

I have discussed scale-out versus scale-up several times in regard to both scalability and reliability. I have pointed out that scale-out is preferable where possible. As I mentioned earlier in this chapter, the presentation fortress is particularly fortunate to have good cluster algorithms in the form of HTTP/IP load balancing. To make the most of the cluster for reliability, however, we do need to build our presentation fortresses appropriately.

Imagine that a browser is making two HTTP requests—R1 and R2—to a presentation fortress. Assume that our fortress is implemented with a cluster of four machines, M1 through M4, and is controlled by an IP load balancer. The basic configuration is shown in Figure 10.5.

Assume that both requests, R1 and R2, are "naturally" headed toward machine M1. I'll take you through the possibilities of M1 going down for the count. M1 could go down at any of five possible moments:

1. Before R1 is received
2. After R1 is received but before R1 is completely processed
3. After R1 is processed but before R2 is received
4. After R2 is received but before R2 is processed
5. After R2 is processed

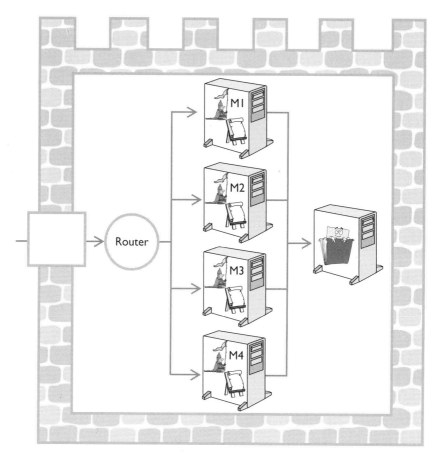

Figure 10.5 Reliability Configuration of a Presentation Fortress

Case 1 (failure before R1 is received) is dealt with by the IP router. In this case the router will recognize that M1 is down and reroute R1 to another machine. Overall, fortress reliability is maintained. Nobody will ever know that M1 went down.

Case 2 (failure before R1 has been completed) is dealt with by the fortress architect, who makes sure that any updates done by the fortress as a result of R1 are transactionally protected. I discussed transaction algorithms back in Chapter 3 (Transactions). If all of the R1 updates are contained within a single transaction, then by the guarantee of transactional integrity, either all of those updates will succeed or none will succeed. Therefore, in the worst scenario you will have to submit R1 again. If M1 is still down when you make that rerequest, the failure will be dealt with as a Case 1 failure.

Case 3 (failure between requests) is an interesting case. R1 has been processed, but R2 has not yet been received. Presumably the overall state of the browser session has been changed as a result of the success of R1. The issue is, where are you storing that browser session state (e.g., an updated shopping cart)? This is where the decisions made by the fortress architect become critical.

I said earlier that there are three places to store the changed browser state: on the browser machine, in memory on the fortress machine processing the browser request, or in the fortress data strongbox.

Storing the entire browser session state on the browser machine itself (either in a field or in a cookie) means that the entire session state must be passed into the presentation fortress with every request. This is not very efficient.

Storing the browser session state in memory (or even on a local disk) on the fortress machine causes reliability problems. If the machine goes down between requests (Case 3), you have lost the browser session state and the browser client must restart the session.

The right place to store the browser session state is the software fortress's data strongbox. Now if M1 goes down between requests, there is no problem. M2 can pick up where M1 left off. Remember, the data strongbox is not local to any single machine in the presentation fortress. It is a resource shared by all machines in the fortress.

You might ask what happens if the machine hosting the data strongbox goes down. This is a much different problem, and either we decide not to worry about this, or we use techniques specialized for high database reliability. These techniques include Redundant Array of Independent Disks (RAID) algorithms to protect the disk drives and tightly coupled backup cluster algorithms to protect the machine itself. These are standard techniques in the database industry, and nothing about them is in any way specific to software fortresses.

Storing the browser session state in the data strongbox is good, but not enough. You still need to store the key to that session state someplace.

The *session state key* is the information the fortress machine needs to find the specific session state being stored in the data strongbox. The session state key can't be stored in the data strongbox without a recursive problem being created (where is the key to the key to the session state stored?). It can't be stored on the machine processing the request, because if it is lost, so is the session state itself (the data may now be locked safely away, but we have lost the means of finding it!).

The session state key must be stored someplace on the browser machine. You can put it in a cookie. You can put it in a browser form field. You can try to convince the browser to let you open a data file (good luck!). How you store it is less important than where you store it. It must live someplace on the browser machine.

This means, of course, that the session state key must be passed in with every request from the browser to the presentation fortress. But wasn't this one of my objections to storing the session state itself on the browser?

It was, but session states represent a lot more data than session state *keys*. The key need be only large enough to uniquely identify the true data to the data strongbox. In the overall scheme of things, the overhead of passing in session state keys with each browser request isn't worth worrying about.

The remaining two failure cases can be considered variants on problems that are already solved. Case 4 (M1 goes down while processing R2) is just a variant of Case 2 (M1 goes down while processing R1). Case 5 is a variant of Case 1 if R2 is the last request, or a variant of Case 3 if there will be an R3.

10.1.5 Integrity

The remaining architectural issues relating to presentation fortresses have to do with internal integrity. How easy is it to mess up the state of the fortress?

Part of this we have already dealt with. We don't have to worry about a partial update of fortress data, for example, if the fortress dies while processing a request. (Why? Because we have transactional protection, as discussed in the preceding section.) But other problems may occur.

Suppose, for example, that the browser sends a request R1 that is "naturally" headed for machine M1 in the fortress cluster, and that M1 dies just before it receives the request. The browser eventually gets bored waiting for a response and sends R1 again. We'll call this version of R1 R1A. But now it turns out that M1 didn't die; it was just out getting coffee. M1 returns and receives both R1 and R1A. Now what happens?

What happens depends on exactly what R1 looks like. If R1 was a request to find out what time of day it is, it probably will do no harm to process both R1 and R1A. But suppose R1 is a request to withdraw 1,000 dollars from your savings account. You might have problems with that request being processed twice!

What is the difference between one request that asks for the time of day and another that withdraws 1,000 dollars from your savings account? This is an interesting theoretical problem that is dealt with most extensively by Pat Helland's fiefdom model for software architectures.

Helland defines requests by whether or not they are what he calls *idempotent*. He defines an idempotent request as one that can be executed multiple times with the same result as one would get if it were executed once. In other words, as long as the request is processed more than zero times, it doesn't matter how many times more than zero it is processed.

One of the tricks to designing integrity into a presentation fortress is designing all requests to be idempotent. This means recognizing, at design time, when a request is not idempotent and then changing it to an equivalent version that is idempotent. I suspect (but have not proved) that all nonidempotent requests have an idempotent equivalent. In fact, most probably have many idempotent equivalents.

Let me give you an example of a metamorphosis from nonidempotent to idempotent. Consider a request to withdraw money. A nonidempotent request simply asks for 1,000 dollars to be withdrawn from account 100. An equivalent idempotent version includes a request ID that is assigned by the browser. This request ID can then be checked by the presentation fortress to make sure the request hasn't already been processed. If the presentation fortress gets two requests with the same request ID, it discards the duplicates. With the idempotent version, you can send duplicates all night without doing any harm.

Note that the idempotent version is not free. You need to assign request IDs in your browser form. You have to design a system to assign request IDs, verify uniqueness, and store their histories. All of this needs to be designed by somebody. Guess who?

10.2 Web Service Fortresses

A Web service fortress shares many characteristics with a presentation fortress. Both act as security buffers protecting your enterprise. Both act as gateways to the outside world. Both receive their requests over the Internet.

There is one major difference between the two fortress types: A presentation fortress receives its requests from browsers. A Web service fortress, on the other hand, receives its requests from programs.

Because the presentation fortress is receiving its requests from a browser, you can start with the assumption (security concerns aside, for the moment) that it is your code making the request. It is not your code running inside your presentation fortress, but it is your code nevertheless. In his fiefdom architecture, Pat Helland calls this code *emissary code*. Because the emissary sending the request is written by the same group that wrote the guard receiving the request, there is no need for strong standards documenting the requests that are accepted by the presentation fortress.

Keep in mind that from a security perspective, you never assume that the request really came from your code (security Rule 6, earlier in this chapter). But this is a different issue. From a documentation perspective, you can assume that the typical presentation fortress request is coming from something you have written that has been offloaded to the browser.

A Web service fortress is different. There is no assumption that it is receiving its requests from anything you wrote. For this reason you need to be able to describe exactly what your fortress can do in a way that a program outside your organization can understand. You must also adhere to some recognized standards as to exactly how the request will be made and transmitted, and the responses returned.

The standards that are defining Web service fortresses (or just Web services, for those who are not yet proponents of the software fortress model) are the SOAP family of standards.

I have already discussed SOAP in the context of heterogeneous synchronous drawbridges. Although there is widespread agreement within the industry today that SOAP is *the* solution, there is very little agreement in the industry as to exactly what problem SOAP is supposed to solve. I hope that the software fortress model will help clarify exactly when SOAP should be used and what problems it should be used to solve.

SOAP can contribute solutions for two problems: The first SOAP-amenable problem is how to accept programmatic requests from outside the enterprise. Included in this is all the peripheral issues, such as describing what requests you're willing to accept, making some delivery guarantees, and perhaps even adding a pinch of security (just for old time's sake). Because systems outside of the enterprise are the least trusted of all systems, we insist that these requests go through a no-man's-land. We implement this no-man's-land as a Web service fortress.

The other SOAP-amenable problem is to provide a heterogeneous synchronous drawbridge between two fortresses (probably business application fortresses) inside the enterprise. We can't use homogeneous synchronous drawbridges (our first choice) because the fortresses are running on different technology bases. Because both systems are inside the fortress, they are relatively trusted (relative to an outside fortress). For such fortresses we may not insist that such communication go through a no-man's-land.

In the future, SOAP will probably find itself taking part in not only heterogeneous *synchronous* drawbridges, but heterogeneous *asynchronous* drawbridges, as message queue-like technologies begin to incorporate SOAP support natively.

10.2.1 J2EE versus the .NET Approach

At this point in time, there seems to be little disagreement among the vendors on their support for the SOAP technologies. If there is any argument, it is over who is embracing SOAP more, how deeply SOAP is being placed in the technology, and how transparent the use of SOAP is. On the basis of the vendors' use of SOAP, there is no obvious reason for choosing either J2EE or .NET for a Web service fortress.

Although SOAP does not provide a compelling reason for choosing between J2EE and .NET, it is more helpful in choosing between the various J2EE vendors. At this point there are only three enterprise-credible J2EE vendors: IBM, Sun, and BEA. Of these, IBM is the clear leader in Web services. Until recently, Sun was arguing that SOAP-like standards aren't even necessary, and BEA has so far taken a back seat to Sun.

Virtually all of the critical SOAP standards are, as of now, a joint development effort between IBM and Microsoft. Microsoft deserves credit for originating the SOAP concept, and IBM deserves credit for giving the technology credibility within the enterprise space. Given IBM's leadership in this area, it should probably be a top contender among those companies who plan to use SOAP and J2EE heavily.

10.2.2 Technology Overview

Recall from the discussion on synchronous drawbridges (Chapter 5) that SOAP is a mapping protocol that describes how a method request can be represented as a string (an XML string, not that it matters). That stringified method request then needs to be transmitted from the requestor to the requestee by means of component-like surrogates. For a Web service fortress, requests are transmitted typically via HTTP.

Before I cover the different standards, let me go through the sequence of events that occurs as a message goes from the requestor through

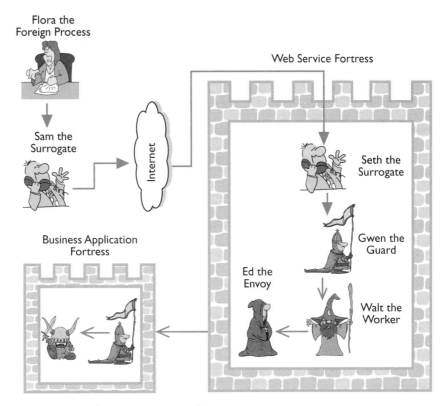

Figure 10.6 Web Service Fortress Characters

the Web service fortress and eventually on to a business logic fortress. The characters involved in this drama are shown in Figure 10.6.

These characters have the following functions:

- Flora is a foreign process that wants to make a request of a Web service fortress.
- Sam and Seth are both SOAP surrogates.
- Gwen is an incoming guard.
- Ed is an envoy.
- Walt is the worker that runs the logic of the Web service fortress.

Let's go through the flow of information from Flora the foreign process through the Web service fortress and on to the back-end business application fortress. Let's assume that Flora's request is to withdraw 500 dollars from account number 1000. To simplify, we won't worry about idempotency (a topic discussed earlier in this chapter).

Flora wants to request the withdrawal, but she doesn't know anything about SOAP. Her software vendor has provided her with the ability to create a SOAP surrogate. A *SOAP surrogate* is a surrogate that knows how to make remote fortress requests using the SOAP protocol and the HTTP delivery mechanism. So Flora asks Sam, her SOAP surrogate, to withdraw 500 dollars from account number 1000.

Sam packages the request as a SOAP string and ships it to the Web service fortress. The request is picked up by Seth, another SOAP surrogate. Seth unpacks the SOAP string and determines that the request maps to a method supported by Gwen, the incoming guard. Gwen is a native component. Seth sends a component-style method request to Gwen.

Gwen decides to accept the request. She passes the information on to Walt the worker bee, the one who knows how to process the request. Note that processing the request probably means routing it to a business fortress elsewhere within the enterprise.

Walt now decides which fortress will get the request and which drawbridge he will use. He determines that the necessary drawbridge is the one presided over by Ed the envoy. Ed packages Walt's request and sends it on to his (Ed's) drawbridge. The infogram will be sent on to the business fortress that has the knowledge (and data) to process the withdrawal request.

Ed's drawbridge is a standard software fortress drawbridge. It can be asynchronous heterogeneous, asynchronous homogeneous, synchronous heterogeneous, or synchronous homogeneous. I discussed the characteristics of each of these drawbridges in Chapters 4 through 6.

Given this sequence of events, we can start to understand how the various standards of the SOAP family play together.

At the lowest level, we need a standard algorithm for representing a request as a string, and we need a standard transport protocol. As already discussed, SOAP defines the stringification algorithms, and

HTTP is the likely transport protocol (at least, in the Web service fortress scenario). SOAP thus allows Flora the foreign process to make a request on one of the enterprise business systems mediated by Walt the Web service fortress worker bee. Most importantly, SOAP allows Flora to make this request without knowing anything whatsoever about the business system, including the technology base on which it is built, the language in which it is programmed, or even the operating system on which it runs. The only thing Flora needs to know is that SOAP requests are accepted.

A SOAP request string has a complex format. There is no way that Flora (or more precisely, Flora's programmer) will be able to construct a SOAP string. So, to allow Flora to make the SOAP request in a natural way, the vendor of Flora's technology base will make the use of SOAP totally transparent to Flora. To do this, the vendor will provide tools to automatically generate Sam the SOAP surrogate. From Flora's perspective, Sam just looks like a normal component with normal methods. Little does Flora know or care that Sam packages his methods as SOAP strings and transmits them using HTTP. Nor does Flora know anything about Seth, Sam's counterpart in the Web service fortress.

But how do these tools automatically create Sam? The building of Sam is driven by the definition of Seth. So to build Sam, the Sam-generating tool needs at least the following information:

- Where in Internet space does Seth live?
- What requests is Seth willing to receive?
- What is the exact format of these requests?
- What information will Seth return?
- How will errors be handled?

Furthermore, the Sam-generating tool needs this information in a standard format that the tool can automatically read. This format must be independent of the platform on which Seth lives because the Sam-generating tool will probably be running on a platform other than the one supporting Seth. So we need not only a standard for making the request of Seth (which we have, SOAP), but also a standard for describing what these requests will look like.

In other words, we need a standard for describing the requests that the Web service fortress is willing to accept on behalf of the enterprise.

The standard that describes what requests will be accepted by a Web service software fortress is the *Web Services Description Language* (*WSDL*). WSDL contains all of the information that the Sam-generating tool could possibly need to create a fully functional Sam that can work with Seth.

If you think that the SOAP format is complicated, wait until you see WSDL. The purpose of WSDL is to allow tools to generate SOAP surrogates automatically so that you are protected from all the complex mysteries of SOAP. But who will protect you from the far more abstruse mysteries of WSDL?

Just as the vendors will provide tools to "consume" WSDL (i.e., create SOAP surrogates corresponding to WSDL documents), they will also provide you with tools to generate WSDL documents automatically. How this is done is not defined by any standard. When you're evaluating different vendors, one of the things you should look at is how well they shield you from both WSDL and SOAP.

A likely scenario for creating a WSDL document is that you will define an interface for a native component using a vendor-specific GUI tool. A compiler option will indicate that you really want this component to support SOAP. When the tool sees the SOAP option set, it will automatically create both the SOAP receiving surrogate (Seth) and the WSDL document that defines Seth and that will ultimately form a template for Sam.

There is still one more problem. How does Flora's system find the WSDL document that defines the SOAP requests that enable her tool to create Sam, who can then talk to Seth?

A general rule in computer science says that you never pass up the opportunity to create another standard—if possible, more than one. In the case of finding WSDL documents, we have been blessed with not one but two standards.

Universal Description, Discovery and Integration (UDDI) is a relatively mature standard that allows one to find random WSDL documents spread across the Internet universe. Maturity, in this case, does not equate to value. So far there has been virtually no use of UDDI. The reason, I believe, is that UDDI is oriented toward finding WSDL documents for "new" collaborators—that is, collaborators with whom you have never worked before. In my experience, finding new collaborators isn't hard, and we don't need a standard that solves this problem. What we really need are standards oriented toward collaborators we already know about. Finding them isn't hard; working with them is. Given the mistaken premise of UDDI, I think we will see what little use it is getting eventually die out. Therefore I won't discuss UDDI further.

The other standard for finding WSDL documents is known as *Web Services Inspection Language (WS-Inspection)*. As of press time, WS-Inspection is still in draft state, so it is too early to know if it will make it. However, like most of the successful Web service–related standards, this is a joint effort by the only two vendors that anybody cares about in the enterprise space: IBM and Microsoft. It thus seems likely that this standard will eventually become a permanent feature of the Web service landscape.

WS-Inspection differs from UDDI. Whereas UDDI allows you to find *any* vendor, including those you never heard of, that supports a specific service, WS-Inspection is less grandiose. It only tries to solve the problem of working with known collaborators. It allows you to go to a *specific* Web site and discover the Web service fortresses the organization supports and the WSDL documents that describe those fortresses.

10.2.3 SOAP Problems

Lest you think that SOAP will solve all of your problems, let me reassure you. SOAP, as it exists today, lacks many of the features we would expect from a serious messaging backbone. Many of these problems are under attack by various standards, but it will likely be years before these standards are finalized and implemented.

Here are some of the issues you can expect to see with SOAP for the near future:

- There is no guarantee that a SOAP message will ever be delivered. And there is no guarantee that if it is delivered, it won't be delivered multiple times. Thus it is critical that all SOAP messages be idempotent. (Idempotency was discussed in Section 10.1.)

- There is no way to tell who is on either side of the message. There is no way for Flora the foreign process to know that her message is being delivered to Walt the Web service worker bee, and there is no way for Walt to know that the message really came from Flora.

- There is no privacy with SOAP. Both messages and replies are transmitted in clear text over the Internet. Not only can *they* read the message, *they* can change it on route.

It could be argued that these missing features are requirements not of the stringification algorithm (SOAP), but of the underlying transport protocol (e.g., HTTP). And, in fact, some of these features are provided by HTTPS. However, the general consensus in the industry is that SOAP should be enhanced to include these types of functionality.

10.2.4 Scalability

Scalability is generally less of an issue for Web service fortresses than for presentation fortresses for several reasons.

First, few people are actually using Web service fortresses. As I have discussed, the more common use for SOAP is as a heterogeneous synchronous drawbridge technology within the enterprise, and even here, it is still in its infancy.

Second, most presentation fortresses perform far more work than do most Web service fortresses. The scalability demands for a Web services fortress are therefore much lower. To start with, figuring out how to interpret the incoming request is much more demanding for a presentation fortress than for a Web service fortress. Add to this the work of managing browser state (a problem most Web service fortresses don't need to worry about) and creating a beautiful presentation (another issue that doesn't concern the Web service fortress). In contrast, the Web service has to do little other than check security (a function also required of the presentation fortress) and route the request to a business fortress. Not exactly a hard life!

Still, it is possible to design your Web service fortress in such a way that it can't scale. The most common problem is not so much a scalability problem as it is a general performance problem. In other words, it's not that you can't *increase* the number of users on your system, it's that you can't get even *one* user to work successfully.

When single-user performance is a problem for a Web service fortress, the likely cause is an architectural flaw in the design of the drawbridge to the fortress. The common flaw is creating the drawbridge interface with too fine a granularity, meaning that poor Flora the foreign process needs to make too many SOAP requests to get any work done. SOAP, especially SOAP delivered with HTTP, is a very expensive protocol and should be used sparingly.

The best solution to single-user performance problems is to look carefully at the drawbridge requests. The requests should be designed to be coarse-grained, self-contained, and idempotent. It is almost always better to send in more information in fewer infograms than less information in more infograms.

On the remote chance that you have an overwhelming demand for your Web service fortress, you will use a similar approach to scaling out as you would for your presentation fortress—that is, IP load-balanced, loosely coupled clusters.

10.2.5 Security

Given what little help we get from the SOAP protocol, the security issues for Web service fortresses look a lot like those for presentation fortresses. With minor modifications, the 11 rules for protecting a presentation fortress apply to Web service fortresses as well. Let's go through them.

The first four rules are pretty much unchanged. Rule 1 (firewall in front) and Rule 2 (firewall behind) apply equally well to Web services. Rule 3 (keep up with patches) also applies, but the reality is that the vendors probably won't release nearly as many patches for your Web service fortress as they will for your presentation fortress. In any case, keep up with whatever they do send. Rule 4 (run on a minimal system) also works for Web service fortresses. You want to accept SOAP requests, period.

Rule 5 (validate user input) is similar for both fortress types. You still need to validate input, for the same reasons. You need to guard against process hijacking, and you need to make sure you don't accidentally pass through unintentional commands to the trusting fortress critters who live farther down the food chain.

Rule 6 (no assumptions about request origins) is probably less of a problem for a Web service than for a presentation fortress because the Web service architect harbors no illusions about where the request came from.

Rule 7 (guard the connections) is exactly the same for the Web service fortress. Secure sockets, one of the ways of guarding the presentation fortress, is a good candidate for Web service fortresses as well. Eventually guarding the fortress may become less of a problem as more and more security is built directly into the SOAP protocol.

Rules 8 through 11 are the fallback rules, those that assume intruders will eventually gain control of your precious Web service fortress. All four rules are the same for Web services as for presentation fortresses. Rule 8 (minimal permissions) protects a hijacked Web service fortress, Rule 9 (stage on a safe server) guarantees recovery, Rule 10 I will discuss in a moment, and Rule 11 (use a software fortress architecture) is just a generally good way to live life.

Rule 10 (don't store anything of value in the fortress) deserves some specific discussion. This rule is really the whole reason for having a Web service fortress.

Many companies are thinking of using Web service technologies to allow collaborators to access their business systems directly over the Internet. I believe that this is much too risky because it is almost impossible to fully protect a system connected to the Internet. Once *they* break into such a system, *they* have full access to confidential data, proprietary algorithms, and trusted accounts.

On the other hand, collaboration over the Internet is an intriguing possibility (still a somewhat remote possibility, as things stand today). Web service fortresses represent a compromise position, allowing collaboration while still managing (but unfortunately, not eliminating) your security risk.

10.2.6 Reliability

Scale out for reliability, just as you do with your presentation fortress. It is actually easier to make a Web service fortress reliable than to make a presentation fortress reliable, mainly because it is harder to screw up state management.

For a presentation fortress, the state of the requestor is the state of the browser, and browsers seem to have a natural propensity to holding on to long-term state. Of course, the assumption that the presentation fortress should care about the browser's state is more psychological than technical because, as we all know, browsers also communicate with a stateless protocol (HTTP). That doesn't seem to stop us from expecting the poor overworked presentation fortress to find a way to manage the browser's state.

For a Web service fortress, the state of the requestor is the state of the foreign process. People understand that this request is going to go through SOAP and that SOAP is a naturally stateless protocol (one SOAP request remembers nothing about the previous SOAP request). Therefore, nobody asks the Web service fortress to maintain the state of the foreign process.

10.2.7 Integrity

Like the presentation fortress, the Web service fortress is transactionally protected against internal failure. And again, the main challenge is making sure that all requests are, as Pat Helland would say, idempotent. There is nothing new to add here.

Summary

We have now completed our first stop on the software fortress tour. We have covered the two fortress types that are Internet intermediaries. The major points are these:

- Presentation fortresses deal with browser clients.

- Web service fortresses deal with foreign processes.

- Both presentation and Web service fortresses act as security buffers between the outside world and your precious computing systems.

- As of press time, Microsoft's .NET technologies have several important advantages for the presentation fortress. There are no obvious differentiators for the Web service fortresses, although IBM does seem to have taken an early lead among the J2EE vendors.

- Scalability of Web service and presentation fortresses is achieved through IP load balancing and loosely coupled clusters.

- Security is paramount for Internet fortresses. The general approach is to guard the fortresses the best you can and then assume you will fail.

- Make sure your presentation fortresses manage browser state in a way that is consistent with scaling out the cluster.

- Make all of your requests idempotent.

- Hope that the powers that be get around to improving SOAP before you have to use it (especially from the security perspective).

- For your Web service fortress, plan to use SOAP for formatting requests, WSDL for describing them, and WS-Inspection for making your WSDL documents available.

CHAPTER 11

Business Application Fortresses

Business application fortresses are the bread and butter of your enterprise. These are the fortresses that actually make you money. They process your account withdrawals, your stock purchases, and all your other purchases. They deserve your respect and gratitude.

If your business application fortresses are designed well, your enterprise will run smoothly. If not, you will have problems. Badly designed business application fortresses result in enterprise systems that perform poorly, scale sluggishly, and fail frequently. When I examine sickly enterprise systems, invariably I find the underlying disease in the business application area.

Design errors in business application fortresses are particularly pernicious. Often the problems do not become apparent until huge amounts of coding have been completed. By then the cure, if it exists at all, is tremendously expensive. So it is critical to design these fortresses correctly from the beginning.

11.1 Foundation: Components and COMWare

Business application fortresses are usually built on two related foundation technologies. The first is distributed components. This is the same distributed-component technology that I discussed in Chapter 5 (Synchronous Drawbridges), and it maps exactly to the technology used by homogeneous synchronous drawbridges. The second foundation technology is a technology I refer to as *component-oriented middleware (COMWare)*.

COMWare was first introduced long before .NET by Microsoft under the name Microsoft Transaction Server (MTS), then it was adopted by Sun to be J2EE's EJB technology, and then finally it was released once again by Microsoft under the name COM+. COMWare is a layer above components, so let me start by reviewing how components work.

As I discussed in Chapter 5 (Synchronous Drawbridges), a *component* is a blob of software defined by an interface and distributed over a network. Clients make requests on these components through intermediaries called *surrogates*. These surrogates handle the details of the communication, allowing the client programmer and the component programmer to focus on their little application worlds.

Two processes communicate with each other. The *client process* is the one in which the client, or caller, resides. The *component process* is the one in which the hardworking instances of the component reside.

In a standard component system the client code is responsible for managing the life cycle of the component instances. The client controls when the component instance is created, how long the component instance is used, and when the component instance is finally destroyed. Invisible to the client is the fact that surrogates are created, used, and destroyed along with component instances. Figure 11.1 illustrates the life cycle of a component.

When components are being used in the context of a business application fortress, the client and the component instance are running inside the same fortress (although probably not in the same process). The client is one of two things: either the guard or another component compatriot.

In fact, the guard itself may well also be a component. The guard's client is the guard process, the one whose responsibility is to constantly loop and check the drawbridge for messages. When the process finds a message, it sends the message to its guard component, which does the usual guardy stuff—namely, approving the messages and passing them on to the appropriate fortress workers. Figure 11.2

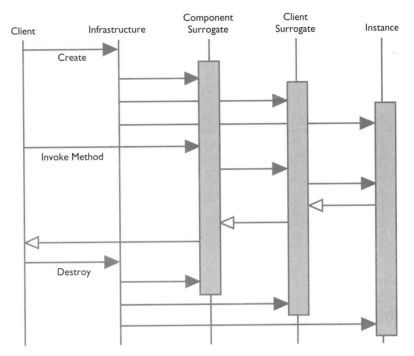

Figure 11.1 Component Life Cycle

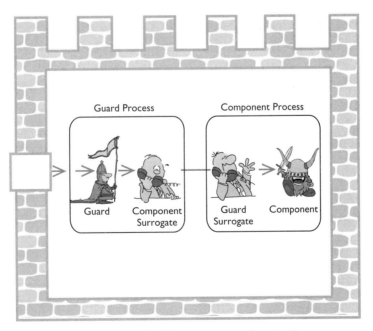

Figure 11.2 The Entities within the Business Application Fortress

shows how the guard process, the guard, the various components, and the surrogates are related.

Component-oriented middleware provides another layer of functionality beyond the distributed capabilities of components. COMWare works by intercepting the method request as it passes between the two surrogates, as shown in Figure 11.3.

This point at which the COMWare system intercepts the method request is what I call the *point of interception*. In a normal component system, one without COMWare, the method request moves directly from one surrogate to the other. In COMWare, the interception point provides an opportunity for the infrastructure to add value to the method delivery in the form of a series of value-added algorithms.

COMWare was originally developed within the context of three-tier, rich client–oriented systems. It was heavily influenced by the technology known as transaction processing monitors (TPMs). Some of the original goals of COMWare are no longer relevant to a fortress architecture, but some are still important. In this chapter I will discuss COMWare technologies from a software fortress perspective.

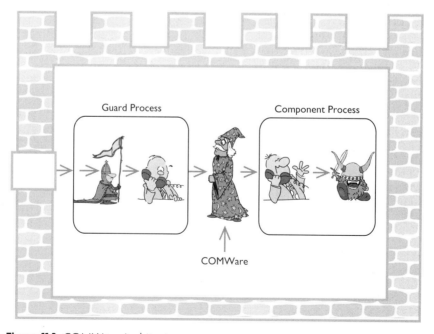

Figure 11.3 COMWare Architecture

Of the various functions of COMWare, three stand out as relevant to software fortresses:

1. Role-based security
2. State management
3. Transaction boundary management

The first of these, role-based security, I discussed already in Chapter 7 (Guards and Walls). It is an important function, but I feel that I have given it due coverage. In this chapter I will discuss only state management and transaction boundary management. In turns out that these two topics are closely related.

11.1.1 State Management

State management is managing the component state. The *component state* consists of any data needed by the component to process its request. If the component is a savings account in a banking operation, the component state might include information such as the account ID, current balance, and account password.

In theory, state information can be stored in three different places. It can be stored in the memory associated with a specific component instance (similar to how state is stored in object-oriented systems). It can be stored in the data strongbox (which, for a business application fortress, is invariably a database). Last and, it turns out, least, it can be stored "someplace else."

It is a rare business application fortress developer who does not attempt to come up with a "someplace else" to store state. The temptation is almost irresistible. Caches in memory are a particularly tempting "someplace else" because they perform so well. Do not succumb to this temptation. It is very difficult to create a "someplace else" and get it right.

In this book I will explore only the component instance memory and the strongbox as places to store component state. Both sites are used, but at different times. The real issue of state management is how to manage the movement of state between instance memory and the data strongbox.

Plans for state migration are an important part of any business application fortress design. If you don't migrate state often enough, you end up with poor reliability, scalability, and integrity. If you migrate too often, you end up with poor performance. Fortunately, COMWare provides some technology and, perhaps more importantly, a model for dealing with state migration. It all revolves around transaction boundary management, which is the second of the three functions we look to COMWare to provide.

I'll take a break, then, to look at transaction boundary management, and then return in Section 11.1.3 to the issue of state management.

11.1.2 Transaction Boundary Management

Oddly enough, COMWare has very little to do with transactions. It has a lot to do with something closely related to transactions—namely, transaction boundary management. I discussed how transactions (including distributed transactions) work in Chapter 3 (Transactions). Briefly, there are two types of transactions: tightly coupled and loosely coupled. I will discuss only tightly coupled transactions in this chapter, so I will call them just transactions.

There are also single-resource and multiple-resource transactions. As I discussed in Chapter 3, whereas single-resource transactions can be coordinated by the transactional resource itself, multiple-resource transactions require the help of a distributed transaction coordinator (DTC). From the perspective of transaction boundary management, it doesn't much matter who the coordinator is, so I will generically refer to whoever is coordinating the transaction as the transaction coordinator.

If the transaction coordinator is to successfully group together a bunch of database updates into one all-or-nothing package, she must know which updates are to be included in that package. Where does she get this vital piece of information? You tell her. How do you tell her? With BeginTransaction and Commit calls. The transaction coordinator assumes that all updates between BeginTransaction and Commit are part of the same transaction package. Therefore, Begin-Transaction and Commit form what I call the *transaction boundaries*.

Although programmers have been using BeginTransaction and Commit calls forever, this approach turns out not to be the best way to define transaction boundaries. At least, it's not the best way for components. And since components are the guts of the business application fortress, it is also not a good way to define transaction boundaries for business application fortresses.

The problem is that components often find themselves used in varying situations, with varying transaction semantics. Take, for example, a banking component called SavingsAccount that supports a method called withdrawFunds. The withdrawFunds method will have to do a bunch of database updates that need to be transactionally protected. In the traditional approach, this code would be written as follows:

```
BeginTransaction:
Do the first database update
Do the second database update;

...
Commit;
```

But what if the Accounts business application fortress were designed as shown in Figure 11.4. What problems might this pseudocode cause?

As Figure 11.4 shows, there are two ways the SavingsAccount component might be used. One is as part of an account transfer. The other is as part of a simple withdrawal. When the withdrawal is a simple withdrawal, the pseudocode works fine. But when the withdrawal is part of the account transfer, a problem arises. Rather than have a money transfer that is transactionally protected, we have, in effect, not one tightly coupled transaction, but two totally independent transactions. One of these transactions withdraws. The other deposits. The two hard-coded transaction boundaries (BeginTransaction and Commit) force this independence.

Because the two transactions are independent, there is no way to be sure that money won't be withdrawn, and then not deposited, or vice versa. This isn't a good way to do money transfers. It is a bad situation when only half of a money transfer occurs!

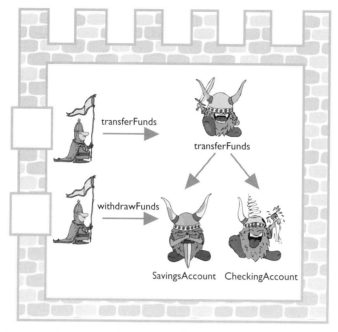

Figure 11.4 Accounts Business Application Fortress

The problem is that hard-coded transaction boundaries are not very flexible. Every time we do a withdrawal, we hit BeginTransaction which starts a new transaction boundary. To solve this problem, we need a more fluid notion of transaction boundaries. In the banking system, for example, we would like the transaction boundaries to surround the withdrawFunds method when we're doing a simple withdrawal and to surround the transferFunds method when we're doing a money transfer.

COMWare systems give us this greater flexibility. COMWare allows us to define which methods require transaction and then itself creates the appropriate transaction boundaries that will give us the desired transaction semantics.

The exact algorithm differs depending on the transaction requirements of each method, but I'll illustrate it with the most common setting: requires-transaction. This setting means that the workload inside the method *does* require transaction protection but does *not* require its own transaction boundary. In other words, if this method (say, withdrawFunds) is called from within another method (say, transferFunds) that has its own transaction, then this method (withdrawFunds) will piggyback off of the other method's transaction (the one belonging to transferFunds). On the other hand, if the method (withdrawFunds) is not being called from within a method that has a transaction in play, then a transaction needs to be started.

I call this algorithm *automatic transaction boundary management*. Automatic transaction boundary management occurs where all COMWare algorithms occur, at the point of interception, between the two surrogates.

At the incoming point of interception, the COMWare system checks if there is a transaction in progress. If there is, it piggybacks off of that transaction. If there isn't, it starts a new transaction.

At the outgoing point of interception (the point at which the method is about to return to the calling surrogate), the COMWare system checks whether this method, at the incoming point of interception, started a new transaction or just piggybacked off of an existing transaction. One of these two things must have happened. If the incoming point of interception decided to piggyback, then the outgoing point of interception does nothing. If the incoming point of interception decided to start a new transaction, then the outgoing point of interception ends the transaction.

Assuming that both the transferFunds and the withdrawFunds methods are defined as requires-transaction, the following sequence occurs during a transfer operation:

1. Somebody outside the fortress requests a transfer.
2. The guard accepts the request and invokes the transferFunds method.
3. COMWare intercepts the request.
4. COMWare notices that transferFunds is one of those methods that requires a transaction.

5. COMWare notices that no transaction is in process.

6. COMWare starts a new transaction.

7. The transferFunds method is invoked.

8. The transferFunds method does its work within the context of the new transaction.

9. The transferFunds method invokes withdrawFunds.

10. COMWare intercepts the request.

11. COMWare notices that withdrawFunds is one of those methods that requires a transaction.

12. COMWare notices that there is already a transaction in progress, so it piggybacks off of that transaction.

13. The withdrawFunds method is invoked, and it does its work within the same transaction as the one in which transfer-Funds did its work.

14. The withdrawFunds method concludes.

15. COMWare intercepts the return.

16. COMWare asks if the transaction in which withdrawFunds did its work was started by withdrawFunds. It determines that withdrawFunds was working within a higher-level transaction (that of transferFunds, not that that matters to COMWare).

17. The withdrawFunds method returns to its caller, which is the remaining part of the transferFunds method.

18. The transferFunds method returns to its caller, the guard.

19. The return is intercepted by COMWare.

20. COMWare asks if the transaction in which transferFunds did its work was started by transferFunds. It determines that transferFunds was the starting point for the transaction. It therefore concludes the transaction.

The net result is that transferFunds and withdrawFunds do their work within the same tightly coupled transaction. If you work through the case where withdrawFunds is called from within a simple withdrawal operation (no transfer), you will find that the same algorithm ensures that the withdrawFunds workload is done within its own tightly coupled transaction. So the exact same withdrawal code works, regardless of the context in which it runs.

Automatic transaction boundary management is one of the nice features of COMWare. To make use of it, though, you must design your business application components appropriately. The key to the design is understanding that the transaction boundary management algorithm, like all other COMWare algorithms, works at the point of interception.

The point of interception, remember, occurs between the two surrogates, which means that it occurs at component-level method invocations. The implication, then, is that automatic transaction boundary management can occur only when a method is invoked, and that for the algorithm to work, the component-level methods must be designed so that each is a potentially self-contained transaction.

11.1.3 State Management Revisited

What does it mean to design your component-level methods to be self-contained transactions? It means three things. First, none of the transaction workload spills outside that method. Second, the method's workload does not include more than one transaction. And third, the component's state is managed according to the unforgiving rule of transactional integrity.

The idea that the method's workload is exactly one transaction can be summarized as the golden rule of a business application component. This rule states that the method *is* the transaction. Those of you who are familiar with my writing on three-tier systems (before my conversion to software fortresses) will recognize the similarity between the golden rule of a business application component and the golden rule of the middle tier.

The similarity between these two "golden rules" is no coincidence. The rules governing the business application fortress are very similar to the rules governing the middle tier in three-tier architectures.

Although the middle tier and the business application fortress are similar, they are not identical. For example, some capabilities of

COMWare that are critical to middle-tier systems are not relevant to business application fortresses. Instance management is one such example. In addition, the approach to scalability in middle-tier systems, which focus primarily on homogeneous rich clients, is much different from the approach in business application fortresses, which focus primarily on heterogeneous asynchronous gateways.

Let's get back to state management. As I said, we need to make sure that the state is migrated, not too much, not too little, but "just right." Well, now I am in a better position to tell you what *just right* means. It means "just right according to the rule of transactional integrity."

The *rule of transactional integrity* governs the migration of data between the data strongbox and the business application component. It governs both directions of data migration: from the component to the data strongbox, and from the data strongbox to the component. Even though I am discussing the rule of transactional integrity, don't forget the other rule, the golden rule of a business application component—that the method *is* the transaction—which will also soon play a major role.

The first part of the rule of transactional integrity governs the migration of data from the strongbox to the component. This part of the rule states that any strongbox data needed by a component's transaction must be acquired from the strongbox *within* that component's transaction. Because the method and the transaction are identical (the golden rule), the rule for transactional integrity in effect tells us that all strongbox data needed by the method must be acquired *within* the method. It can't be acquired earlier and cached. It can't be remembered from earlier method invocations. Any data that is not acquired *during* the current method (or a lower-level method) is not trusted.

The second part of the rule for transactional integrity governs the migration of data from the component back to the strongbox. This part of the rule states that any strongbox data that was changed by the current transaction must be flushed back to the strongbox *before the transaction commits*. Again, within the context of the golden rule, this tells us that any data changed from within this method must be flushed before the method completes.

The penalty for ignoring the rule of transactional integrity is severe. If you base your business logic on data that was not read in sometime after the start of the transaction, that data may be stale (i.e., no longer the same as the data in the database). This situation occurs when another user has changed the database data since you last read it. If you don't store your changed data back to the database before your transaction completes, then when you do finally store it, you may overwrite somebody else's data.

You can see that the algorithm used by COMWare to manage transaction boundaries has two profound design implications. The first implication is that it forces us to design each of our component-level methods as if they were self-contained transactions, even though we know that the actual transaction boundary *may* be bubbled to a higher level by the COMWare system at runtime.

The second implication is that state migration must be managed from within the component method. All reads must occur *after* the method begins. All flushes must occur *before* the method terminates. Why must state migration occur within the method? Because the rule of transactional integrity tells us how state must migrate vis-à-vis transaction boundaries, and the golden rule tells us that the transaction boundaries are the same as the method boundaries.

One last word of warning: All methods are not equal. In particular, not all methods are component-level methods. In fact, the vast majority of methods in the world are *not* component-level methods; they are object-level methods. I discussed the difference between components and objects in Chapter 1 (Introduction).

Do not confuse object-level methods with component-level methods. If you apply the design principles I have discussed in this chapter to object-level methods, you will have big problems. On the other hand, if you *don't* apply these design principles to component-level methods, you will also have big problems. Be sure you understand the difference between these two fundamentally different concepts.

11.2 Leveraging Clusters

In Chapter 9 (General Fortress Issues) I discussed the overall best approach to both reliability and scalability. The basic lesson was to use clusters to scale *out* everything except the data strongbox, to scale *up* the data strongbox, and to design for reliability around the clusters. The design of component-level methods will go a long way to allowing your business application fortress to leverage clusters.

The golden rule (the method is the transaction) tells us that the method will be the unit of error control. In other words, if anything in the method fails to commit, everything in the method will fail to commit. If you call a method and it fails, it is safe to invoke it again. This principle assumes that all of the method's workload updates either transactional resources (resources that will ultimately be tied together into a temporary transactional partnership) or ephemeral resources (resources that are about to evaporate anyway and nobody cares much about).

The idea that it is always safe to reinvoke a failed method is not the same as idempotency, in the sense that I discussed it in Chapter 10 (Internet Fortresses). *Idempotent* means that it is always safe to reinvoke even a successful method. Here we have a much weaker notion of reinvoking. It is safe to reinvoke only a failed method. One could also design business application component methods to be idempotent, but the cost/benefit ratio of an idempotent intrafortress request to a business application component would probably not be favorable. Idempotency across the Internet is an entirely different matter.

Methods that follow the golden rule *and* the rule for transactional integrity are naturally cluster friendly. I already discussed the use of clustering indirectly in Chapter 6 (Asynchronous Drawbridges)—that is, clustering through use of the drawbridge as a cluster controller. Another possible approach is to use the guard as a cluster controller, as shown in Figure 11.5.

There are two ways the guard can serve as cluster controller. The first is through technology that works in conjunction with the COMWare system to automatically provide clustering on your behalf. An example of such a technology is Microsoft's Application Center

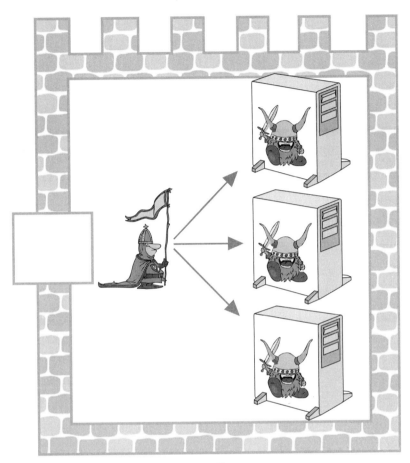

Figure 11.5 The Guard as Cluster Controller

Server component load-balancing capability. The other way is through writing your own clustering algorithms, which is easier than it sounds. The advantage of the first approach is that you get a rich set of cluster management tools along with the necessary algorithms. The advantage of the second approach is that you get algorithms tailored to your specific needs.

Let me take you through the general algorithm used by the guard. Everything here assumes that you have followed both the golden rule and the rule for transactional integrity. The algorithm is independent of the type of drawbridge associated with the guard. This description of the algorithm assumes that the method being called by the guard is the method that defines the transaction boundary, as discussed earlier in this chapter. In this discussion I'll assume the configuration shown in Figure 11.5:

1. The guard receives the infogram.
2. The guard chooses a cluster member.
3. The guard makes a component method invocation on the remote process on that machine.
4. If the invocation is successful (including the implicit transaction), then the guard is happy and everything is done.
5. If the invocation is not successful, then the guard chooses another machine and reinvokes the method on the remote process on that machine.

Various optimizations are possible. Rather than just choose a random machine to receive the method invocation, the guard can constantly poll the different machines on the cluster to see who is most available. The guard can note that the unsuccessful machine is down and request that corrective action be taken. The important point here is that proper management of transaction boundaries and state yields a close synergy of methods, transactions, reliability, and scalability in the business application fortress.

One final issue is worth discussing before I leave clusters for good. This is the age-old question of how much business logic to put in the components and how much to put in the database. All of the major database vendors support the equivalent of stored procedures. A *stored procedure* is a way of putting some or all of your business logic in the database. Stored procedures allow you to build components that are a mere veneer on top of the database. According to the database vendors, this is the preferred architecture for enterprise systems.

The main problem with this architectural approach is that it is cluster unfriendly. As I discussed in Chapter 9 (General Fortress Issues), databases do not scale out well. Currently, the only algorithms we have for scaling out databases use partitioned databases. Partitioned databases are databases with tables that span machines. Any partitioned database must be very carefully designed for partitioning.

Even slight errors in partitioning parameters can have huge implications for how the databases will scale. It is also very difficult to reconfigure a bad configuration later.

Because each of the multiple machines housing the partitioned database contains a different subset of the data, they are not a true cluster. A true cluster is made up of identically configured and loaded machines. Because they are not a true cluster, the machines housing a partitioned database offer absolutely nothing in the way of reliability. If one machine does go down, it can't call on its siblings for backup.

Even the scalability of partitioned databases is questionable. One of the reasons a cluster is so easy to scale out is that more machines can easily be added at the drop of a hat. Because every machine is identically configured and loaded, the overall system doesn't care if there are four or ten machines; it can dynamically adjust its work-load management algorithms as needed. This is not the case with partitioned databases. If you need to spread the database over a larger group of machines, you have a major, major reconfiguration project on your hands.

Given the difficulties in using and administering partitioned databases, I recommend that they be avoided wherever possible. They do not have any of the qualities that make cluster architectures attractive.

Some people might be confused by my statements that database machines cannot use clusters effectively. There is another use of the term *clusters* that database machines do support. This is the idea that two (or more) machines are tightly coupled, with one (or more) machines acting as a redundant machine for the other. I refer to this type of cluster as a *tightly coupled cluster*, as opposed to the loosely coupled cluster that I was discussing earlier.

Tightly coupled clusters have few of the advantages of loosely coupled clusters. In fact, the only advantage of tightly coupled clusters is that they improve overall reliability of the database. They do so, however, at a much higher cost than loosely coupled clusters do. They also do so without any of the benefits of scale-out workload management.

This does not mean you don't want to use tightly coupled clusters. In fact, if you want a highly reliable database, you have no choice but to use them. These are the *only* types of clusters that databases support and the *only* way to achieve high reliability in a database. The point here is that you generally want to base as much of your overall workload as possible on loosely coupled clusters rather than tightly coupled clusters. You do that by moving as much of your workload as possible from the database machines, which support only tightly coupled clusters, to the component machines, which support loosely coupled clusters quite nicely.

What does this discussion have to do with using stored procedures? Well, if you can't scale *out* the database, your only other alternative is to scale it *up*. Remember, from Chapter 9 (General Fortress Issues), scaling up means replacing your small, cheap machine with a big, expensive machine. Replacing machines, especially for databases which, by their very nature, contain huge collections of data, is a time-consuming and difficult process. You want to avoid having to go through this exercise as much as possible.

How do you avoid the time-consuming machine switches required for scaling up your database? Simple. You keep the load on the database machines as light as possible. One way you keep the load light is by avoiding having those machines do anything they don't absolutely need to do. And one thing they don't absolutely have to do is execute stored procedures. By moving the business logic into components, you allow the databases to do the one thing they do well: store data.

Of course, you will still have to scale your business logic, but once you have organized your business logic into well-designed components with proper transaction boundaries and well-managed state, you have a good scale-out architecture for at least that part of the fortress. You will still need to scale up your database, but now that the database is nothing but a data storage engine, its scalability requirements have been dramatically reduced.

One cautionary note here: I am not against *any* use of stored procedures. Occasionally you will run into situations in which the business logic needs to chug through large volumes of data. Then the alternative to running the business logic in the database is transferring all of that data to a component machine. If data transfer exceeds the cost of running the business logic, then for that specific bit of business logic you may actually decrease the overall load on the database machine by running the logic as stored procedures. The decision as to whether or not to use stored procedures should be based on minimizing overall database load. If you can move any of the workload off the database machine, do so.

11.3 .NET versus the J2EE Approach

Given everything going on in the business application fortress, you might expect huge differences between Microsoft's .NET and Sun's J2EE architecture. In fact, you will find vendors disagreeing with many of my recommendations in this chapter (and for that matter, this whole book). The disagreement is not because of differences in the two technologies. It is due to the fact that these vendors are basing their recommendations on a traditional three-tier architecture (or even worse, a client–server architecture), whereas I am basing my recommendations on a software fortress architecture.

As far as the discussion so far in this chapter is concerned, there is no difference whatsoever between J2EE and .NET. Transaction boundary management, security, scalability, and reliability all work exactly the same in the two technologies.

The important business application fortress technology differences between .NET and J2EE are in these areas:

- Language approach
- Cost
- Platform support

Let's look at each of these.

11.3.1 Language

J2EE and .NET have a similar language architecture. Source code is transformed into running business application fortress components as follows:

1. A programmer creates source code conforming to the rules of a particular programming language.
2. A translator transforms the source code into a low-level language.
3. The low-level language is packaged into a deployable unit.
4. A runtime infrastructure is asked to run the deployable unit.
5. Before running the deployable unit for the first time, the run-time infrastructure compiles the low-level language into binary code.

As you would expect, Microsoft and Sun use different terms to describe the various players. Sun calls the low-level language *Java bytecode*; Microsoft calls it *Microsoft intermediate language* (*MSIL*). Microsoft calls the deployable unit an *assembly*; Sun calls it a *Java Archive* (*JAR*) file. Sun calls the runtime infrastructure the *Java Virtual Machine* (*JVM*); Microsoft calls it the *Common Language Runtime* (*CLR*).

The only substantive difference between the two language architectures has to do with the design of the low-level language. Whereas Sun's Java bytecode has been designed specifically for Java, Microsoft's MSIL has been designed to support any programming language. The result is that J2EE is effectively a closed language architecture, accommodating Java and little else. Microsoft's .NET is more of an open language architecture, usable with any programming language that has an MSIL translator. Such languages include FORTRAN, COBOL, Smalltalk, Eiffel, and many others.

Both approaches have advantages. Programmers who want to use nothing but Sun-approved Java will be happy only with the J2EE architecture. Programmers who want to use other languages and don't particularly care if Sun has approved their language choice will be happier with the .NET approach.

Microsoft's .NET does support two Java derivative languages: J# and C# (pronounced "jay sharp" and "cee sharp," respectively). Of these two, J# is the more Java-like, but I consider C# the preferred choice. J# is a language in which Microsoft has little interest, so it is at higher risk for future support. C#, on the other hand, is a more modern language, a language in which Microsoft has invested heavily and a language backed by an independent standards body (unlike either J# or Java). The syntax of C# is close enough to Java that Java programmers can learn it readily.

11.3.2 Platform Support

The various J2EE vendors and Microsoft have taken two different approaches to platform support. The J2EE vendors have generally taken a platform-agnostic approach, so if one writes to IBM's WebSphere J2EE implementation, for example, it will readily port to any operating system on which WebSphere runs, including the Windows platform. Microsoft, on the other hand, has built .NET for Windows and for Windows only. Microsoft has submitted portions of .NET for independent standardization, and non-Windows versions of pieces of .NET will likely someday become available. Even when this happens, however, it is highly unlikely that a major .NET business application fortress will be able to port easily to a non-Microsoft version of .NET, and it is equally unlikely that Microsoft will ever develop a non-Windows version.

The nonportability of .NET across platforms has an analogy in the J2EE space. Generally the lack of portability is not a cross-platform issue as much as it is a cross-vendor issue. Porting from one vendor to another is just as difficult in the J2EE space as it will likely be in the .NET space. Even though J2EE claims to be a vendor-agnostic platform, in reality any serious J2EE business application fortress application would need to leverage so many vendor-specific features that porting that application from one vendor (say, IBM's WebSphere) to another vendor (say, BEA's WebLogic) would be very difficult.

11.3.3 Cost

The final point is cost, which has two aspects. One is development cost. The other is cost per unit of work (say, the cost of processing an infogram in a business application fortress).

It is difficult to compare development costs because there are no widely accepted standards for making these measurements. However, Microsoft generally gets high marks for its development tools. In addition, developers I have spoken to who have built for both .NET and J2EE generally seem to believe that .NET is much easier to use. No doubt, however, the J2EE vendors will disagree with this assessment.

The cost per unit of work is a little easier to quantify. We do have good standards for measuring cost per unit of work. One of those most relevant for business application fortresses is the venerable TPC-C benchmark, which measures the cost of running database-intensive transactions, which are typical of a business application fortress workload. Using this benchmark and others, and talking to many people who have implemented running systems, I believe that the unit-of-work costs will be about one-tenth as much on a .NET system as on a J2EE system running on a non-Windows platform, and about one-fifth as much as a J2EE system running on either a Windows or an Intel Linux platform.

There are two ways you can look at this. You can ask how much a unit of work (say, processing an infogram) costs on the two platforms. According to my predictions, if it costs 10 cents in .NET it will cost 50 cents in J2EE/Windows and a dollar in J2EE/non-Windows. You can also ask how many units of work you can process for a given cost—say, on a 500,000-dollar system. My predictions indicate that if 500,000 dollars buys you 10,000 units of work per minute on J2EE/non-Windows, that same 500,000 dollars will buy you 20,000 units of work per minute on J2EE/Windows and 100,000 units of work per minute on .NET/Windows.

Summary

Here are the main points of this chapter:

- The business application fortress design is critical to your overall enterprise architecture.
- Business application fortresses are built on components and component-oriented middleware (COMWare).
- The main benefits of COMWare are automatic transaction boundary management and fortress wall reinforcements through role-based security.
- The automatic transaction boundary management algorithms lead to the golden rule: Component-level methods should be self-contained transactions.
- The golden rule implies that state should be read in and flushed out within the method.
- Components following the golden rule and managing their state correctly will be amenable to high levels of reliability and scale-out scalability through the use of loosely coupled clusters.
- Be careful to distinguish between object-level methods and component-level methods.
- Avoid putting unnecessary workload in the form of stored procedures in the database.
- Use .NET where low cost is important.
- Use .NET where support for non-Java-like languages is important.
- Use J2EE where support for official Java is important.
- Use J2EE technologies where non-Windows platform support is important.

CHAPTER 12

Legacy, Service, and Treaty Management Fortresses

In Chapters 10 and 11 I covered in reasonable depth three of the most common types of software fortresses: Web service fortresses, presentation fortresses, and business application fortresses. In this chapter I will take a briefer look at the remaining fortress types: legacy, service, and treaty management fortresses.

12.1 Legacy Fortresses

Legacy fortresses wrap existing prefortress systems and allow them to work within the context of an enterprise fortress architecture.

There are arguments in favor of keeping existing systems and arguments in favor of discarding them. On the keep side, existing systems usually work and often represent huge investments. On the discard side, existing systems are often difficult or impossible to modify, they often run on expensive mainframe configurations, and they are sometimes designed in ways that make them rather hostile to enterprise-level collaboration.

I usually take a conservative approach to legacy systems. If the system can be wrapped relatively easily in a legacy fortress architecture, then I recommend this approach. Once the legacy system is snuggly wrapped, it can always be reimplemented, should a rewrite prove justifiable.

Some legacy systems can be wrapped easily; others cannot. The deciding factor is usually whether the legacy application follows a three-tier architecture or a client–server architecture. Three-tier architectures usually wrap well. Client–server architectures, with their intermingling of user interface and business logic, are usually difficult to wrap.

A typical three-tier application is shown in Figure 12.1. It has all of the following characteristics:

- The user interface is cleanly separated from the business logic.
- The system can be configured so that the user interface can be run on a machine different from the one that runs the business logic, and both can run on machines different from the one that stores data.
- System resources, especially database connections, are owned exclusively by the business logic. No system resources are owned, controlled, or managed by the user interface logic.

If all of these conditions are true, your legacy system can rightfully call itself a three-tier architecture and you can probably wrap it comfortably into a legacy software fortress. If not, you still may be able to accomplish wrapping, but the results will be problematic and the technical aspects more daunting. In this discussion I will deal only with systems that are already three-tier systems.

A three-tier system already has a well-defined plan for communication between the presentation tier and the business tier. If it is a Microsoft system, it is probably using ASP or ASP.NET on the presentation tier, COM+ on the middle tier, and DCOM as the linkage between the two. If it is an older Unix application, the middle tier may be a Tuxedo application. If it is an older IBM application, the

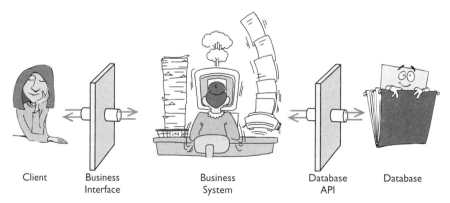

| Client | Business
Interface | Business
System | Database
API | Database |

Figure 12.1 A Three-Tier Application

middle tier is probably running CICS. All of these technologies have well-defined communications channels for moving information between the presentation and middle tiers.

To wrap any of these legacy applications, follow these steps:

First, build an impenetrable wall around the fortress using standard wall techniques, as described in Chapter 7 (Guards and Walls). Place a guard inside the wall, as described in the same chapter. The guard will communicate with the legacy application using the communications channels that had been used between the presentation tier and the middle tier.

From the legacy middle-tier application's perspective, the guard replaces the presentation tier. Because the legacy application was built with a formal three-tier architecture, the middle-tier portion should know nothing whatsoever about the presentation tier. Whether there is a guard or a presentation tier, as long as the communications expectations are met, the middle-tier logic can't tell the difference.

Second, define a drawbridge for the guard to protect, using any of the standard drawbridge techniques described in Chapters 4 through 6. This drawbridge will now be the "official" enterprise-level communications channel for the legacy fortress.

An overview of the process of converting a three-tier legacy application into a legacy fortress is shown in Figure 12.2.

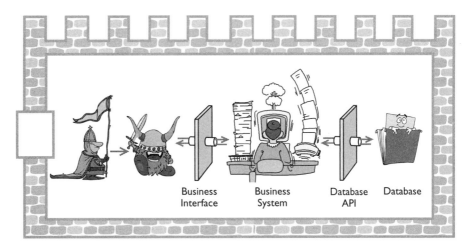

Figure 12.2 Converting a Three-Tier Legacy Application

12.2 Service Fortresses

The term *service fortress* refers to a miscellaneous assortment of fortresses that provide shared functionality that is needed by multiple fortresses within the enterprise.

Many people confuse service fortresses with linked libraries. A *linked library* can be either shared (meaning that the same binary is shared by many processes) or unshared (each process has its own binary). A linked library may be written in an object-oriented programming language.

A service fortress differs from a linked library in that it also represents a significant amount of shared data. It is the data strongbox more than the shared functionality that defines the service fortress. The rule of thumb, then, is that if only functionality needs to be shared across the enterprise, the implementation should be a linked library. If the functionality also needs to share significant amounts of data across the enterprise, the implementation should be a service fortress. Sometimes the distinction between shared libraries and service fortresses may seem arbitrary.

Linked libraries and service fortresses are not mutually exclusive. For example, a service fortress that is providing compensatory transaction management (a topic I will discuss in more detail shortly) could also provide a library used to request transaction management. In this case the library is linked to the donor fortress and becomes, in whole or in part, the envoy. Recall that the envoy is the code responsible for preparing the request on the donor side and passing it over the drawbridge to the receiving guard.

When the envoy is implemented as a linked library, the drawbridge between the two fortresses becomes an implementation detail of the service fortress. In general, only the envoy and the guard need to agree on the drawbridge, and both, in this scenario, are provided by the same party.

The most common service fortresses, in my experience, are those dealing with broadcasting, data sharing, security, and loosely coupled transaction management. Most are likely to be fortress veneers on a purchased technology. I'll take a look at each of these in turn.

12.2.1 Broadcast Service Fortresses

Broadcast service fortresses can broadcast information to many other fortresses. In a credit card system, a broadcast fortress could be used to broadcast information about stolen credit cards. In an insurance corporation, a broadcast fortress might disseminate information about new policies. In a manufacturing environment, a broadcast fortress might be used to solicit bids for subcontracted materials and components.

The most common broadcast model considers two types of fortresses: those that create information, often called *publishers*; and those that want to hear about that information, often called *subscribers*. The broadcast fortress receives the information generated by the publishers and makes sure that it is sent to the various subscribers. Figure 12.3 shows how publishers, subscribers, and broadcast fortresses are related.

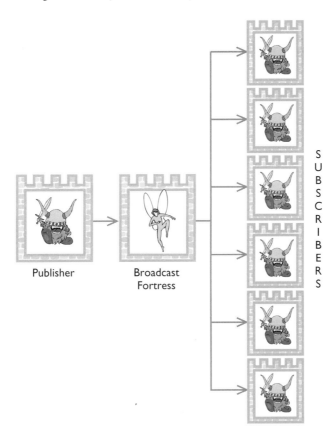

Figure 12.3 A Broadcast Fortress and Its Users

12.2.2 Data-Sharing Fortresses

Data-sharing fortresses share information throughout an enterprise.
A data-sharing fortress is usually just a fortress overlaid on a shared
database, and technically it may be just the database. My own
preference is not to use data-sharing fortresses because they
make ownership of the data difficult to manage. But in some cases
sharing a certain amount of data might make sense. Figure 12.4
shows how a data-sharing fortress might be related to others in
the enterprise.

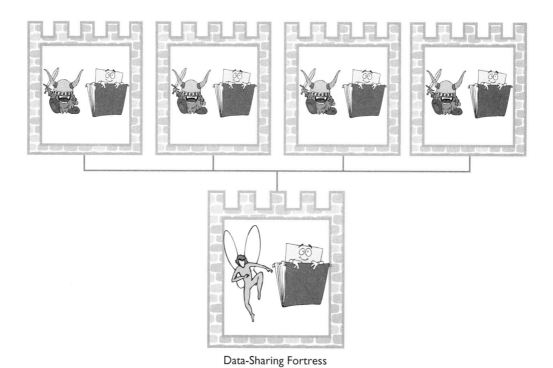

Data-Sharing Fortress

Figure 12.4 A Data-Sharing Fortress and Its Users

12.2.3 Security Fortresses

Most security systems are based on a trusted authority. I discussed the main approaches to security in Chapter 7 (Guards and Walls). The two most common types of systems are shared-key systems, like Kerberos, and public/private–key systems, like Secure Sockets. Both types depend on trusted authorities, although the role of the trusted authority is quite different for each. In both cases, the ultimate goal is to create and transport a temporary shared key that can be used as a basis for securing the drawbridge connecting two or more fortresses. Figure 12.5 shows the relationship between a security fortress and its clients.

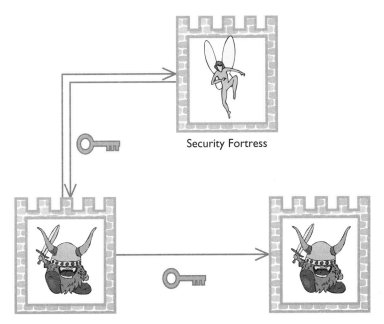

Figure 12.5 A Security Fortress and Its Clients

12.2.4 Loosely Coupled Transaction Management Service Fortresses

A *loosely coupled transaction management (LCTM) service fortress* manages transaction-related communication, particularly that communication needed to coordinate loosely coupled transactions. Because the work of an LCTM fortress can be relatively complicated, I'll look at it in more depth.

I discussed the general ideal of transactions in Chapter 3 (Transactions), both the tightly coupled (strong transactional guarantee) and loosely coupled (weak transactional guarantee) variety. I also pointed out that we don't allow tightly coupled transactions to cross fortress boundaries, even if technically we are allowed to do so.

Let's consider an example of where an LCTM fortress might come in handy. Suppose I wanted to set up the ObjectWatch Web site to allow clients to sign up for classes through a browser-based interface. I know that most people who take my classes are high-level architects or CTO types. I also know that even though I teach classes in perhaps 20 locations throughout the world, most of the students will be traveling to the class and will therefore also need a hotel room.

Given that most students will need a hotel, I decide to negotiate a favorable rate with a major hotel for each workshop and allow students to book the hotel at the same time that they book the seat in the class. Suddenly my system is rather complicated because I have various outcomes to consider.

Suppose Kate wants to take the upcoming workshop in Paris, a city in which we have negotiated a special package with the Star Plaza. She decides she wants both the workshop seat and the hotel room. Our system must be able to handle either of the following possibilities:

- The Paris workshop could have a seat available, and the Star Plaza could have a room available.
- Either the Paris workshop or the Star Plaza or both could be sold out.

Overall, several fortresses need to coordinate their work as follows:

- The ObjectWatch CustomerGateway presentation fortress will deal with Kate's browser.

- The ObjectWatch WorkshopBooking business application fortress will book Kate's workshop seat.

- The hotel's PartnerGateway Web service fortress will accept programmatic Internet requests for room bookings. There will probably be other back-end hotel business application fortresses behind this one, but that is not my concern.

- The bank's PartnerGateway Web service fortress will accept programmatic Internet requests for credit card charges. Like the hotel's fortress, this fortress will have other back-end fortresses that don't concern me.

- The ObjectWatch PartnerGateway Web service fortress will accept programmatic Internet responses from ObjectWatch partners.

A fortress overview document (FOD) maps out the overall relationships of these fortresses. I described FODs in Chapter 2 (Diagramming Software Fortresses). A FOD for the hypothetical ObjectWatch (my company) system might include the figure shown in Figure 12.6.

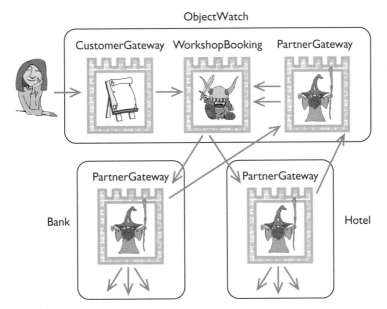

Figure 12.6 Hypothetical ObjectWatch Architecture

Kate's browser will be hooked up to my CustomerGateway fortress, which will be hooked up to my WorkshopBooking fortress. The CustomerGateway fortress will communicate with my Workshop-Booking fortress to book Kate a workshop seat. To book a seat, the WorkshopBooking fortress needs to communicate with a bank's PartnerGateway fortress (to charge Kate's credit card) and the hotel's PartnerGateway fortress (to book Kate's room).

The fortress communications are shown in the SAD (sequence–ally diagram) in Figure 12.7. SADs were first discussed in Chapter 2 (Diagramming Software Fortresses). As a reminder, in Figure 12.7 PF stands for *presentation fortress*, BAF for *business application fortress*, and WSF for *Web service fortress*.

Most of the time, the communication between fortresses is boringly routine:

1. Kate enters her information.
2. The system checks if a workshop seat is available. It is.
3. The system checks if a hotel room is available. It is.
4. The system charges Kate's credit card and tells Kate her seat is reserved.
5. The system books the workshop seat.

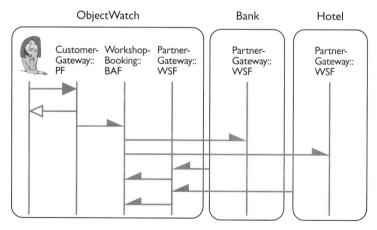

Figure 12.7 SAD for ObjectWatch Architecture

6. The system books the hotel room.
7. The system tells Kate she has a confirmed seat and hotel room.

But a million things can go wrong, any of which turn this routine sequence of interactions into a bewildering minefield of error conditions. For example, between the time the PartnerGateway fortress told us there was an available room and the time we actually booked the room, the hotel could sell out. Now we have sold Kate a workshop seat she doesn't want (because she has no hotel room) and we have already charged her credit card!

We can solve this problem by introducing another fortress whose only roles are to keep track of how each of the other fortresses is doing in terms of successfully accomplishing its workload, and to make this information available for each of the participating fortresses.

This fortress is the LCTM (loosely coupled transaction manager) software fortress. It plays a role similar to that played by a distributed transaction manager (DTC) in a tightly coupled multiple-resource transaction, as described in Chapter 3 (Transactions). It lets each one of the fortresses with responsibility for its piece of the overall loosely coupled transaction know how the loosely coupled transaction as a whole is making out. If, for example, the PartnerGateway fortress fails to book the seat, the LCTM fortress will deliver the bad news to the WorkshopBooking fortress so that it can release Kate's seat.

Widely accepted standards for LCTM fortresses would be great. If such standards existed, it would be possible to construct workflows between fortresses very easily, as long as each one knew how to work with the same LCTM fortress. The closest we have to an accepted standard for LCTM fortresses is something called the Business Transaction Protocol (BTP), which has recently been adopted by a group called the Organization for the Advancement of Structured Information Standards (OASIS).

BTP as a standard has problems. First, it is overly complicated. It tries to solve every possible coordination problem rather than solve the typical problems in a straightforward manner. Second, although the BTP authors include many important companies (such as Sun and Oracle), the two most important companies in the area of Web service transactions (IBM and Microsoft) are conspicuously missing. Third, the standard is barely off the press. It is still in version 1.0, and as I write this, it was finalized less than six months ago. If the standard survives at all, we can expect major changes over the next few years as the comfortable academic world of theoretical white papers meets the unforgiving dog-eat-dog world of the watch-your-back Internet.

Although BTP is far from universally accepted, it is still a good basis for discussion. Using the BTP terminology, then, I will describe in general how an LCTM fortress might work.

First let me introduce some BTP terms from the perspective of software fortresses. I will list them in an order that allows one term to be defined in relationship to others:

Business transaction. A *business transaction* is a group of tasks that need to be coordinated in a loosely coupled fashion. In my example, the combined task of booking both a workshop seat and a hotel room is considered a business transaction.

Coordinator. The *coordinator* is the one coordinating the communications between the fortresses with respect to the business transaction. In my example, the coordinator is the LCTM fortress.

Initiator. The *initiator* is the one starting the transaction. In my example, the initiator is the CustomerGateway fortress that starts the transaction on Kate's behalf.

Context. A *context* is the information uniquely identifying a specific transaction. The context flows with the workflow as part of the infogram passing over the gateway(s). Different fortresses use the context to know which transaction they are currently processing. In my example, Kate would have a unique transaction context that would be different from, say, Mike's. When the CustomerGateway fortress asks the WorkshopBooking fortress to book a seat, it includes in the request the information describing Kate's context.

Create. *Create* is a message from the initiator to the coordinator asking it to create a new context. In my example, the CustomerGateway fortress would ask the LCTM fortress to create a new context for Kate's workload.

Enroll. *Enroll* is a message from a software fortress to the controller that it wants to participate in the business transaction. When the fortress receives an infogram, it examines the accompanying context to see if it has already notified the controller that it is part of this transaction. If not, it enrolls at that time. In my example, the WorkshopBooking fortress would enroll with the LCTM fortress upon receiving the "book room" request from the CustomerGateway fortress, as would the PartnerGateway fortress upon receiving the "book hotel" request.

Confirm. *Confirm* is an instruction from the initiator to the coordinator (LCTM) that the transaction is ready to finalize. In my example, the CustomerGateway fortress will tell the LCTM fortress to confirm the transaction once both the WorkshopBooking and the PartnerGateway fortresses have indicated that they have accepted their respective bookings.

Cancel. *Cancel* is an instruction from a particular fortress that the transaction has been canceled. The fortress issuing the cancel request can be the initiator or any of the participants. The *cancel* request is the opposite of a *confirm* request. In my example, the WorkshopBooking fortress might be told to cancel the transaction if the PartnerGateway fortress could not book the hotel room.

The sequence of completing the business transaction (booking both a workshop seat and a hotel room) looks like this:

1. Kate enters her information into the ObjectWatch CustomerGateway fortress.

2. The CustomerGateway fortress passes the request to the ObjectWatch WorkshopBooking fortress.

3. The WorkshopBooking fortress asks the LCTM fortress to create a context for Kate.

4. The WorkshopBooking fortress books a seat using Kate's context.

5. The WorkshopBooking fortress asks the bank's PartnerGateway fortress to bill Kate's credit card using Kate's context.

6. The bank's PartnerGateway fortress agrees to do so.

7. The PartnerGateway fortress (or a downstream bank fortress) enrolls with the LCTM fortress using Kate's context.

8. The WorkshopBooking fortress asks the hotel's PartnerGateway fortress to book a hotel room using Kate's context.

9. The PartnerGateway fortress agrees to do so.

10. The PartnerGateway fortress (or a downstream hotel fortress) enrolls with the LCTM fortress using Kate's context.

11. The WorkshopBooking fortress tells the LCTM fortress to confirm (finalize) the business transaction using Kate's context.

12. The LCTM fortress asks each of the fortresses that had previously enrolled with Kate's context to prepare to finalize the transaction. Each agrees or refuses.

13. If each fortress agrees, the LCTM fortress tells each in turn to confirm (finalize) the transaction.

14. Each fortress assumes that what it has done on behalf of Kate's context is now finalized.

15. The LCTM fortress tells the WorkshopBooking fortress that the business transaction was successfully completed.

All of this may seem complicated, but from the perspective of any single fortress, there isn't too much to it. Here is the algorithm from a participating fortress's perspective:

1. The fortress is asked to do something using Kate's context.

2. The fortress enrolls with the LCTM fortress using Kate's context.

3. The fortress does whatever it does (e.g., book a room).

4. The fortress is told to prepare the transaction using Kate's context.

5. The fortress decides it is either willing or not willing to do so.

6. The fortress is told either to confirm or to cancel the transaction using Kate's context.

Notice how close all of this is to the way in which transactional resources coordinate with a distributed transaction coordinator, as

Table 12.1 Comparison of Tightly Coupled and Loosely Coupled Transactions

Functionality	Tightly Coupled	Loosely Coupled
Work unit	Transaction	Business transaction
Coordination	DTC	LCTM fortress
Participant	Transactional resource	Software fortress
Algorithm	Four-phase commit	Modified four-phase commit
Transactional guarantee	Strong	Weak

discussed in Chapter 3 (Transactions). In fact, the algorithms are almost identical. The LCTM fortress is very similar to a distributed transaction coordinator (DTC). A participating fortress is very much like a transactional resource. Table 12.1 compares the two systems.

The last item in Table 12.1 is the critical differentiator between the coordination of a business transaction (loosely coupled transaction) by an LCTM fortress and the coordination of a tightly coupled transaction by a DTC. The difference is in the degree of the transactional guarantee.

When asked to commit a tightly coupled transaction, a transactional resource, such as a database, makes a strong guarantee that it will either commit the work (make the work absolutely permanent) or roll it back (make the work absolutely disappear). There is no middle ground.

A software fortress coordinated by an LCTM fortress has a great deal of leeway in its interpretation of commit/confirm or rollback/cancel. A hotel might interpret a commitment to hold a room as just a commitment to hold *any* room, not necessarily the one that was promised. Or it might interpret the commitment as just a promise to find a room in any hotel in the same city.

The interpretation by the fortress of what *commitment* means is not the problem of the LCTM fortress. However, it may be an important factor in the willingness of other fortresses to form collaborative relationships with that fortress.

The BTP may or may not become a widely adopted standard for LCTM fortresses, or even for transactions spanning the Web. In any case, it is representative of the communications and treaties that must occur among fortresses that want to define overall business transactions, fortresses that want to be part of those transactions, and fortresses that will be needed to coordinate the overall communications among the interested parties.

12.3 Treaty Management Fortresses

Treaty management fortresses manage complex relationships among usually three or more fortresses, typically business application fortresses. I discussed the general idea of treaties in Chapter 8 (Treaties). A treaty is an agreement by two or more fortresses to work together and a description of the terms that will govern the overall collaborative relationship. Simple treaties can usually be managed directly by the participating fortresses themselves. More complex treaties often benefit from having specialized fortresses, called treaty management fortresses, orchestrate the collaboration.

Treaty management fortresses are usually based on commercial products. Probably the best-known products in this area are TIBCO's ActiveEnterprise, WebSphere MQ Integrator, and Microsoft's BizTalk Server. None of these products use the term *treaty management* to describe their functionality. Instead, they like to think of themselves as being at the core of the enterprise. Any of them would show the relationship between their product and the rest of your enterprise as something similar to Figure 12.8.

I don't envision these technologies (such as BizTalk) as being the center of your universe. Instead, I see them as having a less pretentious role—that of holding specific collaborations together—for several reasons.

For one, there is no reason for every system in the enterprise to plug into the treaty management technology. When using the software fortress model, we can plug into the treaty management technologies only those systems that need to have a collaborative relationship

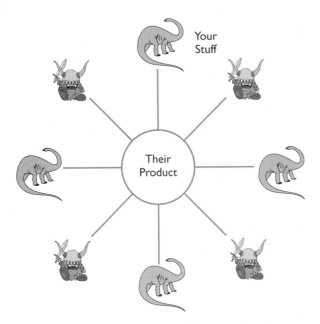

Figure 12.8 Treaty Management from a Vendor's Perspective

managed by that particular technology, thereby avoiding the overhead for the systems that do not have such needs. Systems that either do not collaborate or collaborate only through simple treaties have no need to use treaty management technologies.

Thinking in terms of treaty management rather than enterprise core gives us the flexibility to choose different treaty management technologies for different treaties. TIBCO's high-end ActiveEnterprise is overkill for hooking together a half-dozen fortresses that will be working with less than, say, a few thousand infograms per hour. Such a modest treaty could easily be managed with Microsoft BizTalk Server at a much lower overall cost. So my picture of these technologies looks like Figure 12.9, in contrast to the vendor's picture shown in Figure 12.8.

The most common functions provided by treaty management technologies are these:

- Drawbridge translation (both data and protocol)
- Loosely coupled transaction management
- Workflow management

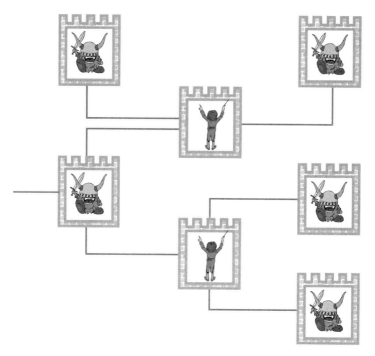

Figure 12.9 Treaty Management from a Software Fortress Perspective

Drawbridge translation refers to the bridging of drawbridges that are naturally incompatible with each other. The incompatibility can be in the infogram itself, in the protocols used to transfer the infogram, or both.

Loosely coupled transaction management is a topic I have covered several times. I described it earlier in this chapter as a possible service fortress. When treaty management technologies are being used, the framework for loosely coupled transaction management is usually included as part of the technology.

Workflow management refers to the coordination of infograms, usually infograms delivered over asynchronous drawbridges, which I discussed in Chapter 6 (Asynchronous Drawbridges). When you have a lot of fortresses throwing asynchronous infograms at each other, it can become pretty confusing as to whose turn is next. The treaty management products can help make sure that work is flowing in the proper order.

When a treaty management product is being used, it is necessary to create what these products often call a *connector*. A connector is a subsystem that knows how to pass messages between the managed system (usually a business application or legacy application) and the managing technology (e.g., BizTalk). From the perspective of software fortresses, the managed system is a fortress ally, a connector is an envoy, and the messaging technology linking together the manager and the managed system is a drawbridge.

Summary

In this chapter I have discussed different technologies that cover a wide area. I have discussed wrapping legacy systems into legacy fortresses. I have discussed a somewhat random collection of fortresses that, for lack of a better common term, are described as service fortresses. And I have discussed treaty management fortresses, fortresses that can manage collaborations.

The main area in which standards may be emerging is loosely coupled transaction management (LCTM). LCTM is an important area because it defines how fortresses that are working together within a particular treaty can let each other know about the failure or success of their part of the workload. At this point, the best bet for an LCTM standard is the BTP work by OASIS, but this work is premature.

Software Fortress Design Review

I am going to be optimistic. I am going to assume that you have decided to use the software fortress methodology and that you have created your first high-level design. Now you are ready to take this design into a design review. What should you look for in the review?

In this chapter I give you a list of 25 questions you should ask during any software fortress design review. This list is not all-inclusive; it merely represents the state of the art today. As we gain more experience with this methodology, the list will grow. I hope that you are one of those who will contribute to the next revision of this list.

I'll divide these questions into three groups. The first group is for enterprise-level managers and relates to a high-level organizational look at the overall software fortress architecture. The second group of questions is for the enterprise-level architects and relates to drawbridges and the relationships between fortresses. The third group of questions is for fortress-level architects and relates to the design of individual fortresses.

13.1 Group One: Enterprise Overview Questions

The questions in this first group are targeted at those who are responsible for managing the overall software development process.

Question 1: Do we need a software fortress architecture?

As much as I believe in the software fortress model, it clearly isn't for every software venture. As I said earlier in this book, the software fortress model is a serious architecture for large-scale enterprise systems. If you're working with three other programmers to build the next-generation word processor, I can't imagine this architecture helping you, and it may well introduce many problems. This architecture is for the enterprise environment. It is for building systems that involve hundreds of programmers organized in more or less autonomous groups.

Question 2: Do we all have the same understanding of the software fortress methodology?

It is important that everybody, including the CTO, the architects, and the developers, has a common understanding of what the software fortress methodology is. This is not to say that everybody will be involved in planning enterprise-level fortress relationships, but everybody needs to understand the basic ideas and terminology so that communication is facilitated.

You can take two important steps to ensure that everyone involved is on the same page. First, make this book required reading for everybody. I have purposely tried to keep the book at a level and length where it can be read in a weekend. With volume discounts, this is a cheap investment. Second, appoint one person to be the software fortress advocate within your organization. If your organization is large enough, appoint a small group of people to serve as software fortress resources. These people will eventually serve as the start of a corporate knowledge pool about software fortresses and will become valuable resources for future designs.

Question 3: Have the requirements for each fortress been clearly articulated?

As you start to think about which technologies you will use for each fortress, you need to understand the requirements for each of those fortresses. These requirements may well affect decisions you make not only about fortress technologies, but about how you approach treaties and drawbridges.

You should assign a weight to each requirement. You are likely to find that different requirements conflict with each other. For example, a fortress might require the lowest possible unit-of-work cost and also need to be run on Unix. These are conflicting requirements. Low unit-of-work costs greatly favor Microsoft's .NET technologies, whereas running on the Unix platform greatly favors J2EE technologies. You must decide which of the two conflicting requirements is more important to you.

At the very least, for each fortress you should identify requirements with respect to unit-of-work cost, platform, and scalability.

Question 4: Have our fortresses been partitioned with organizational boundaries in mind?

Remember that a fortress is not just a collection of cooperating technologies; it is a collection of cooperating people working closely together. If you have a fortress that depends on two different groups who usually do not work together, do not report to the same person, and are suspicious of each other's work, you need to rethink your design. Don't try to force people into artificial constraints. Be realistic. Fortresses are more adaptable than people.

Question 5: Are our fortresses organized around natural trust boundaries?

Hopefully the importance of a fortress as a trust boundary is obvious by now. Remember, trust is not just a technical issue; it is also an organizational issue. Some fortresses may draw more suspicion than others, but every request originating outside the fortress should cause trepidation.

Question 6: Have we really made enterprise-level decisions at the enterprise level and fortress-level decisions at the fortress level?

Enterprise-level architects should work at the enterprise level, and fortress-level architects should work at the fortress level. They shouldn't unnecessarily get in each other's way by making inappropriate decisions at inappropriate levels.

For example, it is *not* appropriate to decide at the enterprise level whether to use Microsoft's .NET or IBM's WebSphere. This is a fortress-level decision. It *is* appropriate to decide at the enterprise level which J2EE vendors are acceptable alternatives.

It is *not* appropriate to decide at the enterprise level whether tightly coupled transaction boundaries will be managed automatically by the fortress infrastructure or whether they will be hard-coded—a topic I covered in Chapter 11 (Business Application Fortresses). It *is* appropriate to decide at the enterprise level how compensatory transactions will be managed.

Question 7: Have we confused objects, components, and fortresses?

Confusion of objects, components, and fortresses is probably one of the most common reasons for failures in fortress and related architectures.

An *object* is an artifact of object-oriented programming. Object-oriented programming is one (not the only) technique we can use to implement algorithms. An object is therefore a unit of implementation. In Java, an object is an instantiation of a Java class. For .NET, an object is an instantiation of a class defined in one of the .NET languages, such as C#.

A *component* is an artifact of a component packaging technology. Component packaging is one of the ways we package compiled code together, identify remotely accessible interfaces to that code, and assign processes in which that code will run. A component usually encompasses some significant business functionality, such as an account. Ultimately, a component is a unit of packaging and distribution.

In Java, a component is typically an Enterprise JavaBean. In .NET, it is typically a COM+ component. Although COM+ pre-dated what most people think of as .NET, it still provides the component packaging technology for .NET. Most component technologies do not assume that the software systems they are packaging are implemented with objects (Java being the notable exception).

A *software fortress* is an artifact of the software fortress model. It is an organization of software systems along common trust boundaries. A software fortress is therefore a unit of organizational functionality. The concept of a software fortress is independent of the packaging technology used to package and distribute the underlying systems within the fortress. You can just as easily create a fortress around Enterprise JavaBean components as you can around COM+ components.

Question 8: Have we identified all of the security issues?

Enterprise security is one of the most obvious features of the software fortress model, but it is up to you to identify the security concerns of your architecture. There is no such thing as a perfectly secure fortress. The best you can do is make the cost of breaking into your fortresses greater than the value of the resulting break-in. For some systems you need to leverage every possible resource, encrypting every request, authenticating every infogram source, and authenticating every authenticator. For others, you can get by with basic operating system authentication. You need to use an appropriate security defense. To determine what an appropriate defense is, you must start by understanding both the risks and the costs of break-ins.

13.2 Group Two: Enterprise Architecture Questions

The questions in this second group are targeted at the enterprise-level architects, those who are responsible for making sure the different fortresses work together as a single, well-oiled machine.

Question 9: Do we have the right number of fortresses?

Be sure you have the right number of fortresses. If you have too many, you will have various problems:

- You will spend too much time on interfortress communications. Drawbridge communication is relatively slow compared to intrafortress communication.
- You will sacrifice transactional protection for closely related work. Transactions should not flow across drawbridges.
- You will find it hard to scale your system. Cluster algorithms logically work best at the fortress level.

So you don't want to have too many fortresses. But you also don't want to have too few fortresses. Too few fortresses, in the extreme, is no fortress architecture at all!

Question 10: Are all drawbridge requests idempotent?

Make all of your drawbridge requests idempotent. I discussed the idea of idempotency in Chapter 10 (Internet Fortresses). In theory, idempotency is a drawbridge feature that is most important for presentation and Web service fortresses because of the high (relative) rate of drawbridge failure for those types of fortresses. However, all drawbridges have some risk of delivery failure. The best protection you have is to design your drawbridges so that all requests are idempotent. Then if there is ever a question as to whether a request was delivered, the request can be delivered a second time without risk.

Question 11: Are all drawbridge requests for substantial work?

Many people think the software fortress architecture will not perform well because of the cost of drawbridge communications. They are right about the cost of drawbridge communications, especially as compared to the relative speed of component-to-component communications, or the lightning speed of object-to-object communications. However, these people are missing the point. It is not the cost of the drawbridge communications that is significant. It is the ratio of the cost of the drawbridge communications to the cost of processing the work request.

Let me give an example. Is 10 milliseconds for a drawbridge delivery expensive or not? It depends. If it takes 200 milliseconds to complete the work request, then the cost of the drawbridge adds only 5 percent. If it takes 1 millisecond to complete the work request, then the cost of the drawbridge adds 1,000 percent.

Do not use a drawbridge for idle chatter! Sending one 500-byte infogram will cost about the same as sending one 50-byte infogram and about one-tenth the cost of sending ten 50-byte infograms. Make every request count. Design your fortresses so that you send more information in fewer infograms. Do not try to improve overall performance by eliminating fortresses; instead, improve performance by eliminating infograms (or at least get rid of as many as you can).

Question 12: Do we have any tightly coupled transactions across fortresses?

Never allow a tightly coupled transaction to span a drawbridge. As I discussed in Chapter 3 (Transactions), a tightly coupled transaction guarantees that a collection of updates will be done either en masse or not at all. You should use tightly coupled transactions frequently within the fortress, but they should never be allowed to leave the fortress. If they do, then an unlucky fortress is going to be forced to hold open database locks until another lazy, worthless fortress decides to return from its coffee break. This is serious violation of the prime directive, which is, of course, that the fortress is the trust boundary.

Question 13: Are all drawbridges heterogeneous asynchronous?

For drawbridges, I strongly favor the heterogeneous asynchronous flavor. I discussed this in Chapter 6 (Asynchronous Drawbridges). However, the use of heterogeneous asynchronous drawbridges is not a hard-and-fast rule. It is not uncommon, for example, to find a homogeneous synchronous drawbridge connecting a presentation fortress to a back-end business application or treaty management fortress. But there is no question that the preponderance of synchronous communications in the world today is due much more to ignorance than to technical necessity. If you are in a design review, subject every drawbridge that is not heterogeneous asynchronous to a serious cross-examination as to why it was designed the way it was.

Question 14: Does all interfortress communication pass through drawbridges?

Make sure all interfortress communication passes through drawbridges. Keep in mind that the technology doesn't enforce this rule. Technically, there is no reason that the presentation fortress couldn't make a component-style method invocation directly to a business application component. It would probably even be faster to do so. Do not succumb to this temptation. Communication needs to pass through well-defined and monitored ports, which is the role of the drawbridge and the guard. Make sure the walls of the fortress are designed in such a way that direct communication through the fortress walls is impossible; no holes in the ceiling, no back doors, no trap doors, no hidden tunnels.

Question 15: Have we considered all of the risk factors inherent in our presentation and Web service fortresses?

Do everything you can to protect your Internet fortresses. Review the security recommendations I made in Chapter 10 (Internet Fortresses). Take them as a basic starting point. Assign security specialists at your company who keep up with current threats.

Keep in mind that it is ultimately impossible to protect either presentation or Web service fortresses. If somebody wants badly enough to break into them, chances are they can. So look at your presentation and Web service fortresses very carefully. Ask yourself what the implications will be when the horrid ones do penetrate these fortresses. What damage could *they* do to your Web site? How difficult would it be to fix the damage? What proprietary data and algorithms could *they* look at? Do these fortresses contain information that would allow *them* to penetrate deeper into your enterprise?

13.3 Group Three: Fortress Architecture Questions

The questions in this third group are targeted at the fortress-level architects, those who are responsible for the individual fortresses.

Question 16: Are we considering fortress-appropriate technologies?

You wouldn't believe how much time is spent by presentation folks arguing about which is better: COM+ (a .NET technology) or EJB (a J2EE technology). Similar hours are wasted by business application folks arguing about the merits of ASP.NET versus JavaServer Pages.

If you are a presentation programmer, COM+ and EJB are technologies that are totally irrelevant to your life. You should be debating ASP.NET versus JavaServer Pages. If you are a business application fortress person, you are in exactly the opposite situation.

One of the advantages of the software fortress approach is that it helps partition the confusing collection of software technologies into manageable segments. When you're looking at different technologies, first understand to what fortresses they belong. Then consider them only if they are relevant to your type of fortress. Ignore them otherwise.

Question 17: If we must use a synchronous drawbridge, do we have an asynchronous back end?

As I said earlier, my preference is for heterogeneous asynchronous drawbridges. I also pointed out that this option is not always desirable, especially when you're connecting to an Internet fortress. If you find yourself in a position where you really need a synchronous drawbridge, try to back it up with an internal asynchronous communication as soon as possible.

One good strategy is to have the guard accept the synchronous request. Then the guard breaks up the request into two segments. The first segment is the part of the work request that must be done synchronously. That part is done, and the result is returned to the requesting fortress. Once the synchronous portion of the request has been completed and the result returned, the guard makes an internal asynchronous request for the remaining work.

For example, suppose you're writing a system to process credit cards for stores. You have a presentation fortress that accepts Web requests to process a credit card and a business application fortress that does the credit card processing. Keep in mind that the store has an impatient customer waiting for a cashier to complete the purchase.

The cashier fills in the credit card and customer information on the browser (using emissary code) and sends that information to the presentation fortress. The presentation fortress validates the input information and ensures that the request is authenticated, as well as it can. Then it sends the request to the business application fortress.

The business application guard accepts the information en masse and splits it into the synchronous segment and the asynchronous segment. The synchronous segment is the segment that must be completed before the guard can send a return infogram back to the presentation fortress.

Let's say that the only information the presentation fortress really needs back is an authorization code. The synchronous segment will then include the following steps:

- Verifying the customer information
- Checking that the purchase is within the customer's credit limit
- Assigning a unique authorization code to this particular purchase

The asynchronous segment is the actual posting of the sale to the customer account. This does not need to take place immediately; it can be done in five minutes or even five hours.

Figure 13.1 illustrates this architecture.

The ideal situation, then, is to use an asynchronous drawbridge wherever possible. Where it is not possible, back up the synchronous

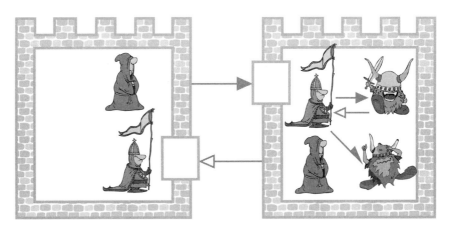

Figure 13.1 Synchronous Drawbridge with Asynchronous Back End

drawbridge with an internal asynchronous request as soon as possible, encompassing as much of the overall workload as possible.

Question 18: Are we using more than one technology base within a single fortress?

Using more than one technology base within a single fortress will cause you many integration problems. J2EE and .NET are not exactly compatible stablemates, and neither are the programmers who work in those technologies. This rule is true even when two J2EE-based technologies are being used—say, IBM's WebSphere and BEA's WebLogic. You can use them both, but keep them out of each other's face. One fortress, one technology.

Question 19: Have we designed a scale-out architecture?

Sooner or later, if you're lucky, you will have to accommodate a lot of users. Or maybe if you are not so lucky. Therefore you need to plan a strategy for increasing your workload capability. As I have discussed, there are two approaches: scale-up (replacing your small machine with a large machine) and scale-out (getting more small machines and managing them as a loosely coupled cluster). The best approach is to use both. Scale *up* the data strongbox, and scale *out* everything else. Because most data strongboxes don't require a lot of scaling (and even if they do, there aren't many architectural issues in doing so), you can focus your energy on scaling out everything else.

The approach of scaling up the data strongbox and scaling out everything else has the advantage of dovetailing nicely with improved reliability. It has the disadvantage of requiring that you design your system appropriately. I have discussed the scale-out architectural requirements in the fortress-specific chapters (Chapters 10 and 11), but in general the most important requirement is the incorporation of a load-balancing algorithm, such as IP load balancing or asynchronous drawbridges. Make sure that you have planned your architecture so that it is consistent with the scale-out approach.

Question 20: Have we designed a fortress architecture that can leverage loosely coupled clusters for reliability?

Assuming that you built your system to scale out using loosely coupled clusters, you are very close to getting high reliability for free (well, for very low cost). I have discussed the architectural requirements in the fortress-specific chapters, especially Chapters 10 and 11, but the most important requirements have to do with state management, transactional integrity, and idempotency. Being sure you understand these issues, design your fortresses properly to leverage loosely coupled clusters not only for scalability but also for reliability.

Question 21: Have we designed adequate security for each of our guards?

Building good guards is probably the toughest job in the software fortress architecture. The guards need to deal with encryption, authorization, authentication, and a seemingly unlimited number of other security-related issues. One could write a book just on guard design. The task is very specialized. Go through an exhaustive review of everything the guard is expected to protect against and how the guard will do this.

Question 22: Have we built effective walls around the fortress?

Having good guards is of little value without good walls. The walls are what guarantee that the guard will be used. Many technologies can be leveraged to provide automatic fortification of the walls. If this is a business application fortress, use the role-based security that is part of your component infrastructure to ensure that components inside the fortress accept requests only from other processes inside the same fortress. Use data strongbox (database) security to deny access to processes outside of the fortress.

During your design review, try to imagine how someone might be able to break through the wall, decide if the risk is great enough to protect against, and if so, make sure you have taken adequate precautions.

Question 23: Are we using only homogeneous synchronous communications within the fortress?

In general, asynchronous technologies are too slow for communications inside the fortress. The major exception to this rule is when you are creating a back end for a synchronous drawbridge, in which case you will want to make a single asynchronous request inside the fortress. I discussed this topic earlier, in Question 17. The typical intrafortress communications technology should be homogeneous synchronous.

There is no reason for having heterogeneous synchronous intrafortress communications because heterogeneous synchronous is slower than homogeneous synchronous, and it provides no benefit other than its support for heterogeneity. Heterogeneity is never an issue inside the fortress, as I discussed in Question 18.

Question 24: Do all of our outgoing communications pass through envoys?

It is much easier to maintain a fortress if all outgoing communications pass through envoys. The envoys protect the business logic from changes in the drawbridge technologies and, to some extent, from changes in the treaty. With envoys, the business logic need understand nothing about the underlying interfortress communication system.

Question 25: Is all of our data being stored in the data strongbox?

This seems like a silly question. Where would you store data other than in a data strongbox? In fact, however, too many programmers think they can write a more efficient database than the database vendors can. They believe they can optimize the transactions, do better caching, or do faster disk I/O. Do not allow this. Databases are highly specialized. It is too easy to write a caching algorithm that works fine for one machine but then corrupts the database when that one machine turns into a cluster. My advice is simple: Use the data strongbox. Don't write your own. Buy one from a vendor that knows what it's doing.

Summary

I have given you a lot of questions to ask, but I think you will find the answers to be important in helping you understand your overall software fortress architecture. They will also help you head off serious problems before they become deeply entrenched in your systems. Keep in mind that the list isn't all-inclusive. When you find some good questions of your own, let me know what they are. You can find me at the ObjectWatch Web site (www.objectwatch.com).

Case Study

Now let me try to tie together the different ideas I have presented. There is nothing like a good case study to check the validity of ideas. I'll choose an example that most readers will be able to relate to: a Web-based retail operation. I can't cover every possible capability one might want from such an operation, but I will at least go through some basic scenarios that should be enough to see what a software fortress architecture might look like in practice, and I will cover enough of the design process to give you an idea of the trade-offs you might be called upon to make.

14.1 The Problem

The case study is a large Internet store. I want customers to be able to make purchases through browsers. I also want to create a close relationship with my vendors. I will let my vendors check for themselves to see how much of their inventory I have on hand. Doing this will allow my vendors to make good predictions about when I am likely to need to reorder. Vendors will be allowed to look at only the inventory items that they provide. Vendors will request inventory information programmatically.

14.2 First-Pass Design

I will start by trying to identify some possible fortresses. Because customers will be using browsers, I know that I will have at least one presentation fortress. Vendors will be coming into my system programmatically, so I know I will need a Web service fortress. I also know that I will have at least one business application fortress to process the requests. So far, I am up to three fortresses. But how many business application fortresses should I have? And what about treaty management and service fortresses?

Let me start by identifying the functionality that I think needs to be in the system someplace:

1. **Customer gateway**: sending catalog information, accepting browser requests, and preparing the order information
2. **Vendor gateway**: accepting SOAP requests from vendors
3. **Vendor management**: processing vendor requests and checking inventory
4. **Order management**: processing customer orders
5. **Customer information**: remembering billing, credit card, and other customer-specific information
6. **Inventory information**: tracking my store's inventory
7. **Shipping**: preparing an order to ship to the customer
8. **Credit card processing**: interfacing with the external credit card companies
9. **Security**: making sure the vendor request is coming from an authorized company

Having both a vendor gateway (that accepts the SOAP requests) and a vendor management fortress (that processes the vendor requests) may seem odd. But keep in mind that the Web service fortress provides a critical security buffer, and that buffer shouldn't contain any proprietary information.

For my first pass through the system, I will create a fortress for each of the major pieces of functionality that I have enumerated here. This is not unlike how I might approach an object-oriented design session. From this first pass I get the following fortresses:

1. CustomerGateway::Presentation Fortress
2. VendorGateway::Web Service Fortress
3. VendorInventoryCheck::Treaty Management Fortress
4. OrderManagement::Treaty Management Fortress
5. Customer::Business Application Fortress

6. Inventory::Business Application Fortress
7. Shipping::Business Application Fortress
8. CreditCardProcessing::Business Application Fortress
9. Security::Service Fortress

In addition to the fortresses, I will have two treaties: one that governs how the fortresses work together to process a customer order (which I'll call ProcessOrder), and one to process a vendor inventory check (which I'll call CheckInventory).

Let's get an overview of what form this enterprise system might take. Figure 14.1 shows a fortress–ally diagram (FAD) for my new enterprise.

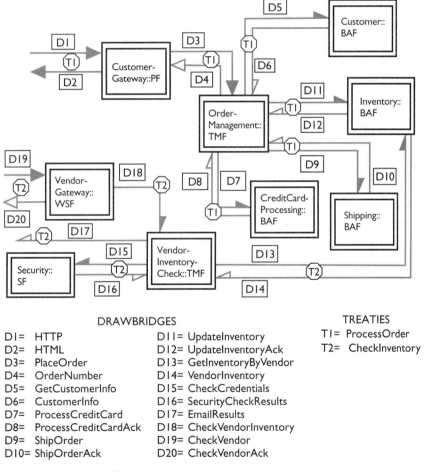

DRAWBRIDGES		TREATIES
D1= HTTP	D11= UpdateInventory	T1= ProcessOrder
D2= HTML	D12= UpdateInventoryAck	T2= CheckInventory
D3= PlaceOrder	D13= GetInventoryByVendor	
D4= OrderNumber	D14= VendorInventory	
D5= GetCustomerInfo	D15= CheckCredentials	
D6= CustomerInfo	D16= SecurityCheckResults	
D7= ProcessCreditCard	D17= EmailResults	
D8= ProcessCreditCardAck	D18= CheckVendorInventory	
D9= ShipOrder	D19= CheckVendor	
D10= ShipOrderAck	D20= CheckVendorAck	

Figure 14.1 Fortress–Ally Diagram

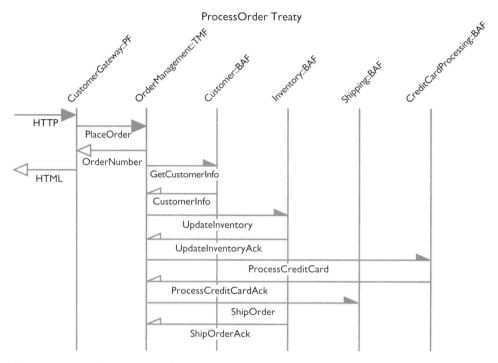

Figure 14.2 SAD for ProcessOrder

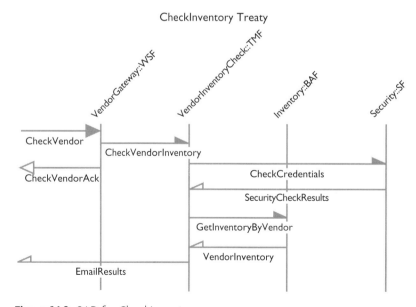

Figure 14.3 SAD for CheckInventory

The FAD shows a lot of detail, so I'll step back a few paces and look at a couple of sequence–ally diagrams (SADs). Figure 14.2 shows the SAD for my system's ProcessOrder treaty, and Figure 14.3 shows the SAD for my system's CheckInventory treaty.

14.3 Second-Pass Design

My SADs are starting to make me a little nervous. A lot of inter-fortress communication seems to be going on, especially for the ProcessOrder treaty. I know that interfortress communication is expensive. Even though I notice that most of the communication uses asynchronous drawbridges, which is good, the sheer volume of it is starting to seem overwhelming. I am starting to wonder if I can consolidate my fortresses.

My starting point for possible fortress consolidation is to notice which fortresses are involved in which treaties. Fortresses that are used within only a single treaty are good candidates for consolidation, although there may still be organizational reasons for keeping them separate. Table 14.1 shows an analysis of which fortresses are used within which treaties.

Table 14.1 Treaty/Fortress Relationships

	Treaty	
Fortress	ProcessOrder	CheckInventory
CustomerGateway	X	
VendorGateway		X
OrderManagement	X	
Customer	X	
Inventory	X	X
Shipping	X	
CreditCardProcessing	X	
VendorInventoryCheck		X
Security		X

This analysis indicates that the Inventory fortress is the only fortress that is used in both treaties. Because inventory management seems very organizationally specialized and because the functionality is needed by both treaties, it seems reasonable to keep it a separate fortress. I decide to collapse the remaining treaty fortresses as much as possible while still maintaining my security buffer for the untrusted browsers and SOAP requests.

In my next pass I decide to consolidate the Customer, Shipping, and CreditCardProcessing fortresses into the OrderManagement fortress. Because OrderManagement is no longer orchestrating other fortresses as much as taking over their functionality, I change its type from treaty management (TMF) to business application (BAF). I similarly consolidate Security into VendorInventoryCheck because Security is used only to process a vendor request.

After this consolidation, I can redraw my FAD as shown in Figure 14.4. Notice how much simpler things are starting to look!

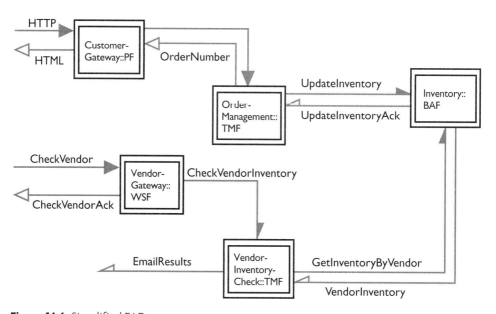

Figure 14.4 Simplified FAD

Breaking up the new FAD into the two enterprise treaties gives us the TADs (treaty–ally diagrams) shown in Figures 14.5 and 14.6. Each treaty now seems quite manageable.

My official fortress count is now down to five: CustomerGateway (PF), OrderManagement (BAF), Inventory (BAF), VendorGateway (WSF), and VendorInventoryCheck (BAF). Creating fortress–ally-responsibility (FAR) cards will give me a handle on the major

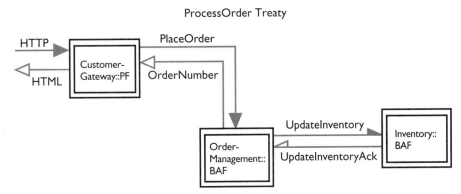

Figure 14.5 TAD for ProcessOrder

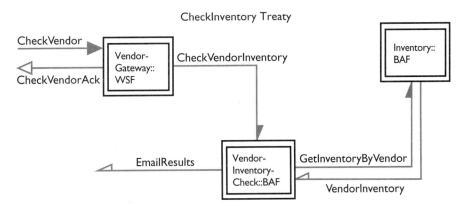

Figure 14.6 TAD for CheckInventory

functions of each. The FAR cards for all of these fortresses are shown in Figure 14.7.

Fortress: CustomGateway::PF	
RESPONSIBILITIES	**ALLY**
Receive order request from browser	
Queue up order	OrderManagement
Return order number	

Fortress: OrderManagement::BAF	
RESPONSIBILITIES	**ALLY**
Receive customer order	
Process customer order	
Update inventory	Inventory

Fortress: Inventory::BAF	
RESPONSIBILITIES	**ALLY**
Manage inventory	
Update orders	OrderManagement
Program Inventory list by vendor	VendorInventoryCheck

Fortress: VendorGateway::WSF	
RESPONSIBILITIES	**ALLY**
Receive vendor inventory request	
Queue up request	VendorInventoryCheck
Return acknowledgment	

Fortress: VendorInventoryCheck::BAF	
RESPONSIBILITIES	**ALLY**
Process vendor inventory request	
E-mail results back to vendor	Inventory

Figure 14.7 FAR Cards

Treaty: CheckInventory	
RESPONSIBILITIES	ALLY
Manage vendor interaction	VendorGateway
Manage processing of request	VendorInventoryCheck
Program inventory list by vendor	Inventory

Treaty: ProcessOrder	
RESPONSIBILITIES	ALLY
Manage browser interaction	CustomerGateway
Process customer order	OrderManagement
Update inventory	Inventory

Figure 14.8 High-Level TAR Cards

In a very high-level treaty overview, we can also look at the treaty–ally–responsibility (TAR) cards, which are shown in Figure 14.8.

14.4 The ProcessOrder Drawbridges

Now that I have a good overview of what fortresses I have and how they will work together, my next goal is to understand the drawbridge requirements better. I'll start with a SAD for the ProcessOrder treaty and look specifically at each drawbridge interaction. The overall SAD for ProcessOrder is shown in Figure 14.9.

Now let me start going through the drawbridges. The first ProcessOrder interaction occurs between the browser and the CustomerGateway fortress. This interaction is specifically governed by CustomerGateway code running on the browser. As I discussed in Chapter 10 (Internet Fortresses), this is what Pat Helland calls emissary code.

The next drawbridge crossing occurs over the Place Order drawbridge, used by the CustomerGateway fortress to send an order for processing to the OrderManagement fortress. The SAD shows a synchronous drawbridge. You might wonder why I'm using a synchronous drawbridge

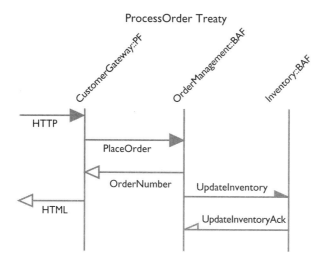

Figure 14.9 New SAD for ProcessOrder

in light of my emphasis on asynchronous drawbridges. And in fact, I do believe that we can probably design the OrderManagement fortress so that the overall order flow is asynchronous relative to the CustomerGateway fortress. But then why not use an asynchronous drawbridge?

The reason for the synchronous drawbridge is that I assume I want to let Claire, the customer, know two things before she leaves my Web site. First, I want her to know that her order has definitely been received into my processing queue. Second, I want to assign her order an ID so that she can return to my Web site and check on her order's progress. Although I haven't specified this functionality at this time, I assume it will be a straightforward extension of my basic architecture.

So I have conflicting goals. On the one hand, I want to process the order asynchronously relative to Claire sitting at her browser. As I discussed in Chapter 6 (Asynchronous Drawbridges), asynchronous processing gives me good load balancing and reliability, or at least good potential for these things. On the other hand, I don't want Claire to leave until I have at least assigned the order ID. This implies the need for a synchronous drawbridge. How do I resolve this problem?

The standard design technique, discussed in Chapter 13 (Software Fortress Design Review, Question 17) is to build a synchronous drawbridge façade to an asynchronous fortress. I would probably build this façade using a synchronous technology between the Customer-Gateway fortress (the presentation fortress) and the guard for the OrderManagement fortress (the business application fortress). Then I would have a synchronous communications request between the guard of the OrderManagement fortress and the internal worker who assigns the order ID. The worker bee returns the order ID to the guard, who returns it to the presentation fortress, who can then send it back to Claire. Once the order ID assignment has been made, the guard can continue with the rest of the order processing. This part can be done asynchronously, as Figure 14.10 shows.

The drawbridge that accepts the request from the CustomerGateway fortress is titled PlaceOrder. I have said that this is a synchronous drawbridge, but I haven't said yet whether I would use heterogeneous or homogeneous technology. In general, I prefer to use the same technology base for the presentation fortress as for the business application fortresses to which it is connected. The main reason is that some synchronous connection between the two is often necessary, and the most efficient synchronous drawbridges

HTTP

HTML

Figure 14.10 Synchronous Drawbridge Façade and Asynchronous Fortress

are of the homogeneous type. Therefore, I would probably make the PlaceOrder drawbridge a homogeneous synchronous drawbridge.

As long as we're dealing with drawbridges connecting the Customer-Gateway and the OrderManagement fortresses, we might as well look at the gateway used to return the order number to the CustomerGateway fortress. The rule of thumb here is that when we have a drawbridge whose role is to return information from a synchronous drawbridge, it will be of the same type as the original drawbridge. If the original drawbridge (PlaceOrder) is homogeneous synchronous, then so will be the return drawbridge (OrderNumber).

As I have already discussed, all synchronous drawbridges are based on component systems. One way to implement the PlaceOrder and OrderNumber drawbridges is to have a dual function of envoy and guard on both sides of the fortress, as Figure 14.11 shows.

There is one more question. What kind of asynchronous technology do we use to communicate between the incoming guard of the OrderManagement fortress and the second worker bee, the one who will start off the asynchronous order processing? My answer is simple: Who cares? Let the fortress architect worry about that. It isn't my problem. *I* am an Enterprise-Level Architect. *I* have bigger fish to fry.

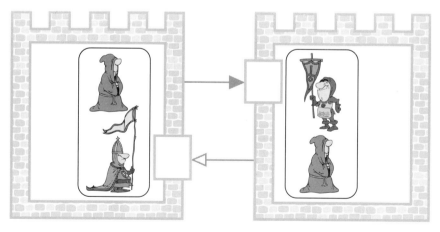

Figure 14.11 Component-Based Implementation of Synchronous Drawbridge

Speaking of bigger fish, let's look at the drawbridges connecting the two business application fortresses (OrderManagement and Inventory) that are involved with order processing. The Inventory fortress accepts the request through its UpdateInventory drawbridge and returns the answer through the OrderManagement's UpdateInventoryAck drawbridge. (*Ack*, by the way, stands for "acknowledgment," and just means that the request has been completed.) This flow is most clearly shown in Figure 14.9.

But wait! What the heck does "returns the answer" mean? The SAD in Figure 14.9 shows the UpdateInventory drawbridge as an asynchronous drawbridge (that's what the half-arrow means). How does an asynchronous drawbridge "return" anything? Isn't the whole point of *asynchronous* that the requestor goes along doing whatever it chooses *without* waiting for an answer?

Yes and no. Keep in mind that the requestor here is not the normal kind of requestor. It is not a person. It is not a component. It is not even a process. It is a *fortress*. A fortress consists of many different processes, including processes that can check message queues for incoming messages and process them independently of whatever else is happening in the fortress. The asynchronous return represented by UpdateInventoryAck is like the next iteration in a workflow system.

14.5 The CheckInventory Drawbridges

Now I'll turn my attention to the drawbridges used by the CheckInventory treaty, starting with the VendorGateway fortress. Figure 14.12 shows the SAD for CheckInventory.

Superficially the CheckInventory treaty looks like the ProcessOrder treaty, as you can see by comparing Figure 14.12 to Figure 14.9. Both treaties involve three fortresses. Both feature an asynchronous relationship with the Inventory fortress. However, this is where the similarities end.

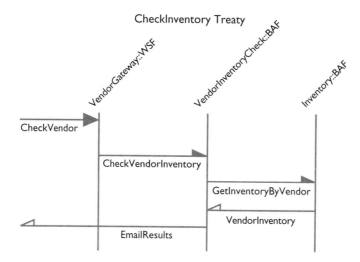

Figure 14.12 New SAD for CheckInventory

The first difference is at the gateway level. The incoming request to the CustomerGateway fortress originated with emissary code—that is, code that is properly owned by the fortress itself, although it is running on the browser—notwithstanding the ever present suspicion that the request could have originated with a rogue system. The incoming request to the VendorGateway fortress, on the other hand, certainly did *not* originate with code that had anything to do with my fortress.

Although I may not know much about the originator of the incoming request, I can make two reasonable assumptions. First, there won't be just one originator; there will be many. All of my vendors will be using this portal to get information about their inventory status. Given that there will be so many vendors, it stands to reason that at least some of them will be using a different technology for their fortresses than I am using for mine. Therefore I must assume that the drawbridge is heterogeneous. My second assumption is that at least some of these vendors will need to be using the Internet to connect to my system. Given today's state of technology, this scenario implies SOAP requests delivered via HTTP.

Although SOAP/HTTP is a synchronous drawbridge technology, as I discussed in Chapter 5 (Synchronous Drawbridges), I really don't need this gateway to be synchronous. I don't plan to return anything to the requestor, at least not from this fortress. I also don't expect the bulk of the work to be blocking. If I could figure out how to deliver SOAP over HTTP asynchronously, I would do so. But like it or not, SOAP over HTTP is basically a synchronous drawbridge.

Why don't I expect the bulk of the CheckInventory work to be blocking? The answer is apparent in the SAD (see Figure 14.12). The VendorGateway fortress is just a SOAP veneer for the VendorInventoryCheck fortress, where the real work will be done. And the drawbridge connecting the VendorGateway and VendorInventoryCheck fortresses is CheckVendorInventory. This is an asynchronous drawbridge (as indicated by the half-arrowhead in the SAD). So we know the work is going to be nonblocking with respect to the VendorGateway fortress. And well it should be. I like my vendors, but I don't want them interfering with valuable computer cycles that could be better used for processing customer orders. I'll process vendor requests when I have absolutely nothing better to do.

The GetInventoryByVendor drawbridge used by VendorInventoryCheck to access the Inventory fortress is slightly different from the UpdateInventory drawbridge used by OrderManagement. The latter returns just a touch of information—namely, an acknowledgment that the inventory was updated. The former returns quite a bit of information, the entire list of inventory "owned" by this vendor. A logical, heterogeneous approach to packaging this much information is as an XML document.

I have said that the drawbridges owned by the Inventory fortress are asynchronous, but I haven't discussed whether they are heterogeneous or homogeneous asynchronous. If you recall from Chapter 6 (Asynchronous Drawbridges), the homogeneous variety adds precious little functionality to what one gets with the heterogeneous variety, and it does add quite a few limitations. So in general, when I make a drawbridge asynchronous, I almost always make it heterogeneous as well.

This is quite different from the approach I would take with a synchronous drawbridge. When my drawbridge is synchronous, there are compelling reasons to look for homogeneity where it does not unduly restrict my fortress options.

The only remaining communications issue is the return of the inventory information to the vendor. This can't be done synchronously, even though the incoming request came in synchronously. Why not? Because the processing of the incoming request has long ago been completed. So I want to return the information asynchronously. Now you might think that no asynchronous technology works across the Internet and is technology agnostic. But if you did, you would be wrong. There is such a technology, and if you are reading this book, you probably use it almost every day of your life. This technology is e-mail. So I decide I will e-mail the final result back to the vendor. If I don't get around to sending out the e-mail until 2:00 in the morning, I don't think my vendor will complain.

14.6 Guards

We can get a good handle on the guard issues by following information flow from the browser to the CustomerGateway fortress to the OrderManagement fortress to the Inventory fortress, as shown in Figure 14.9. All of the guards in this system will be variants of guards that we will encounter within this sequence.

The single hardest guard issue we run into is, coincidentally, the first: validation of the HTTP request. You might ask why we're worried about validating the HTTP request. After all, this request is coming from emissary code—that is, code that was written by the same team that wrote the CustomerGateway fortress. But that is part of the problem. HTTP requests can come from anywhere.

The guard should check all input fields for two things: buffer overflows and illegal characters. Both of these are topics I discussed in Chapter 7 (Guards and Walls), so I won't repeat that discussion here. Note that problems with both buffer length and illegal characters can be handled by emissary code, so in a sense what I'm really worrying about is hackers skirting my emissaries. Because it is trivial for hackers to do so, I must take this possibility seriously.

Once I am convinced that I'm receiving a valid HTTP request from one of my emissaries, I can start to deal with the next problem: Is this request coming from somebody who is authorized to use my system? This is a more difficult problem to attack in the presentation fortress, namely because we run into conflicting security demands.

On the one hand I want the presentation fortress to validate the user. To do this, I may need to store passwords and sensitive user information in the presentation fortress's data strongbox. I could then design my guard to check the password input field and the user name, and validate these against information in the data strongbox.

On the other hand, storing passwords and sensitive user information in the presentation fortress's data strongbox is, in itself, a security problem because anyone who succeeds in hijacking a presentation fortress process will have access to all of this information. After all, the whole reason we have a presentation fortress is to keep our proprietary business logic "offline" relative to our Internet connections.

Good guard design requires balancing these two concerns, recognizing in advance that there is no perfect solution. For example, I could store encrypted user passwords on the presentation fortress. However, I would also have to store a private key on the presentation fortress, which in itself would be a tempting hacker target.

I could pass through the user ID and password to the back-end Order-Management fortress. However, at least temporarily I would have to store unencrypted user IDs and passwords in presentation fortress memory that is potentially available to a hijacked presentation fortress process.

I could set up my emissary to do public/private–key encryption of the user ID and password at the emissary. I could then pass this encrypted information to the OrderManagement fortress and let it do the decryption and authentication. However, this approach limits my users to those for whom I have a trusted public key. Not many of my standard users will have bothered to register with public/private–key systems, although such an approach might be workable on the Web service fortress side.

In any case, the guard authentication algorithms will be standard authentication algorithms that are a specialized topic in their own right. This is one of the reasons I emphasize consolidating security responsibility into a single point of contact.

Having discussed the CustomerGateway guard, I can turn my attention to the OrderManagement guard, the one defending the Place-Order drawbridge. This guard wants to ensure that it is receiving requests only from the CustomerGateway fortress. Depending on what authentication choices we made in CustomerGateway, we may need to include some authentication logic in the PlaceOrder guard as well.

As I have said, I prefer to use a single technology base for both presentation fortresses (e.g., CustomerGateway) and the connected business application fortresses (e.g., OrderManagement) where possible. If I am using a synchronous gateway (which is what I have shown in the SAD for the ProcessOrder treaty), then I will be making that gateway homogeneous. Homogeneous synchronous gateways are invariably based on native component technology, such as .NET Remote Binary Protocol in the Microsoft system, or RMI/IIOP in a Java system. One nice thing about homogeneous synchronous gateway technologies is that they include some useful built-in guard mechanisms. One of these is the ability to make sure that the PlaceOrder guard accepts requests only from specific processes, such as the one containing the outgoing guard in the CustomerGateway fortress.

The final guard I'll look at is the one in the Inventory fortress guarding the UpdateInventory drawbridge. The UpdateInventory drawbridge is a heterogeneous asynchronous drawbridge, as shown in Figure 14.9. As such, it is most likely based on a message queue technology, such as IBM's MQSeries or Microsoft's MSMQ. Either of these technologies includes the ability to set permissions on the underlying message queue, which can theoretically make it impossible for nonauthorized processes even to send messages to the GetInventory-ByVendor guard.

This analysis covers only three of the various guards, but the rest are just variants. The GetInventoryByVendor guard of the Inventory fortress, for example, is a variant of the UpdateInventory guard of the same fortress. The CheckVendorInventory guard of the VendorGateway fortress is a variant of the HTTP guard of the CustomerGateway fortress.

Summary

In this chapter I have given an example of how one might approach a real problem using the software fortress model. The most important lessons in this chapter are these:

- Plan on several iterations when developing a software fortress architecture. Even with a relatively simple problem, I used two iterations.

- Use the TADs and SADs to help you analyze the overall complexity of your architecture.

- Don't get carried away in creating software fortresses. Software fortresses are not objects. You don't need many of them. Unless there is a good reason for having functionality in different fortresses, don't do it.

- Drawbridge communication is expensive. Don't do too much of it, and when you do do it, make it count.

- When you must use a synchronous drawbridge, do as little of the work as possible synchronously.

- When using asynchronous drawbridges, use heterogeneous technologies. There just isn't enough benefit (at least today) with the homogeneous asynchronous drawbridges.

- When using synchronous drawbridges, use homogeneous technologies where possible because they offer more guard support (at least today) than do the heterogeneous synchronous technologies.

- Treat all input to a presentation or Web service fortress with great suspicion.

- Authentication in a presentation or Web service fortress is a tough problem, and you will probably have to live with some trade-offs.

CHAPTER 15

Postlude

In this book I have covered the basics of the software fortress model. I have discussed the terminology, documentation techniques, various technical approaches, and major software fortress types. In this chapter I summarize the most important points, give you some guidance in choosing software platforms, and tell you the main things that I think are wrong with the software industry (perhaps this will serve as a wake-up call!).

15.1 Ten Important Points about Software Fortresses

Let's start by reviewing the basics of the software fortress model. This much of the model should be familiar to everybody in your organization, from the CTO to the end user:

1. The software fortress is a *trust boundary*. Everybody in the fortress trusts everybody else in the fortress, and nobody in the fortress trusts anybody outside the fortress.

2. The software fortress consists of many close-knit *systems*, *machines*, and *processes*. These systems, machines, and processes work together to solve a significant business problem, such as accounts payable.

3. Every fortress has one or more places where fortress-critical data is stored. These are collectively referred to as *data strongboxes*.

4. Every fortress is protected by one or more systems that prevent communications from being received from the outside world except through approved channels. These protective systems are collectively referred to as *walls*.

5. Fortresses always regard each other with suspicion, but sometimes they must work together despite this suspicion. Fortresses that work together to accomplish a mutual goal are called *allies*.

6. When one fortress makes a request of an ally, it does so over a formal communications channel known as a *drawbridge*. A request passing over a drawbridge is referred to as an *infogram*.

7. When a fortress wants to communicate with an ally, it does so using an internal system called an *envoy*.

8. When a fortress receives a communication from an ally, that communication is subjected to inspection and possibly other security measures (such as auditing) by a specialized system called a *guard*. The guard decides whether to accept the request on behalf of the fortress.

9. Ally relationships are defined by all-encompassing agreements called *treaties*.

10. Fortresses can be characterized by the kind of work they do. There are at least six major types of fortresses: business application fortresses, presentation fortresses, Web service fortresses, treaty management fortresses, service fortresses, and legacy fortresses.

15.2 Ten Reasons to Adopt the Software Fortress Model

Your enterprise will face a significant learning curve, should you choose to adopt the software fortress model. Why do I think this learning curve will pay off? Here are my top ten reasons:

1. The software fortress model gives everybody in your organization, including managers, architects, users, and developers, a common language and a common vision for understanding how to build systems that can work together.

2. The software fortress model helps you understand the complex relationships among the many discrete systems that make up your enterprise.

3. The software fortress model recognizes the relationship between the political and technical boundaries of your organization.

4. The software fortress model provides you with specific modeling tools based on industry standard techniques for documenting your overall enterprise system.

5. The software fortress model gives you a methodology for getting software systems to work together, even when those software systems are built on completely different technology bases.

6. The software fortress model defines appropriate levels for you to make technology choices, giving your enterprise tremendous flexibility in choosing the best possible technology for each specific problem.

7. The software fortress model helps you evaluate technologies by focusing on only those capabilities that are relevant either to a particular fortress type or to a particular function within the fortress.

8. The software fortress model helps you protect your enterprise from attack over the Internet by defining a security buffer between the Internet and your enterprise systems.

9. The software fortress model gives you a simple yet highly effective model for overall enterprise security based on the complementary functions of preventing entry (walls) and allowing entry (guards).

10. The software fortress model is a clear, simple, and safe model for flowing transactions through your enterprise.

15.3 Ten Rules for Software Fortress Design

Of course, software fortresses work well only if your overall design is sound. What are the most important design rules for a software fortress architecture? Here are my top ten:

1. **At the enterprise level, focus on treaties**. Use treaty–ally–responsibility (TAR) cards to get an overview of which fortresses play which parts in which treaties. Pay close attention to the sequence–ally diagrams (SADs), which are very helpful for gaining an understanding of how fortresses will work together and for identifying performance problems.

2. **Define fortresses with the right amount of granularity**. If you have thousands of fortresses, you have most likely confused fortresses with components, or even worse, with objects. If you have only one fortress in a thousand-person organization, you have probably confused fortresses with enterprises. A good rule of thumb is one fortress for every 20 to 50 employees, and one for every purchased system.

3. **Look carefully at your walls**. There should be only one possible way into a fortress: through a secured drawbridge. Firewalls, database security, role-based security, and access control lists are some of the technologies you can use to reinforce your fortress walls. You should also run your fortresses on stripped-down systems. Every unnecessary feature of the operating system is a potentially forgotten passageway into your fortress. Use as many layers of protection as you need to defeat likely intruders who are knocking against your fortress walls looking for weak spots. Make sure nobody can get into the fortress except through a drawbridge.

4. **Look carefully at your guards**. If your walls are working well, then your guards are your last defense against the miscreants of the world. Ask yourself these questions:

   ■ How do you know an infogram is coming from where you think it's coming from?

   ■ Could somebody have read or tampered with an infogram en route?

- Could somebody have captured an infogram en route, and then replay it later?
- Might you be called upon later to prove that you really did receive an infogram that the sender denies having sent?

Put your best security specialists on guard design and implementation.

5. **Make sure nobody can exit the fortress except through an envoy**. Envoys protect the internal fortress workers from becoming entangled in the sometimes complex details of preparing infograms and placing them on drawbridges. Envoys also protect the fortress workers from inevitable changes in the drawbridges.

6. **Design infograms to be resilient**. Some drawbridges, such as those based on message queues, have reliable delivery. Others, such as those based on HTTP, have unreliable delivery. Even the most reliable drawbridges cannot protect against implementation failures in the receiving fortress. The best protection against interfortress communications anomalies is designing the infograms to be highly resilient. A resilient infogram is one that, without causing problems, can be sent over and over again (i.e., is idempotent) and can be received in any order (i.e., is communicative).

7. **Design your fortresses to scale**. My preference is to use a scale-out design for everything I can in the fortress. A scale-out design is based on loosely connected clusters of small, cheap machines. I like such clusters because they give an excellent cost/performance ratio and provide high reliability. The one part of the fortress that typically does not scale out is the data strongbox, especially when it is implemented with a database. Fortunately, through proper fortress granularity, careful state management, and judicious use of stored procedures, we can minimize the need to scale the data strongbox at all.

8. **Use only loosely coupled transactions across fortresses**. Keep in mind that a loosely coupled transaction is not much of a transaction at all. It is really just some kind of an agreement between two or more fortresses to let each other know

if their portion of the treaty workload failed. Usually this agreement is mediated by an independent body, either a treaty management fortress or a specialized service fortress that might be called a compensatory transaction manager or a business transaction manager.

9. **Use tightly coupled transactions only within the fortress**. A tightly coupled transaction is a "real" transaction, one that involves absolute guarantees by the various transactional resources that they will either all commit or all roll back. This agreement is mediated by a distributed transaction coordinator (DTC). To make this guarantee, the resources typically need to maintain locks. We never allow a resource outside our fortress to determine when, if, and for how long we will hold resource locks. Therefore, distributed transaction coordinators are not shared across fortresses; they live strictly within only one fortress.

   Tightly coupled transactions are relevant mostly within business application fortresses. Such fortresses are typically implemented with component technology, either COM+ in the Microsoft space or Enterprise JavaBeans in the Java space. Both technologies provide automatic transaction boundary management algorithms that help considerably in building well-behaved components.

10. **Use asynchronous drawbridges wherever possible**. Asynchronous drawbridges provide workflow averaging, nonblocking workflow, and high reliability. Where you absolutely can't use an asynchronous drawbridge, then at least back up the synchronous drawbridge with an internal asynchronous rerouting as quickly as possible.

15.4 Ten Controversial Ideas within the Software Fortress Model

As I write this, the basic ideas of the software fortress model have been presented in person to thousands of managers, architects, and developers and in writing to tens of thousands more. The acceptance of the model is enthusiastic. However, I have noticed that certain questions, uncertainties, and controversies seem to pop up over and over. This is probably a good place to deal with them. Here are the most common ten:

1. **Performance doesn't count**. I have stated in this book several times that performance doesn't count. I have made this statement in two contexts: (1) drawbridge performance and (2) overall fortress performance.

   In the context of drawbridges, the cost of transporting an infogram is generally white noise in the background. Or at least it will be, if everything else has been well designed. Consider a donor fortress D working with an allied recipient fortress R. If D needs to work with R, it should make a very small number (preferably a number that looks a lot like *one*) of infogram requests, so the cost of transporting those infograms should be small compared to the work R will be performing once the infograms have been received. If R does very little work after receiving the infogram, or if D needs to send many infograms to get its workload processed, then one of these issues, and not the cost of transporting a single infogram, will be the performance problem.

   In the context of fortresses, performance does count, but not as much as overall design. In my experience, implementors are notoriously unreliable when it comes to predicting performance problems. They often spend a great deal of time trying to optimize areas that ultimately make little or no difference to overall fortress performance. In a business application fortress, for example, overall performance will be dominated by the cost of the distributed transaction coordination, so trying to optimize a variable in a *for* loop is almost certainly a waste of time. Implementors are generally better off building with only minimal regard to performance, and then looking for bottlenecks and fixing them after the fact. These bottlenecks are almost never where they would have been predicted.

2. **Put security *only* in the guard**. The idea of putting security only in the guard runs counterintuitive among people who

have been trained to build security in depth, meaning to build it into every layer of a system. In fact, building security everywhere is the same thing as building security nowhere.

Very few developers have the skills necessary to manage security well. You are lucky if you have a few developers who really understand the issues of security. This is not to malign the typical developer. It is just that security is a very complex issue, and the typical developer has enough to keep track of just building a good business application or browser interface.

Security is a specialized area. By putting security in the guard (and only the guard) we can be sure that nothing arrives in the fortress that has not been subjected to the most rigorous inspection. Should your fortress find itself under a new attack, one not anticipated in your initial design, you have only one place you need to go to deal with the situation. Should security requirements change (say, auditing is suddenly required), you can add it in one location and have it enabled for the entire fortress.

3. **Organizational boundaries are related to fortress boundaries**. Some people question my supposition that the software fortress boundary should in some way reflect organizational boundaries within the enterprise. They point out that organizational boundaries tend to shift over time.

   In my experience, fortress responsibilities tend to shift en masse when organizations are reorganized. In any case, I don't consider alignment of organizational and fortress boundaries to be an absolute rule; it's just that organizational boundaries tend to be natural trust boundaries, and it is usually most natural if the two boundaries (organizational and technical) align.

4. **Tightly coupled transactions shouldn't cross fortress boundaries**. As I write this, there are two significant efforts under way to standardize Web service transactions. One of these is sponsored by Microsoft, IBM, and BEA, and in their proposal, they suggest that tightly coupled transactions

should be allowed to travel over SOAP. Within the context of a software fortress architecture, the implication is that these companies believe that tightly coupled transactions should be allowed to cross fortress boundaries.

The only reason I can imagine enabling such functionality would be to allow different technology bases (such as Java's J2EE and Microsoft's .NET) to work within the same tightly coupled transaction. However, it is highly unlikely that J2EE and .NET would coexist in the same fortress. I am in favor of using both, but not in favor of mixing them in the same fortress. Assuming that we will have only one technology within a fortress, there is no reason to carry tightly coupled transactions over SOAP. SOAP is strictly a heterogeneous drawbridge technology.

Some unusual situations might be able to take advantage of tightly coupled transactions over Web services. However, I believe that the potential danger is much greater than the potential benefit. In my view, this proposal is fatally flawed. Hopefully by the time you read this, the only transactions that will be widely accepted over SOAP will be the loosely coupled variety.

5. **We need fortresses within fortresses**. Some people have suggested that they would like to use a construct of a fortress within a fortress. This idea can also be described as allowing recursive fortresses, an approach that seems to be particularly attractive to the academic community. I see this concept as a variant of the argument that we shouldn't put all of our security eggs in the guard basket. The reason for allowing fortress recursion would be to allow many layers of security. My arguments in favor of single security focal points also argue against allowing recursive fortresses. I realize this idea is controversial, but as yet I have not seen a compelling case for allowing fortress recursion.

6. **The software fortress model should always be used**. Some people argue that, for many software enterprises, the software

fortress model is overkill. I agree. I see this model as applicable to large enterprise systems, such as at banks, investment houses, or insurance companies, typically built by at least hundreds of different developers. However, I have been surprised by the number of people who see this model as offering value to software enterprises for which I had never envisioned using it. For example, the military establishment seems drawn to the basic fortress security model. So this model may gradually become more widely used than I had envisioned, but I can't imagine that it will ever be used to the ubiquitous extent, say, of object-oriented programming.

7. **Turn off database security**. Turn off database security? What, are you crazy? OK, if it will make you feel better, we don't really turn off database security; we use it only as a way of reinforcing the fortress walls, of making sure that outside processes are not allowed to access the database. Database security was designed for client–server systems. It didn't work for three-tier architectures. It doesn't work for software fortress architectures.

8. **Don't share databases across fortresses**. This is a tough one because large companies have shown somewhat of a trend to consolidate all database operations into a single group and to think of data as a corporate resource. I still prefer the architecture in which each fortress owns its own data.

   There are several possible compromise positions. One is that the database is centrally owned but partitioned so that each partition is controlled by one fortress. Another compromise is that we use another service fortress, one that is a consolidated data storage fortress. This is definitely an area where some may feel the need to make adjustments to the software fortress model.

9. **Give scale-out priority over scale-up**. Many organizations have found that managing clusters of small machines is more difficult than managing a small number of large machines. I still prefer the scale-out approach because of the reliability gains. However, many organizations find that they get great

reliability using scale-up. In any case, I don't consider the choice of scale-up versus scale-out an essential feature of the model.

10. **The model hasn't been proven**. Some people object to the software fortress model on the basis that it hasn't been proven. This is true. The model is still very young. However, I would point out that some critical features of the model have been proven, albeit in different contexts. For example,

   - The idea that database centric security does not work has been known for two decades, since the advent of transaction processing monitors.
   - The idea that asynchronous communications can provide workflow averaging, nonblocking workflow, and high reliability has been known since message queues were first released.

I would also mention that although this model has not been proven, it doesn't exactly have any competition. What are you going to do? Surely you have figured out that what you're doing now is not working! And nobody else is offering anything (and if they are, it hasn't been proven either).

Furthermore, I would point out that the concepts have been presented over and over to many of the top software architects in the world, none of whom have found problems with the main ideas you have been reading about, other than the issues I have discussed in this section. Even here, debate focuses on the details (e.g., is scale-out really better than scale-up?), not the fundamentals of the software fortress approach.

And finally, I might even argue that the software fortress model *has* been proven. One of the responses I frequently hear when presenting the software fortress model is that it corresponds closely to the way in which many organizations are building systems today. One of the things some people like about the model is that it formalizes an approach they feel they have already been using.

15.5 Ten Considerations for Evaluating J2EE versus .NET

The two main technology contenders for running your enterprise are Java 2 Enterprise Edition, known as J2EE, and Microsoft's .NET. A major advantage of the software fortress model is that you don't have to choose between them, at least at an enterprise level. But within the fortress, I still prefer the simple world of homogeneity. So as you plan your fortresses, you will need to choose one or the other approach. How do you choose? Here are the top ten considerations that I think should guide your decision:

1. **Do you need to run this fortress on a non-Windows platform?** Once you have decided that you must run a fortress on a non-Windows platform, .NET is out of the picture. Although versions of .NET are coming out for non-Windows platforms, as of this writing none of these are ready for prime time. So if you must run your fortress on Unix or Linux, look to a J2EE solution.

   It is worth asking yourself why you think you need to run the fortress on something other than Windows. If the reason is that you think other platforms are more secure, more scalable, more reliable, or less expensive, you are probably wrong. There is little evidence that other platforms have any advantages in any of these areas.

   Of course, you might prefer a non-Windows platform for other reasons. For example, your code base may already run on another system and there is no advantage to be gained by porting it to Windows. You may already have Unix machines that you can leverage in your new fortresses.

   Bottom line: Use .NET for Windows, and J2EE for anything else.

2. **Is cost of the fortress important?** Predicting fortress costs can be a bit complicated, but for cost-critical systems it is well worth the exercise. Let's say we have a fortress F that is built with technology T. Assume F can be built up in incremental

units of T_U, where each increment costs T_D dollars. If F is built with scale-out fortresses, then it might cost T_D dollars to add another machine to the cluster. If F is built with scale-up fortresses, then D is the additional cost of the next biggest machine. Assume that each T_D dollars adds the ability to process T_U units of work per minute. Assume that F is going to be asked to process a peak workload of P infograms per minute and an average workload of A infograms per minute. Got that? Let me review:

- F is the fortress we're trying to build.

- T is the technology we're using.

- T_D is the dollar cost per incremental unit of adding new pieces of T.

- T_U is the number of units of work per minute that each T_D dollars adds.

- P is the peak workload (in infograms per minute) that F will be asked to process. P is independent of T because people outside the fortress will be shoving P at you, like it or not, regardless of what T you choose.

- A is the average workload (in infograms per minute) that F will be asked to process. Like P, A is independent of T.

We are almost ready to calculate the unit-of-work costs, but we are missing one piece of critical information. Can you see what it is?

The missing piece of information is the nature of the drawbridge over which F will be receiving its infograms. This is important because if the drawbridge is asynchronous, we will need enough multiples of T_U to accommodate A. If the drawbridge is synchronous, we will need enough multiples of T_U to accommodate P. Because P is typically at least an order of magnitude bigger than A, the drawbridge makes a big difference.

The overall cost of building F with technology T using a *synchronous* drawbridge will be $A \div (T_U \times T_D)$. The cost of building F with technology T using an *asynchronous* drawbridge is

$P \div (T_U \times T_D)$. These calculations are all a bit approximate because they don't include the cost of the drawbridge itself and they assume that the ratio T_U/T_D is linear (an optimistic assumption), but they are a good starting point.

It is difficult to compare T_U and T_D for J2EE and .NET. We have very few benchmarks comparing the two technologies, mainly because the J2EE community specifically defines its benchmarks to preclude participation by .NET. However, from the direct benchmarks we do have, the benchmarks we can extrapolate, and my discussions with people who have used both, I have come to some general conclusions that I believe are valid at least for business application and presentation fortresses, where we have the most data.

For presentation fortresses and business application fortresses, I believe that a good rule of thumb is that the number of units of work you can process, T_U, for a given number of dollars, T_D, is 5 to 10 times higher for .NET than it is for J2EE. This assumption leads to the general prediction that if a fortress costs X dollars to build on .NET, it will cost between 5X and 10X dollars to build with J2EE. Because fortress hardware/software costs are typically in the range of 50,000 to 500,000 dollars, this cost difference can quickly add up. A .NET fortress with a predicted price tag of 500,000 dollars would have a predicted price tag of 2.5 to 5 million dollars if built with J2EE.

As I said, these comparisons are mainly valid for business application and presentation fortresses. It is too early to predict what comparison we might get for other fortress types.

Bottom line: Near as I can tell, cost analyses favor .NET by at least a factor of 5.

3. **Do you need consultants?** If you will be hiring consultants, you will generally find it easier to hire expertise in the J2EE space than the .NET space. The expertise that exists in .NET is mostly in one of two places: small, mom-and-pop consulting organizations of less than 100 people or Microsoft Consulting Services (MCS). MCS is a mere shadow of the IBM

equivalent organization, IBM Global Services. Whereas IBM Global Services is well positioned to come in and run your IT organization from beginning to end, MCS generally serves only in an advisory role, depending on smaller consulting organizations (mostly ones you have never heard of) to do the real work. If you have decided to use IBM Global Services to run your organization, you have also made a de facto decision to use J2EE (and probably Linux), regardless of whether that's the best decision.

Bottom line: If you depend on outside consultants and prefer working with name-brand organizations, you will be better off in the J2EE space.

4. **How much work do you have in the presentation fortress?** The presentation fortress is one of the areas where .NET technologies have some important advantages. ASP.NET, for example, can significantly reduce the time involved in developing presentation fortresses, especially those that have complex and highly interactive presentations. .NET technologies will offer fewer advantages for presentation fortresses that are more data centric.

The ASP.NET technology has four major advantages over the analogous J2EE technology (known as Java ServerPages):

   1. It is much easier to manage browser state, a very tricky issue in Java ServerPages.

   2. It is much easier to figure out what is happening on the browser side.

   3. It is much easier to write browser-independent code.

   4. It is much easier to purchase sophisticated visual controls.

The major disadvantage of ASP.NET is that it depends on Microsoft's IIS (Internet Information Server) to provide an infrastructure in which to run. IIS has a long history of security problems. A careful analysis would show that IIS is no worse off than its competition, but because it is so widely used (and probably because it is from Microsoft), its security problems get much wider publicity than those of other (non-Microsoft) products. Whether the sentiment is reasonable or not, many companies don't trust IIS.

Bottom line: Unless you are IIS-phobic, ASP.NET is a clear winner for developing presentation fortresses.

5. **What connectors do your existing systems have?** Connectors are mostly an issue for treaty management fortresses. These types of fortresses use the .NET technology known as BizTalk Server, or competitor products such as IBM's WebSphere MQ Integrator or TIBCO's ActiveEnterprise (these names seem to change on the drop of a hat, so don't count on them).

All of these products are superficially similar in that they define interfaces that other systems must support to be integrated into their overall framework. From a software fortress perspective, these interfaces effectively define the drawbridge between the treaty management fortress (BizTalk Server and others) and the business application fortress (the ones you have either written or purchased).

These interface implementations are usually known as connectors. For most large purchased systems, connectors must be written by the original system vendor. They are too complex for anybody who is not intimately familiar with the system to attempt.

Unfortunately, there is no standard for these connectors. They are specific to the treaty management technology. So if you are in the lucky position of having to link together systems that already have prebuilt connectors to a particular treaty management technology, that technology will be your best choice for at least the treaty management system working with those systems.

Bottom line: When you need to connect business application fortresses together, choose a treaty management fortress technology that those business application fortresses already support.

6. **What is your existing skill set?** The easiest technology to use is the technology that your developers already know. If they have expertise in Visual Basic, COBOL, or one of the other .NET-supported languages, then .NET will be easier for them to use. If they have expertise in Java, then one of the J2EE offerings will be easier.

   Bottom line: If your developers are very familiar with Java, they will be most productive with J2EE. If not, they will be most productive with .NET.

7. **What is the long-term health of the vendors?** I think it is obvious that Microsoft, as the primary vendor of .NET, and IBM, as the primary vendor of J2EE, are going to be with us for a while. Anybody else is high risk. Sun, which owns the J2EE specifications, is facing tough challenges from both IBM, at the high end, and Microsoft, at the low end. BEA, which at one point I believed would be a major contender in the J2EE space, has just finished a disastrous quarter (second quarter, '02), with revenues down 28 percent over the same quarter in the previous year.

   Bottom line: IBM seems to be a safe bet in the J2EE space, and Microsoft seems to be a safe bet in the .NET space. Anybody else is high risk.

8. **Will you need very high-end databases?** The benchmark that is usually used to measure database performance is the TPC-C benchmark. This benchmark is relevant mostly to business application fortresses, which tend to stress databases to the maximum.

   Vendors are allowed to run the TPC-C benchmark with both clustered and nonclustered configurations. To run clustered configurations, you must partition your database. For most business application fortresses, partitioning databases is not a realistic option. Therefore, when looking at the TPC-C numbers, I tend to give more weight to the nonclustered configurations.

   At press time, the best performance for .NET technologies without partitioned databases is about 300,000 transactions per minute. The best-performing non-.NET systems can achieve 455,000 transactions per minute. If one allows partitioned databases, .NET systems can achieve over 700,000 transactions per minute. As I have said, however, this level of performance is probably not realistic for most applications.

Unfortunately, the 455,000-transaction-per-minute non-.NET systems do not use J2EE. These systems are built on boring, tried-and-true transaction processing monitor (TPM) technologies. J2EE vendors do not participate in this industry standard benchmark, presumably because the performance numbers are too low.

So although you can't get the highest possible performance with nonpartitioned .NET systems, you probably can't with J2EE either. Fortunately, the numbers you can get, the documented numbers for nonpartitioned .NET, are far in excess of what any but the most demanding applications would need. After all, 300,000 transactions per minute is still 432 million transactions per day!

Bottom line: If you are a database user at the extreme high end, you probably can't use either .NET or J2EE. Otherwise, .NET will definitely meet your needs, and probably J2EE will as well (although we have less data to support the latter claim).

9. **How well are Web services integrated into the platform?** Web services are the basis for both Web service fortresses and heterogeneous synchronous drawbridges. SOAP, WSDL, and UDDI are all standards that generally fall under the umbrella term *Web services*. With the likely exception of UDDI, these are all important standards. You need them. But they are too complex to use directly. You need your platform to use these standards but make their use invisible to you. It is hard to evaluate how good a job vendors are doing in this area because the technology is changing fast. However, as you are considering different vendors, think about how you will be using Web services and look for excellent tool support that shields you from the ugly details.

Bottom line: The less you need to know about Web services to use them effectively, the better.

10. **What legacy tools are available for your particular legacy systems?** There are no standards for building legacy fortresses. When choosing platforms for legacy fortresses, consider the options that the vendor provides. What do you need to do to wrap an existing legacy system into a legacy software fortress?

    There is no single right answer here. It will depend on the specific legacy application. In making a decision, you should answer at least the following questions:

    - What footprint, if any, is required on the legacy platform? *Preferred answer*: none.

    - What modifications need to be made to the legacy code? *Preferred answer*: none.

    - What performance does the technology support? *Preferred answer*: higher than you need.

    - How difficult is the technology to use? *Preferred answer: easy.*

    Bottom line: Choose legacy fortress technologies that support your specific legacy fortress needs. There will not be one answer for all legacy fortresses.

15.6 Ten Observations on the State of the Software Industry

One of the reasons that it is so difficult to build enterprise-caliber software systems today is that the software industry is out of touch with enterprise architects. Here are my top ten complaints about the current state of the software industry:

1. **The software industry has no conceptual model for building enterprise systems**. It isn't just that we have no industrywide standards for building enterprise systems. Even the individual companies themselves have no vision for how to build such systems. When you read the "architectural" documents from software vendors, they are invariably advanced

developer manuals. Often it isn't clear that these companies even know what a software architect is, much less how to write for one. I'm not saying that Microsoft, IBM, BEA, and Sun must necessarily adopt the software fortress model (although obviously I think they would be well advised to do so). If they think they can do better, fine. But come up with *something*!

2. **The software industry lacks a coherent vision for flowing transactions through the enterprise**. So far, the industry can't even agree on what the word *transaction* means, so forget having a vision of how one would flow through the enterprise!

3. **The software industry has a confusing hodgepodge of security capabilities and no model for how they should be used**. It seems as if every product has its own idea of security and no concept of how its notion of security relates to that of other products. What is the "role" of role-based security in component systems like COM+ (for Microsoft) or Enterprise JavaBeans (for Java)? How does this role relate to database security? How do both types of systems relate to firewalls? The industry has no idea because it has no coherent vision of what security means or how it should be modeled.

4. **The software industry is wasting time defining portability standards when what we need are interoperability standards**. Efforts like CORBA (from OMG) and J2EE (from the Java consortium) are a monumental waste of time. We don't need standards for portability. Portability means moving a fortress from one platform to another. Nobody does this. We need standards for interoperability, the biggest problem facing enterprise systems today.

5. **The software industry does not differentiate among implementation technologies (such as objects), distribution technologies (such as components), and interoperability technologies (such as fortresses)**. Regardless of which company's programming tools you use, objects and components are virtually indistinguishable. This lack of

distinction exists despite the fact that confusing these technologies is a sure recipe for disaster. Of course, it goes without saying that none of the companies today differentiate between components and fortresses.

6. **The software industry has no concept of the difference between the communications that must occur within a system and the communications that must occur between systems**. If you attend a presentation on message queues led by either IBM or Microsoft, you will learn that everything should be done asynchronously. If you attend a presentation on component technologies, you will learn that everything should be done synchronously. Neither IBM nor Microsoft presents a clear vision for differentiating communications that occur within fortresses (synchronous) from communications that occur between fortresses (asynchronous).

7. **The software industry does not have a common model for interoperability, so different vendors create products that are difficult to glue together**. Progress is slowly being made on this front with some of the new work on SOAP and Web services, but the emphasis here is on *slowly*.

8. **The software industry uses technology-specific terminology for describing what is being done, making it difficult to understand when common approaches are being used**. In Java, business logic is based on "session beans." In Microsoft technologies, business logic is based on "COM+ components." Would you ever guess that these two architectures are virtually identical?

9. **The software industry assumes that interoperability will be solved by the choice of one single technology that will integrate everything**. Everybody in the software industry wants to be at the center of the doughnut, providing the core of the enterprise infrastructure. All software vendors will tell you that if you just make their technology ubiquitous, you will be able to hang everybody else off at the edges and achieve an interoperability utopia. In the real world, there is no single ubiquitous technology. There are a lot of

technologies, and we need to cut, paste, and bridge as necessary to get systems to talk with one another. Once we recognize this fact, we can start to model the requirements to achieve reality-based interoperability.

10. **The software industry frequently provides capabilities that are not only not useful, but downright harmful**. Some examples that come to mind are entity beans (from the Java folks), the transaction Internet protocol (from Microsoft), and "distributed objects" (from just about everybody).

15.7 Where to Go Next

If you haven't already done so, the next thing you should do is sign up for a free subscription to the *ObjectWatch Newsletter*, written and published by me. This publication is your ongoing source for all of the following:

- Updates or changes to the software fortress model
- Information on events related to the software fortress model
- Pointers to new information about the software fortress model

To sign up, send an e-mail to sub@objectwatch.com with the subject line

    subscribe yourName, yourEmail

I never sell or rent the list.

I hope you take advantage of this opportunity to become part of this ongoing dialogue.

15.8 Final Words

I hope you have been convinced to try some of the ideas in the software fortress model. In fact, I hope you have already been trying some of these ideas. As I have said, one of the appealing aspects of this model is that many people feel it is just a formalization of what they have already been doing. This is great news.

There is a lot of room for further work on this model. Regardless of your talents, you are needed. Here are some ways in which you might be able to contribute:

- Contributing case studies of projects built from the ground up with this model
- Writing articles and books on software fortress patterns
- Developing tools to automate software fortress design
- Championing the software fortress model in your organization

Few of us ever have the opportunity to directly influence the future of an important methodology. It is my hope, more than anything else, that this book will enable as many people as possible to help define the future of the software fortress model. This model has the potential to move us as far beyond three-tier/N-tier architectures as three-tier/N-tier architectures moved us beyond client–server systems.

A participant in a recent workshop I gave on software fortresses expressed the idea well. He said it is very exciting to be in on the ground floor of such a promising new modeling approach—late enough to see clearly the enormous potential, but still early enough to be able to influence how the technology evolves.

I hope you will join me in defining this evolution.

Glossary

access control list (ACL) An operating system facility for defining which users are allowed to access which system resources.

ACL See *access control list*.

ActiveEnterprise TIBCO's technology for treaty management fortresses.

Active Server Pages (ASP) Microsoft's pre-.NET programming technology for the presentation fortress, now replaced by ASP.NET.

ally A fortress that works with another fortress to fulfill a common objective.

ASP See *Active Server Pages*.

ASP.NET Microsoft's .NET programming technology for the presentation fortress.

assembly In .NET terminology, a deployable unit of code.

asynchronous component A component that uses an asynchronous communications protocol, such as message queues, for transmitting information. In the J2EE space, these components are called *message-driven beans*. In the .NET space, these components are called *queued components*.

asynchronous drawbridge A drawbridge that makes no promises about when it will deliver its infograms or the order in which it will deliver its infograms, and that returns no information to the sender once those infograms have been delivered. Compare *synchronous drawbridge*.

auditing The guard function of logging infograms.

authentication The guard function of verifying the source of an infogram.

authenticator A trusted party that can be used to verify the identity of other, nontrusted parties.

authorization The process for deciding whether or not a fortress is authorized to do what it is trying to do.

automatic transaction boundary management A feature of component-oriented middleware (COMWare) by which the system automatically determines transaction boundaries.

autosecurity The ability of a system to provide some security features administratively rather than through code.

availability See *true reliability*.

BAF See *business application fortress.*

BizTalk Server Microsoft's product that is the basis for .NET's equivalent of the treaty management fortress.

broadcast To send information from one source to many other places.

broadcast service fortress A service fortress that receives information from one fortress (the publisher) and broadcasts it to a number of other fortresses (the subscribers).

browser client A human being working at a browser. Also called *thin client*.

BTP See *Business Transaction Protocol*.

buffer overflow An attack on an Internet fortress in which a hacker tries to send more data into the infogram than the fortress can handle, thereby overriding memory in the fortress. If successful, the hacker can gain control of the trusted processes within the fortress.

build-big An approach to scalability that attempts to predict the eventual workload of a system and build it on a system large enough to handle that workload from the beginning. Compare *scale-up* and *scale-out*.

business application fortress (BAF) A fortress that processes a major piece of business functionality, such as a human resource system.

business transaction In BTP terminology, a loosely coupled transaction that spans Web services.

Business Transaction Protocol (BTP) The standard proposed by OASIS for coordinating loosely coupled transactions across Web services.

C# A .NET programming language that closely resembles Java. Pronounced "cee sharp."

cancel A request to terminate and undo a transaction (usually loosely coupled) that has been started but not yet committed.

CERT/Coordination Center Formally known as the Computer Emergency Response Team Coordination Center, one of the main organizations that tracks and reports on Internet-based attacks on enterprise systems. The Web site is www.cert.org.

certificate A document that can be used to prove a party's identity.

CICS Customer Information Control System, an early transaction processing monitor from IBM that is still widely used in large enterprise systems.

class One of possibly many object-oriented implementations of an interface.

class–responsibility–collaborator (CRC) cards A design technique that was first described at an OOPSLA conference by Ward Cunningham and Kent Beck in 1989 and became popularized most notably by Rebecca Wirfs-Brock, Brian Wilkerson, and Lauren Wiener in their book *Designing Object-Oriented Software* (1990, Prentice-Hall). *FAR cards* are based on CRC cards.

client One who requests a service from another.

client process The process in which the client, or caller, resides. Compare *component process*.

client–server architecture A software architecture that recognizes only two tiers: one for the combined client/business logic and one for the database.

client surrogate A bit of software that stands in for a client in the component process in a component system. Compare *component surrogate*.

CLR See *Common Language Runtime*.

cluster A collection of similarly configured computers designed so that any given work request can be sent to and successfully processed by any one of them.

cluster controller The process, machine, or other entity of the cluster that decides which machine in the cluster will process the next request.

COM+ Microsoft's infrastructure for the business application fortress. COM+ predates .NET but is still considered part of .NET.

Common Language Runtime (CLR) The runtime infrastructure used by the .NET programming languages. Compare *Java Virtual Machine*.

Common Object Request Broker Architecture (CORBA) An early distributed-component architecture.

complex treaty A treaty that requires the coordination of a treaty management fortress. Compare *simple treaty*.

component The smallest unit of packaging and distribution in component-based systems. Component packaging is one of the techniques we use to package compiled code, identify remotely accessible interfaces to that code, and assign processes in which that code will run. In Java, a component is typically an Enterprise JavaBean. In .NET, it is typically a COM+ component. Compare *object*.

component instance A discrete blob of memory that serves the role of a component and can process requests from a remote client.

component interface A collection of method definitions that a component supports.

component-oriented middleware (COMWare) The technologies represented by EJB and COM+. These technologies were originally intended to be *middle*-tier infrastructures for components (hence their name). They are now used as the infrastructure for business application fortresses.

component process The process in which one or more instances of one or more components lives. See *client process*.

component state The data needed by a component to fulfill a request.

component surrogate A bit of software that stands in for a component instance in the client process in a component system. Compare *client surrogate*.

COMWare See *component-oriented middleware*.

confirm In BTP terminology, the process of letting the coordinator know that the end boundary of the transaction has been reached and that the coordinator should start working with the participants to reach the final transactional end game.

connector The part of an application designed to plug into a treaty management product, such as BizTalk Server.

consensus The third phase of the four-phase commit protocol, which is entered when the transaction initiator informs the coordinator that the end transactional boundary has been reached. In this phase, the coordinator asks the participants how each one feels about its portion of the transactional workload.

context In BTP terminology, information that uniquely identifies a specific business transaction.

coordinator In BTP terminology, the entity that is coordinating the loosely coupled transaction, analogous to DTC for a tightly coupled transaction.

CORBA See *Common Object Request Broker Architecture*.

CRC cards See *class–responsibility–collaborator cards*.

create In the context of a loosely coupled transaction, the request to the transaction coordinator to begin a new transaction and allocate a region of memory to store information about that transaction.

CTO Chief technical officer, the highest position in an IT organization.

database A technology specialized for managing data and processing update requests to that data within the context of a tightly coupled transaction.

database connection A logical connection between a database client (typically a process within a fortress) and the database itself.

database locks A technique in which users are temporarily denied access to specific data. This technique is used by databases to coordinate the conflicting data access requirements of different database users.

data-sharing fortress A service fortress that serves as a shared data repository for two or more other fortresses.

data strongbox Conceptually, the private data storage facilities used by a fortress. A data strongbox can be implemented, for example, with a dedicated database, a logical partition of a database, or a file system.

data tier The back end of a three-tier architecture. This is the tier in which the database resides.

DCOM See *Distributed Component Object Model*.

decryption The process of converting data that had been algorithmically altered to appear garbled back to its original form. Compare *encryption*.

Distributed Component Object Model (DCOM) One of the component protocols used by .NET.

distributed transaction coordinator (DTC) A system that coordinates two or more transactional resources in a tightly coupled multiple-resource transaction.

donor fortress The fortress that is making a request of another fortress. Compare *recipient fortress*.

drawbridge Conceptually, a communications channel that a fortress uses to receive work requests (infograms). A drawbridge can be implemented, for example, with a message queue or a shared logical data partition.

DTC See *distributed transaction coordinator*.

EJB See *Enterprise JavaBeans*.

emissary code In Pat Helland's software fiefdom model, code that runs on the browser to prepare requests for a software fortress.

encryption The process of algorithmically altering data to appear garbled. Compare *decryption*.

enroll The process by which a participant in a transaction (either loosely coupled or tightly coupled) informs the coordinator of its intention to participate in the transaction.

Enterprise JavaBeans (EJB) The J2EE specification that defines an infrastructure for the business application fortress.

enterprise system A collection of software fortresses that collectively run a large enterprise.

envoy A specialized system within a fortress that creates infograms and sends them to other fortresses via drawbridges.

Extensible Markup Language (XML) A standard string-encoding mechanism designed specifically for data.

FAD See *fortress–ally–diagram*.

FAR (fortress–ally–responsibility) card An adaptation of a CRC card that tells us three things about a fortress: its name and type, its responsibilities, and the allies with which it must collaborate to fulfill its responsibilities. Compare *TAR card*.

File Transfer Protocol (FTP) A protocol used to transfer files between machines.

final The fourth phase of the four-phase commit protocol, which is entered when the last transactional participant lets the transactional coordinator know its opinion on the transaction outcome. In this phase, the coordinator informs each of the participants of the transaction as to what the transaction result should be.

firewall A combination of hardware and software systems designed to prevent unauthorized entry into a private network.

FOD See *fortress overview document*.

fortification The wall function of preventing access to a fortress other than through approved channels (drawbridges).

fortress See *software fortress*.

fortress–ally diagram (FAD) A diagram showing the enterprise fortresses and the ally relationships between them.

fortress–ally–responsibility card See *FAR card*.

fortress overview document (FOD) A detailed description of a specific fortress, including any information that a fortress outsider might need to know, such as information about the drawbridges, the high-level algorithms the fortress implements, and the technologies used inside the fortress.

fortress-specific icon A cartoon figure used in diagrams to represent the type of a fortress.

four-phase commit protocol The protocol that is used by most transaction coordinators for either loosely or tightly coupled transactions. The four phases are sleep, meditative, consensus, and final.

FTP See *File Transfer Protocol.*

golden rule of components The rule stating that business component methods should be designed to be self-contained tightly coupled transactions.

guard A specialized system within a fortress that receives requests from a drawbridge and subjects them to a security inspection. Compare *wall.*

heterogeneous Describing two or more dissimilar systems. The term usually refers to the technology base on which the systems are built. For example, a pair of two systems—one built on .NET and the other built on WebSphere—would be considered a heterogeneous pair. Compare *homogeneous.*

heterogeneous drawbridge A drawbridge connecting a pair of heterogeneous fortresses. Compare *homogeneous drawbridge.*

homogeneous Describing two or more similar systems. The term usually refers to the technology base on which the systems are built. For example, a pair of two systems, both built on .NET would be considered a homogeneous pair. Compare *heterogeneous.*

homogeneous drawbridge A drawbridge connecting a pair of homogeneous fortresses. Compare *heterogeneous drawbridge.*

HTML See *HyperText Markup Language.*

HTTP See *HyperText Transfer Protocol.*

HyperText Markup Language (HTML) The standard definition of documents returned to browsers from presentation fortresses.

HyperText Transfer Protocol (HTTP) One of the common protocols used for the transferral of information between browsers and presentation fortresses.

idempotent In Pat Helland's software fiefdom model, describing a request that can be executed any number of times greater than zero with an equivalent result.

IIOP Internet Inter-ORB Protocol, the CORBA component protocol and precursor to the Java RMI/IIOP component protocol.

IIS See *Internet Information Server*.

infogram A request that travels between two fortresses via a connecting drawbridge.

Information Technology (IT) The part of a large enterprise that owns information processing.

initiator In BTP terminology, the party starting the transaction and defining the loosely coupled transaction boundaries.

instance management A feature of component-oriented middleware (COMWare) that shares a single instance of a component among a large number of clients.

integrity A guarantee by a fortress that it never leaves itself in a damaged or incomplete state. Also the process of guaranteeing that an infogram has not been changed en route through a drawbridge.

interface A description of what something can do for you, usually used within the context of objects or components.

interfortress Describing a process that involves more than one fortress. Compare *intrafortress*.

Internet fortress A presentation or Web service fortress.

Internet Information Server (IIS) The part of the .NET technologies that provides an infrastructure for presentation fortresses and sometimes for Web service fortresses.

Internet Inter-ORB Protocol See *IIOP*.

intrafortress Describing a process that occurs entirely within one fortress. Compare *interfortress*.

IT See *Information Technology*.

J2EE (Java 2 Enterprise Edition) A family of specifications, produced by Sun, that define an enterprise architecture and are rooted in the Java programming language.

JAR See *Java Archive*.

Java The programming language used with J2EE technologies.

Java Archive (JAR) In J2EE terminology, a deployable unit of code.

Java bytecode The low-level language into which Java is translated before it is compiled. Compare *Microsoft Intermediate Language*.

JavaServer Pages (JSP) Sun's main specification for programming presentation fortresses.

Java Virtual Machine (JVM) The runtime infrastructure used by the Java language. Compare *Common Language Runtime*.

JSP See *JavaServer Pages*.

JVM See *Java Virtual Machine*.

Kerberos A shared-key authentication system.

LCTM See *loosely coupled transaction management service fortress*.

legacy fortress (LF) A fortress that wraps an existing legacy system that was originally developed without regard to the software fortress model.

LF See *legacy fortress*.

linked library A collection of compiled code that is linked into an executable.

loosely coupled cluster A cluster of machines, usually a large number, that are organized such that if one machine goes down, its work in progress is lost, but new work can be picked up by another machine in the cluster. Compare *tightly coupled cluster*.

loosely coupled transaction A coordination of two or more activities that allows each activity to learn of the failure or success of the others, and to take appropriate remedial action upon failure. Compare *tightly coupled transaction*.

**loosely coupled transaction management (LCTM) service
   fortress** A service fortress that is responsible for coordinating
   loosely coupled transactions that span fortresses.

meditative The second phase of the four-phase commit protocol,
   which is entered when the transaction initiator informs the coordinator that a new transaction boundary has been reached and the
   coordinator has assigned a transaction ID. In this phase, the coordinator is waiting for transactionally aware resources to check in.

message-driven bean See *asynchronous component*.

message queue A communications technology that is the basis for
   asynchronous drawbridges today.

method Usually used within the context of objects or components, a
   specific request that something can do for you.

method invocation A request to a component instance to perform a
   service on behalf of a specific client.

Microsoft Intermediate Language (MSIL) The low-level language
   into which all .NET-supported languages are translated before they
   are compiled. Compare *Java bytecode*.

middle tier One of the tiers in a three-tier architecture. The middle
   tier is typically responsible for tightly coupled transaction processing.

MQ Integrator IBM's technology for treaty management fortresses,
   considered part of its WebSphere product line.

MQSeries IBM's message queue product.

MSIL See *Microsoft Intermediate Language*.

MSMQ Microsoft's message queue product.

multiple-resource transaction A transaction that must be coordinated over two or more transactional resources, such as databases.

.NET Microsoft's term for its enterprise technologies.

.NET language A language that can be used for programming within
   .NET. Most languages (the notable exception is Java) are .NET
   languages.

.NET Remote Binary Protocol One of the component communications protocols supported by .NET.

nonblocking Describing a workload that can be accomplished without blocking the one requesting the work. In the software fortress model, the term is usually used in reference to asynchronous drawbridges.

nonrepudiation A process for proving that a particular fortress made a particular request, especially when the fortress denies having done so.

nontransactional queue A message queue that does not support transactional protection and will not participate with transactional resources in a multiple-resource transaction.

N-tier architecture A three-tier architecture in which the middle tier is subdivided into smaller business systems.

OASIS See *Organization for the Advancement of Structured Information Standards*.

object An artifact of object-oriented programming, which is one (not the only) technique we can use to implement algorithms. An object is therefore a unit of implementation. In Java, an object is an instantiation of a Java class. In .NET, an object is an instantiation of a class defined in one of the .NET languages, such as C#. Compare *component*.

ObjectWatch Newsletter The official newsletter of the software fortress movement, available at www.objectwatch.com.

Oracle Oracle corporation's main database (data strongbox) technology.

Organization for the Advancement of Structured Information Standards (OASIS) One of several software consortia that are trying to define standards for various aspects of Web services. The Web site is www.oasis-open.org.

partitioned database A database that is spread out over multiple physical computers.

persistent queue A message queue that is stored on disk and therefore is not lost in case of system failure. Compare *transient queue*.

PF See *presentation fortress*.

point of interception The point at which COMWare technologies intercept a method request traveling between a client and a specific component instance for the purpose of running a variety of COMWare algorithms.

polymorphic method resolution The ability of an object-oriented or component-oriented system to support multiple implementations of an interface and then choose which of those implementations is appropriate to use at runtime.

poor-man's clustering The use of asynchronous drawbridges to implement many of the features of clusters.

presentation fortress (PF) A fortress that accepts browser requests and prepares to forward them to the corporate empire. The presentation fortress is a browser gateway into the enterprise.

presentation tier The browser-facing tier in a traditional three-tier architecture. This tier typically handles interactions with the browser. Its function is analogous to that of a presentation fortress.

privacy The process of protecting infograms en route through a drawbridge from prying eyes.

private key A secret key, typically used for encryption and decryption, that is shared by a small number of parties (usually two). Compare *public key*.

proxy See *surrogate*.

pseudoreliability The condition in which a fortress is not particularly trustworthy but appears to be so, most likely through the use of asynchronous drawbridges. Compare *true reliability*.

public key A key that is made publicly available for use in encryption and decryption. Compare *private key*.

public/private–key authentication An authentication scheme that is based on public and private keys. Secure Sockets Layer (SSL) is a public/private–key authentication scheme. Compare *shared-key authentication*.

publisher The source of a broadcast. Compare *subscriber*.

queue The carrier of a message in a message queue system.

queued component See *asynchronous component*.

recipient fortress The fortress that is receiving a request from another fortress. Compare *donor fortress*.

reliability A measure of how much a fortress can be trusted to be available when it is needed.

remote method invocation (RMI) Any technology designed to allow component method invocations to be made across process boundaries.

remote procedure call (RPC) A precursor technology to distributed components.

rich client A client system that is built as a stand-alone program.

RMI See *remote method invocation*.

RMI/IIOP Remote Method Invocation/Internet Inter-ORB Protocol, the standard component protocol that is supposed to be used by all J2EE systems. Pronounced "RMI over IIOP."

role-based security A type of security used with components in which users are assigned roles (such as managers or tellers) and then access rights to components, interfaces within components, or methods within interfaces are based on those same roles.

RPC See *remote procedure call*.

rule of transactional integrity The rule dictating how data must move between code that implements business logic and a database. The first part of this two-part rule states that all data used in a transaction must be acquired from the database within that transaction. The second part states that all data that is changed during the transaction must be stored back to the database before the transaction commits.

SAD See *sequence–ally diagram*.

scalability The ability to increase the processing capability of a fortress, preferably without increasing the overall cost per unit of work.

scale-out An approach to scalability in which more machines are added to one or more clusters. Compare *scale-up* and *build-big*.

scale-up An approach to scalability in which smaller machines are replaced with larger machines. Compare *scale-out* and *build-big*.

Secure Sockets Layer (SSL) A public/private–key authentication scheme.

sequence–ally diagram (SAD) An adaptation of the UML construct called class sequence diagram. SADs give more detail about how the various fortresses work together while still fitting in a relatively small space. In a SAD, the heading gives the name of the treaty. Within the treaty, each ally fortress is represented by a vertical line. Interactions between the fortresses are shown with one of three arrows, following conventions similar to those of UML's class sequence diagrams. Full solid arrowheads show use of a synchronous drawbridge. Full hollow arrowheads show a synchronous drawbridge returning information. Half solid arrowheads show use of an asynchronous drawbridge. Typically the name of the drawbridge is written underneath the arrow.

service fortress (SF) A fortress that packages some common functionality and/or data that must be shared across one or more enterprises.

session key The data that is used by a presentation fortress to find, in a data strongbox, the larger body of data that represents the state of a specific browser session. Also called *session state key*.

SF See *service fortress*.

shared-key authentication An authentication scheme that is based on two parties sharing a common secret, such as a password. Kerberos is a shared-key authentication scheme. Compare *public/private-key authentication*.

Simple Object Access Protocol (SOAP) A standard string representation of a request between heterogeneous systems.

simple treaty A treaty that does not require the coordination of a treaty management fortress. Compare *complex treaty*.

single-resource transaction A transaction that involves only one transactional resource.

sleep The first phase of the four-phase commit protocol, in which the transaction coordinator is not paying attention to anything you are doing.

SOAP See *Simple Object Access Protocol*.

SOAP surrogate A component surrogate that uses SOAP to transform a method request into a string.

software fiefdom model Pat Helland's model for enterprise architectures, in which software systems owned by different enterprises treat each other as autonomous computing units.

software fortress A conglomerate of software systems that work together in a tight trust relationship to provide consistent and meaningful functionality to a hostile outside world.

software fortress architecture An enterprise architecture consisting of a series of self-contained, mutually suspicious, marginally cooperating software fortresses interacting with each other through carefully crafted and meticulously managed treaty relationships.

software fortress model A methodology for designing an enterprise system based on software fortresses.

SQL Server Microsoft's main database (data strongbox) technology.

SSL See *Secure Sockets Layer*.

state management The process of managing information that is specific to the donor fortress or requestor of a service.

stored procedure Programming logic that is stored inside and executed from inside of a database.

strongbox See *data strongbox*.

strong transactional guarantee A guarantee that is made in a tightly coupled transaction—namely, that participating transactionally aware resources will all undo their portion of the workload if any other participating transactionally aware resource is unable to complete its portion of the workload and will absolutely guarantee to complete their portion of the workload once they all agree to do so. Compare *weak transactional guarantee*.

subscriber One of the places to which a broadcast will be sent. Compare *publisher*.

surrogate Something that stands in for something else. Also called *proxy*.

synchronous drawbridge A drawbridge that delivers its infogram immediately and does not return control to the envoy until that delivery has occurred. Compare *asynchronous drawbridge*.

TAD See *treaty–ally diagram*.

TAR (treaty–ally–responsibility) card A brief overview of a treaty, including which fortresses are part of that treaty and what their responsibilities are within that treaty.

thin client See *browser client*.

three-phase commit protocol A version of the four-phase commit protocol that does not consider the sleep part of the commit protocol.

three-tier architecture A traditional architecture that consists of a presentation tier, a middle tier, and a data tier. Compare *N-tier architecture*.

ticket A string, typically encrypted, that gives one party permission to do something with another party.

tightly coupled cluster A cluster of machines, usually a small number, that are organized such that if one machine goes down, its work in progress is not lost but rather is automatically picked up by one of the remaining machines in the cluster. Tightly coupled clusters are usually used to protect the database machine from failures. Compare *loosely coupled cluster*.

tightly coupled multiple-resource transaction A tightly coupled transaction in which there are two or more transactional resources and the services of a distributed transaction coordinator are therefore required. Compare *tightly coupled single-resource transaction*.

tightly coupled single-resource transaction A tightly coupled transaction in which exactly one transactional resource is involved, and the services of a distributed transaction coordinator are therefore not required. Compare *tightly coupled multiple-resource transaction*.

tightly coupled transaction A coordination of updates to one or more transactional resources (such as databases or message queues) such that all resources either complete their updates or none of the resources complete any of their updates. Compare *loosely coupled transaction*.

TMF See *treaty management fortress*.

TOD See *treaty overview document*.

TPC-C An industry standard benchmark designed to test high-end database applications.

TPM See *transaction processing monitor*.

transaction A collection of either requests or updates that should be processed as a group, with all either succeeding or failing.

transactionally aware resource Something that knows how to accept groups of updates and guarantee that they are done or not done en masse, and how to participate with an outside entity to coordinate its group of updates with groups of updates to other transactionally aware resources. Often called simply *transactional resource*.

transactional queue A message queue that can behave as a transactionally aware resource.

transactional resource See *transactionally aware resource*.

transaction boundary The point at which a transaction either begins or ends.

transaction boundary management See *automatic transaction boundary management*.

transaction flow The ability of a system to automatically have all of the work in a given workflow be done within the same transaction.

transaction processing monitor (TPM) The original approach to building the middle tier in a three-tier system. TPMs were built to provide highly scalable systems built around a rich-client architecture.

transient queue A message queue that is not stored on disk and therefore is not protected against loss in case of system failure. Compare *persistent queue*.

treaty A defined partnership of two or more fortresses.

treaty–ally diagram (TAD) A subset of a fortress–ally diagram (FAD) that shows only those fortresses participating in a given treaty.

treaty–ally–responsibility card See *TAR card*.

treaty management fortress (TMF) A fortress that is specialized to manage complex treaties.

treaty overview document (TOD) A detailed description of a specific treaty, including any information that a participant in the treaty might need to know, such as information about sequences of fortress interactions, security requirements, transactional expectations, and the synchronicity of the drawbridge.

true reliability The condition in which a fortress is truly up and running when asked to do something. Also called *availability*. Compare *pseudoreliability*.

trust rule A basic rule of fortress design stating that all entities within a fortress trust all other entities within the same fortress, but trust no entities that live outside the fortress.

two-phase commit protocol A version of the four-phase commit protocol that considers the sleep and meditative phases part of the precommit phase and not part of the commit protocol per se.

UDDI See *Universal Description, Discovery and Integration*.

UML See *Unified Modeling Language*.

Unified Modeling Language (UML) An object-oriented design methodology.

Universal Description, Discovery and Integration (UDDI) One of the Web service family of standards that is used to find potential partners, usually partners exposing their functionality through SOAP.

validation The guard function of checking infograms to make sure they don't contain illegal or invalid information.

Visual Studio.NET Microsoft's programmer tools, used primarily for presentation and business application fortresses.

wall Conceptually, a part of the fortress that prevents requests from entering the fortress other than through approved channels. A wall could be implemented as a firewall, through role-based security, through database security, or through ACLs. Compare *guard*.

weak transactional guarantee A guarantee that is made in a loosely coupled transaction—namely, that participants will merely let each other know if they are unable to complete their portion of the workload, and let each participant decide what action, if any, to take as a result. Compare *strong transactional guarantee*.

Web service fortress (WSF) A fortress that accepts programmatic requests over the Internet and prepares to forward them to the corporate empire. The Web service fortress is the programmatic gateway into the enterprise.

Web Services Description Language (WSDL) A standard string format defining, in minute detail, everything there is to know about a Web service.

Web Services Inspection Language (WS-Inspection) A specification for finding WSDL documents and related information on a Web site.

WebLogic BEA's J2EE-influenced enterprise technologies.

WebSphere IBM's J2EE-influenced enterprise technologies.

worker Conceptually, something within the fortress that fulfills part of the overall fortress's responsibility. A worker could be implemented, for example, as a component, a process, or a collection of processes.

workload averaging The use of asynchronous drawbridges to put off peak workloads until times when the system would normally be used lightly.

WSDL See *Web Services Description Language*.

WSF See *Web service fortress*.

WS-Inspection See *Web Services Inspection Language*.

XML See *Extensible Markup Language*.

Index

Note: Italicized page locators refer to tables/figures.

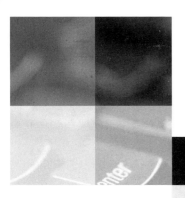

inform**IT**